Curriculum for Young Children: An Introduction

Curriculum for Young Children: An Introduction

Eve-Marie Arce, M. A.
Shasta College

Africa • Australia • Canada • Denmark • Japan • Mexico • New Zealand • Philippines
Puerto Rico • Singapore • Spain • United Kingdom • United States

NOTICE TO THE READER

Publisher does not warrant or guarantee any of the products described herein or perform any independent analysis in connection with any of the product information contained herein. Publisher does not assume, and expressly disclaims, any obligation to obtain and include information other than that provided to it by the manufacturer. The reader is expressly warned to consider and adopt all safety precautions that might be indicated by the activities herein and to avoid all potential hazards. By following the instructions contained herein, the reader willingly assumes all risks in connection with such instructions.

The Publisher makes no representation or warranties of any kind, including but not limited to, the warranties of fitness for particular purpose or merchantability, nor are any such representations implied with respect to the material set forth herein, and the publisher takes no responsibility with respect to such material. The publisher shall not be liable for any special, consequential, or exemplary damages resulting, in whole or part, from the readers' use of, or reliance upon, this material.

Delmar Staff

Business Unit Director: Susan L. Simpfenderfer
Executive Editor: Marlene McHugh Pratt
Acquisitions Editor: Erin O'Connor Traylor
Developmental Editor: Melissa Riveglia
Editorial Assistant: Alexis Ferraro
Executive Production Manager: Wendy A. Troeger
Project Editor: Amy E. Tucker
Production Editor: Sandra Woods
Executive Marketing Manager: Donna J. Lewis
Channel Manager: Nigar Hale

For more information, contact:
Delmar, 3 Columbia Circle, PO Box 15015, Albany, NY 12212-0515;
or find us on the World Wide Web at http://www.Delmar.com or
http://www.EarlyChildEd.Delmar.com

Library of Congress Cataloging-in-Publication Data
Arce, Eve-Marie.
    Curriculum for young children / Eve-Marie Arce.
        p.   cm.
    Includes bibliographical references and index.
    ISBN 0-7668-1278-2
    1. Early childhood education—United States—Curricula.
    2. Curriculum planning—United States.   I. Title.
LB1139.4.H73 2000
372.19' 0973—dc21   99-11642
                                                                   CIP

Contents

Preface

Curriculum for Young Children: An Introduction offers both basic Early Childhood curriculum for entry-level students and a resource for practitioners. The many points of entry into the Early Childhood profession gives rise to classes and in-service groups with great variability in both the work experience and academic readiness of the participants. This book addresses the need of all Early Childhood Education college students to acquire primary skills in curriculum planning. The book is designed to help students understand the *how* of curriculum for preschool-age children, ages three to five years; however, concepts apply to a broader age range of children.

The organization of the chapters allows students to immediately apply ideas as they progress through their coursework. This book does not require students to have completed prerequisite courses in child growth and development or comprehension of theoretical foundations. The seventy Curriculum Activity Guides (CAG) presented in Appendix A both provide practical examples of curriculum experiences and illustrate the information presented in the text. References in the text direct you to each specific activity and complete listings of all CAGs [CAG], and their corresponding page numbers are included on the inside front and back covers and at the beginning of Appendix A. The identification of a goal for each activity purposefully places emphasis on opportunities and experiences for young children, rather than dictating expectations of behavioral objectives.

Extensive consideration has been given to the summary of information framed within the charts in order to simplify the delivery of concepts for students. The charts deliver a large amount of information to students without challenging them to read extensive written narrative.

The first four chapters create a foundation of basic knowledge with a general introduction to the subject of curriculum. Chapters 5 and 6 lead the student through the process of designing curriculum for their own center. These two chapters offer a blueprint for managing curriculum. The next three chapters introduce the student to curriculum content that integrates developmental and curriculum activities. Because there are extensive curriculum resources available, this textbook simply links curriculum development to specific curriculum areas. Chapter 10 summarizes with discussion about professional growth. Each chapter opens with an overview that includes a Curriculum Profile, Chapter Outline, and Study Guide. At the end of each chapter, students will find helpful summary elements, beginning with a brief Review section and a list of Key Terms. The Respond section provides questions and assignments, including options to access information from Early Childhood Web sites, and is followed by a list of references. (Please note that because Internet resources are of a time-sensitive nature and URL addresses may change or be deleted, searches should also be conducted by association and/or topic.) Sensitivity for diversity and children with special needs is threaded throughout the text to nurture an inclusive approach.

The textbook does not depend on any single theory or method; instead, it provides a solid foundation for accessing adaptable, introductory curriculum concepts. *Curriculum for Young Children: An Introduction* defines curriculum for Early Childhood students and practitioners as they prepare and extend suitable experiences for young children with:

- Focus on the "how" of curriculum.
- Introduction to basic curriculum concepts.
- Integrated experiences documented with Curriculum Activity Guides.
- Information summarized in charts.

ACKNOWLEDGMENTS

Any project, especially writing a textbook, is a collaboration of many: students willing to listen; program directors supporting new methods; and colleagues responding with comments and ideas.

I am extremely grateful to the reviewers, whose constructive suggestions and encouragement strengthened the final draft. The reviewers include Elaine Camerin, Ed.D., Daytona Beach

Community College, Daytona, Florida; Theresa Stewart, Ph.D., University of Illinois at Springfield, Springfield, Illinois; Martha Dever, Utah State University, Logan, Utah; Josephine M. Alexander, Mohawk Valley Community College, Utica, New York; and Linda Gamble, University of Maine at Farmington, Farmington, Maine.

I wish to give considerable recognition to a professional friend, Laurie Barton Koukol, whose ideas helped create the foundation for this textbook. Having co-directed the California State University, Los Angeles lab school in the early 1970s, we share a basic commitment to teaching and desire to effectively prepare teachers of young children. We have continued through the years to exchange ideas, refine materials, and conceptualize management of curriculum.

I am indebted to Kathy Barry, teaching colleague in Early Childhood Education at Shasta College, for her dedicated support and assistance. Kathy completed the sample Curriculum Activity Guides, which provide valuable examples of curriculum experiences for young children.

I am appreciative for the professional teaching staff at the Shasta College Early Childhood Education Center who infused the abstract ideas advanced in the textbook into a model program for young children.

Many thanks to the numerous students whose questions and responses stimulated me to rethink and re-explain. I continue to learn about development, teaching, and curriculum from each new group.

Finally, with love and appreciation, I note the understanding and ongoing influence of my family:

- My parents, for giving me a blend of culture and religion.
- My daughters, Cecily and Olivia, for enlightening my perspective about child development and parenting; they are my center.
- My husband, Walt Brooks, for remaining vital during every aspect of the project; a true partner in love, life, and work.

Eve-Marie
Millville, California

CHAPTER 1

Curriculum for Young Children:
As Valuable and As Much Fun As You Make It!

Curriculum Profile

Imagine that you are a visitor to a program for young children. Close your eyes. Visualize that you are walking into the lobby, checking in with the director, and securing a seat in the observation area. Sitting on a raised stool, you can see most of the main room, which is set up for children ages three, four, and five. It is early in the morning, and children are arriving. You can see a staff member greeting children as they arrive and then inviting them to participate in activities available throughout the classroom.

A Dramatic Play area is set up in one corner of the room. Sun is streaming through a window, providing natural light. Equipment and furniture replicate a miniature house, complete with fresh flowers. Children are trying on clothing. Two children are sitting on blocks that look like a car just outside the Dramatic Play area. To the right of this area, four children are pulling blocks from the shelves, which are marked with block shapes. A sign with six happy faces and the words *six friends* marks the entrance to the block area. Various miniature houses, vehicles, and animals wait on the shelves.

You turn to the opposite side of the classroom and spot three tables bordered with shelves. There are four children engaged in various activities at these tables. On the opposite side of the right shelf there is a table with a low carrel providing some privacy. A child with earphones is turning the pages of a picture book. There is one child in the Art area concentrating on dipping a brush into a secured cup of blue paint. Two children pick up aprons in anticipation of participating at the table covered with butcher paper. Next to this Art area is a teacher at a table with three children. The children each have small bowls and are measuring ingredients. They interact with the teacher, who is directing their attention to a large menu chart.

You leave the observation room and begin wondering who organized and planned all of these activities. Who decided what materials would be placed on the tables? How can anyone make so many decisions? How did they know what is best for children? What influenced their choices? How will you be able to make so many decisions about children's activities?

Chapter Outline

Understanding Curriculum
  Curriculum Ideas—Old and New
  The Remarkable Teacher Planning Remarkable
    Curriculum
  Activities—The Core of the Curriculum
  Benefits of Planning and Managing Curriculum
  Technology to Assist Teachers of Young Children
Fundamentals That Shape Early Childhood
    Education
  Defining Early Childhood Education Terms
  The Importance of the Early Experiences
Program Perspectives and Practices
  Theories Influence Curricula
  Types of Programs
Essential Considerations
  Best Practices for Quality Programs
  Strengthening Connections: Harmony, Equity,
    Respect

Study Guide

As you study the sections in this chapter you should be able to:

- Learn how to define the value and benefits of curriculum planning.

- Appreciate the general and differing definitions in Early Childhood Education.
- Recognize the importance of early experiences in the lives of young children.
- Examine the theories that influence curriculum and the types of programs in Early Childhood.
- Become familiar with the concepts of developmentally appropriate and best practices.
- Identify the importance of including harmony, equity, and respect in curriculum development.

UNDERSTANDING CURRICULUM

Curriculum ideas are about you—who you are, what you have done, and how you will impact the lives of young children. Your basic ideas about children evolved from your childhood and adult experiences as a member of a family and community. As you assume the role of teacher, teacher assistant, or director, you will incorporate the growing knowledge of the Early Childhood profession into your own understandings and beliefs. Much of what you learn will validate your understanding of children. Some ideas, however, will change your way of thinking about children and how you will interact with them.

The word **curriculum** refers to learning programs, activities, school subjects, materials, plans, and topics of study. Early Childhood educators define curriculum as all the school-related **experiences** that affect the child. Curriculum involves both planned and unplanned experiences and results from the values and attitudes of the teachers, the staff, the families, and the community. The curriculum is also influenced by funding sources, sponsoring agencies, and state and national legislative policy. The goals of a school will also affect the way the curriculum is planned for young children.

This introduction to curriculum provides you with initial knowledge that will encourage you to develop meaningful experiences for young children. Begin with an understanding of the word *curriculum* (Figure 1–1).

Curriculum Ideas—Old and New

As educators we are continuously searching for improved ways to guide children. Sometimes our ideas agree and sometimes they do not. There are some ideas that we all seem to accept, and these commonalities become established in written definition about Early Childhood Education. Some ideas emerge from previous times, often repackaged, sometimes improved with basic concepts about the purpose of curriculum remaining solid

FIGURE 1–1 Use of the Word—Curriculum

curriculum	a noun	a course of study; a program of studies leading to a particular degree or certificate (Barnhart & Barnhart, 1990)
		Curriculum for young children is the topic of this textbook.
curriculums or curricula	plural	*The teacher tried many different types of curriculums. The teacher tried many different types of curricula.*
curricular	adjective	of or having to do with a curriculum
		Early childhood educators continued to develop their curricular practices.

FIGURE 1–2 Similarities Among Old and New Statements

Words identified in 1957 *Platform of Beliefs,* ASCD	Words identified NAEYC *Developmentally Appropriate Practice,* 1997, NAEYC
. . . needs of the learner	. . . recognizing that children are best understood in the context of family, culture, and society.
. . . fullest possible development	. . . helping children and adults achieve full potential in the context of relationships that are based on trust, respect, and positive regard.
. . . individual differences	. . . respecting the dignity, worth, and uniqueness of each individual.

and applicable. *The Platform of Beliefs,* presented by the Association for Supervision and Curriculum Development in 1957, listed specific words and phrases such as "equal opportunities for all children" and "individual differences." (Hanna, 1972, p. 230). There are similarities among the words found in *The Platform of Beliefs* and in a document titled *Developmentally Appropriate Practice in Early Childhood Programs Serving Children from Birth through Age 8.* This document was initially published in 1987 by the National Association for the Education of Young Children and revised in 1997. The themes that are prevalent in both publications emphasize the importance of each child's needs, individual differences, interests, and the responsibility of the teacher to plan interactive experiences that are based on observation and evaluation (Figure 1–2).

The Remarkable Teacher Planning Remarkable Curriculum

Teachers of young children generate a quiet yet powerful force in our society. The influence of teachers on children occurs during their critical periods of growth and development. That is why it is

so important for you understand the curriculum planning process and how to plan and facilitate the experiences for children enrolled in your program.

Teachers who enjoy their careers with children do not hesitate to state that "a day in the life of a teacher of young children can only be boring if you let that happen." Teaching is fun, exciting, and rewarding, but demands a great deal of commitment and energy.

The need for qualified teachers for young children will continue to increase. The characteristics of a good teacher include creativity, flexibility, sensitivity, and curiosity. "I enjoy young children" is the most frequent response from teachers when they are asked why they chose **Early Childhood Education.** Teaching in Early Childhood center–based settings is also interactive, calling for teachers to relate mutually with the staff, the parents, and the community. Family child care providers create nurturing settings for smaller groups of children.

Interest in children, sensitivity, and college courses in Early Childhood Education will contribute to your ability to plan curriculum. When you complete a class in child growth and development you will be able to more effectively adapt experiences and activities to a specific child's developmental

Teaching young children is an exciting and rewarding career.

level. You will understand that the child's ability to cut with a pair of scissors will depend on his age and current skill. Coursework that requires you to observe children over an extended period of time will prepare you to record and interpret their behaviors and appreciate the relationship between development and curriculum.

Whether you are beginning your career or returning to classes for in-service training, perfecting your curriculum planning skills is essential to your development as an Early Childhood Education teacher. Skills in curriculum planning will give you a sense of predictability, control, and confidence. These are empowering skills that contribute to your ability to provide quality programming.

Knowledge about children that you will acquire in specific course work will be enhanced with knowledge in other topics such as guidance techniques, providing you with the tools to positively affect the lives of young children. You will join the ranks of remarkable Early Childhood educators.

Activities—The Core of the Curriculum

The outcome of thoughtful curriculum planning is a program for young children that provides enriching and appropriate experiences. The experiences offered at preschool and child-care settings are commonly referred to as *activities*. The interaction between the teachers and children create the reality

of the Early Childhood setting, with the activities creating the only concrete part of the curriculum plan. The various activities that are planned and offered to children provide the core of your curriculum. You will hear the phrase *hands-on* used to refer to those activities in which children actively engage in some way. "Hands-on" means that children use their hands, arms, legs, feet, and bodies rather than just listening and observing. You will also hear the word *concrete* describing activities that allow children to use real materials and to actively participate. Painting with marbles is an example of an activity that engages children in a hands-on experience (Curriculum Activity Guide 1 CAG).

Students studying Early Childhood Education frequently comment that they believe that they usually set up the "right activities" in their classrooms but cannot explain why they provide those activities. The ability to select and design appropriate hands-on activities develops with professional preparation courses and experience with planning and implementing experiences for young children. The Curriculum Activity Guides presented in Appendix A detail activities that focus on the needs and interests of young children. This activity planning format calls for teachers to set the stage for varied and multiple experiences. The activities are designed to help young children to become learners through exploration and to adapt to changes within a secure and nurturing environment. Teachers need to know what children can do and what they enjoy doing to help them direct their own learning when given the opportunities to pursue their interests at their stage of development.

Benefits of Planning and Managing Curriculum

Working with young children requires that teachers engage in planning to ensure secure and stable environments because children thrive optimally in secure, stable, and consistent settings. Planning allows us to predict and to prepare for events and the behavior of other people. Planning provides an important sense of predictability, confidence, and positive control. These are important, empowering skills for a teacher of young children. Once you know what is best for children, you will be able to prepare the program and to justify the purpose and value of your plan. Planning for young children acknowledges that to achieve success the plan should be flexible and adaptable and should outline long-term and short-term goals. An unanticipated event, such as the arrival of a moving van at the business next to the school, becomes an exciting addition to the children's day. A well-established plan provides a strong, secure base of activities that allows the inclusion of spontaneous experiences without abandoning predictability and security.

Planning maximizes the use of time efficiently, thereby increasing opportunities for quality interaction among the staff and children. Extra time will benefit children with more individualized attention, stability, and security. A teacher is more efficient with an established yet flexible framework. A teacher who is able to predict the daily, weekly, and monthly flow of activities also increases interaction with the families and staff and the quality for the experience for all. Planning will bring the staff together, requiring that staff meet regularly to collectively map out the way children's needs will be met. The quality of experiences for enrolled children improves with planning because the types of activities can be balanced and planned within different disciplines. Coordination and design of curriculum contributes positively to the administration of the school operation. Coordination among teachers, support staff, and volunteers, all working with a curriculum plan, increases utilization of resources, saves time, supports team building among staff members, and reduces repetitive work. The outcome of curriculum planning is a product that can be used to inform the parents about the experiences their children are enjoying. The curriculum plan is a record for staff, parents, and community (Figure 1–3).

FIGURE 1–3 Benefits of Exemplary Curriculum Planning

Benefits for Children	Benefits for Program
Stability and security	Empower staff
Increase child/teacher interaction	Increase staff efficiency
Balance experiences	Increase resource utilization
Exposure to spectrum of disciplines	Record of activities
Develop competence	Quality experience for all

Technology to Assist Teachers of Young Children

There are many exciting opportunities for teachers of young children as technology changes every aspect of our lives. The quickening pace has a direct impact on education. You are no longer limited by facts, concepts, and ideas available in books. Technology allows us to gather, organize, and utilize the vast quantity of educational knowledge. The word **technology** is commonly used in educational settings to mean the application of a technical, mechanical process. This process most particularly implies application of the personal computer (PC) and related systems such as telecommunications. Schools can fax (send a facsimile of a document over a telephone line); downlink special programs broadcast in other locations; and hook up to the Internet to acquire unlimited information.

Creative use of the computer provides teachers with a means to keep assessment records. A computer file established for each child maintains a running record of observed behavior and other administrative information related to enrollment. It is wise to print out copies of the information entered into the computer and to maintain the hard copy as well as the data in the computer. Access to the Internet provides limitless resources and allows teachers to connect with Web sites that have current information about a subject directly from the field. Teachers can also connect with other early educators on LISTSERVes (online information exchange for professionals) to explore learning topics. "The electronic communities bring together students, teachers, and adults from outside the education area" (Levin, 1996, p. 46).

Management skills, which have always been important to teachers, are becoming more important as the teacher's role in overall program

It is important for teachers to carefully review the potential benefits of technology for children.

planning and evaluation changes. A teacher needs to have the ability to organize and retrieve information about the enrolled children and the experiences in which they engage. You will find that computerized systems are indispensable tools in helping you to organize and manage your program.

The teacher's responsibility traditionally has been to review the technology and select the software that the children use in the school setting. The National Association for the Education of Young Children's *Position Statement on Technology and Children—Ages Three through Eight,* affirms that teachers should look carefully at the potential benefits of technology for children. Checklists provide guides to evaluate technical products, looking specifically at features that affect the children and the teacher (Shade, 1996, p. 19).

FUNDAMENTALS THAT SHAPE EARLY CHILDHOOD EDUCATION

Activities come from the curriculum, which is based on the philosophy and beliefs of directors and teachers. The selection and preparation of activities for a school is based on what the teachers and directors believe about children and how they learn. In most situations, a set of ideas, or **fundamentals,** directs the development of curriculum as well. Fundamentals for Early Childhood (Figure 1–4),

outlines basic ideas that organize curriculum concepts throughout this textbook. No single underlying educational or psychological theory is the foundation for these fundamentals; therefore there is no single underlying theory that directs this information. Rather, this list of Fundamentals for Early Childhood is based on what is generally accepted in the field of Early Childhood Education and what has been found to be useful in teaching students to prepare curriculum. Research has revalidated the lasting effects of early care and the importance of prevention and early intervention (Shore, 1997, p. x). The list of Fundamentals is not static; it presumes that those who use it will engage in a continuing review of the latest research, in the application of current professional practices, and in a commitment to recognize the changing needs of the children and families that they serve.

The Fundamentals offer both a general guide to the student who is new to child development and a conceptual framework for the consideration of the experienced teacher. In the course of time, students and teachers will gather ideas from a variety of sources to shape their own Early Childhood curriculum. These ideas are offered now to help you think about what is important in the field and what you may want to consider as part of your own list of guiding principles. This framework organizes ideas about development, teaching practices, and the importance of families. The value of diversity, balancing curriculum, and observation and assessment are listed as

FIGURE 1–4   Fundamentals for Early Childhood

Fundamental	Explanation
1. Developmental principles for the whole child	Understanding that development of the child is based on interrelated physical, social, emotional, and cognitive domains and not on isolated systems and events.
2. Individual and age appropriate	Promoting an ongoing individualized focus. Recognition of the difference between a child's developmental age and chronological age.
3. Family involvement and appreciation	Understanding and appreciating the families and cultures with respect and sensitivity.
4. Authentic inclusion of children	Valuing curriculum that is sensitive to all children, avoiding separate add-on activities.
5. Observation and assessment—basis	Using observation and assessment as the basis for curriculum planning.
6. Professional accountability	Continuous professional and development experiences review to ensure that program goals support fundaments for Early Education and maintain a balance of activities to meet the needs of enrolled children.

important ideas for quality Early Childhood programs. Together these organized ideas and concepts direct the core of Early Childhood curriculum as presented throughout these pages and is based on interrelated factors, not on isolated systems and events. Ideas about child development should be connected with the planning of children's activities.

Defining Early Childhood Education Terms

Students will learn that the field of Early Childhood recognizes common words that carry different meanings. A simple word such as *theme* causes varied reactions among professionals. Some professionals use the word *theme* to describe an acceptable approach to curriculum. Perceived differences may be a matter of title or word use, or may be real differences in concept and program implementation.

Within a given center or program for young children, the staff and administrators must first agree on the definition of words commonly used. Is the equipment to be placed in the housekeeping corner, doll corner, Dramatic Play area, or Creative Dramatics section of the classroom? The area that is visualized may in fact be the same physical space. It is reasonable to agree also that the area may be referred to with different terms, keeping in mind the importance of communicating clearly to young children.

Professionals in Early Childhood combine terms from research and studies of child development, psychology, educational psychology, and health and medical practices with elements of child care, education, and nursery school experiences. The outcome results in new concepts and theories about behavior and learning.

The Importance of the Early Experiences

Development is about change. Understanding development is understanding how children change over time in their physical, behavioral, and thinking characteristics. "To teach young children well you must study children" (Hymes, 1969, p. 71). Documentation regarding the early childhood years indicates that it is important for all development that follows (Bloom, 1981, p. 67). Recent discoveries regarding the wiring of the brain and critical periods of development validate the significance of the early childhood years, and there is renewed interest in the child's environment and the type of nurturing given (Lindsey, 1998/99, p. 97). Past knowledge is being united with new insights gathered with technologies that allow scientists to study the brain in noninvasive ways. These studies have shown that the brain is affected, not just influenced, by environmental

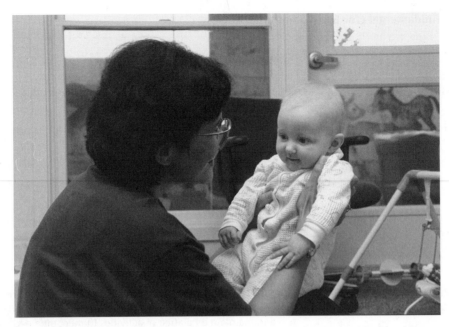

Very young children need nurturing from their caregivers to ensure critical healthy development.

conditions. The environment, beginning before birth, actually determines how the circuitry of each child's brain forms (Shore, 1997, pp. 7, 15, 21).

The youngest children need nurturing and responsive relationships with their primary caregivers during prime times to ensure critical healthy development. The effects of these findings are important to child development and Early Childhood Education. A study by the Family and Work Institute documented that children will more likely attach securely to a child care provider who has completed effective training (Shore, 1977, pp. 27, 60). Research results released by the National Institute of Child Health and Human Development identified that quality child care during the early years, with high levels of positive interaction between the children and caregivers, actually improves the quality of mother-child interactions. The quality of care influences the learning abilities of very young children by affecting their cognitive development and their use of language as well as their interactions and relationships (NICHD, 1997).

Understanding the development of young children has many advantages. The teacher benefits because knowledge increases the teacher's ability to identify childhood learning processes. The teacher becomes capable of identifying these processes for individual children and for specific groups of children. When common and individual learning processes are identified, curriculum for

young children can be appropriately planned. In this way, knowing what children are like, what they do, and how they behave becomes the key consideration for curriculum planning (Cohen, 1972, pp. 24–25).

PROGRAM PERSPECTIVES AND PRACTICES

The visitor described in the Curriculum Profile left the observation area with several questions: Who organizes and plans the activities? Who decides what materials will be placed outside and what materials will be offered inside? How can anyone make so many decisions? The decisions about Early Childhood curriculum will be determined by many factors or program characteristics. For example, the declared purpose of the program narrows the way in which the characteristics influence the experiences planned for young children. Characteristics such as the grouping of children, program philosophies, and goals influence how and what is planned for a program. The learning environment and scheduling formats also influence curriculum-related choices. Staffing is another important aspect of children's programs that influences how curricula take shape. Programs relate directly and indirectly to school models, both models that are popular in Early Childhood now and those that

FIGURE 1–5   Major Theoretical Perspectives

Behavioral	Maintains that environment is carefully controlled and designed to shape the child's behavior. Conditioning such as reinforcement is thought to increase a given behavior. Behavior modification and social-learning concepts are associated with this learning theory.
Cognitive	Describes mental process related to how children develop ability for thinking, logic, and problem solving. Cognitive development refers to changes that occur in stages.
Developmental	Defines child's behavior and sets forth age-range expectations. Child learns through interaction of maturing abilities and environmental opportunities.
Ecological	Child's interaction with family and community within environment cause development.
Maturational	Principles are directed by hereditary factors. Focus on normative characteristics of children and the natural unfolding of behavior.
Psychodynamic	Psychodynamic theory, also called psychoanalytic theory, focuses on psychological characteristics, including personality and emotions. It emphasizes childhood experiences that shape and steer later social behavior and adjustment.

were popular in the past. Trends in Early Childhood practices also influence how and what activities for young children are offered.

Theories Influence Curricula

There are many descriptions about how children develop and learn. The descriptions and explanations vary greatly, and therefore so does the interpretation of a child's behavior. Does a child learn by observing? Does a child learn by responding? Do we know that learning has taken place by observing a child's behavior?

A theory, or particular ideology, explains and predicts the behavior of children. A theory is a collection of ideas, concepts, terms, and statements blended to illustrate behavior. A theory about children gathers concepts and terms to also predict behavior during childhood. There are numerous theories to explain and predict how children behave and learn, and some of them are complementary. Others have contradictory views, and some have many perspectives. Awareness of the basic **theoretical perspectives** (Figure 1–5) will help you to begin to interpret research and apply specific notions about young children. You need to understand that the major theoretical perspectives affect the planning and organization of children's activities.

Jean Piaget's theories and extensive writings about the mental processes of young children gained acceptance among Early Childhood educators. His theory would be classified primarily within the cognitive theoretical perspective, although this stage theory also satisfies the developmental perspective. He emphasized that as preschool-age children mature, they develop thinking connections bit by bit through related and repeated experiences. If you accept Piaget's theory, as a teacher of young children you will provide materials for investigation and conversation to encourage learning. Children's knowledge of the world, Piaget said, lies in their actions (Piaget, 1955, p. 39). A teacher following Piaget's insight will arrange the setting and materials to allow children to actively engage in the activities, encouraging exploration and discovery. An activity titled "Planting Seeds" (Curriculum Activity Guide 2 [CAG]) does just that.

Another theorist, Lev Vygotsky, suggested that children learn by building and layering ideas through social and cultural experiences. A teacher would maximize learning, according to Vygotsky's theory, by offering children opportunities to learn a concept in a variety of ways, especially through communication with adults and other children. Social experience is the tool for mental activity and cooperative learning (Berk, 1994, p. 30). Vygotsky suggested that teachers help children to discover what adults already know, with emphasis on verbal interaction. This directs children toward higher levels of thinking that they might not achieve on their own (Dworetzky, 1996, p. 299). A teacher will guide children to higher levels by arranging for collaborative experiences, particularly with children of different ages. Vygotsky's theory would support the idea of suggesting to children that they find a solution for the growing litter problem on the school's street.

Dr. Maria Montessori's perspective of children has significantly influenced Early Childhood Education. The **Montessori Method,** recognized around the world since Dr. Maria Montessori opened the first Children's House in Rome in 1907, underlies most early childhood strategies practiced today. The primary feature of the Montessori educational approach is to focus on the needs and spontaneous interests of individual children, which she distinguished to be different from those of adults. Montessori detailed a philosophy of child development with a rationale for guidance of young children, ages zero to six. The Montessori Method advises that observation of children provides important insight for teachers to be able to anticipate their needs and desired choices. The Montessori Method also suggests that young children absorb learning during the early, sensitive periods of their development in environments that allow freedom to select purposeful experiences. When children are allowed to direct their own activities and proceed at their natural rate of progress in prepared settings, they learn by doing and further their potential for growth (Orem, 1974, p. 97). Specifically, Montessori stressed that "the primary aim of the new education is the discovery and freeing of the child" (Montessori, 1966, p. 110). She stated that "the first thing to be done, therefore, is to discover the true nature of a child and then assist him in his normal development" (Montessori, 1966, p. 137).

Although Montessori schools may differ, the environments typically meet the individual needs of young children with careful observation of children "at work" and by grouping children of different ages. The proportioned furniture used by Montessori schools increases opportunities for children to become absorbed in their work. Montessori teachers guide with appreciation for the children's sensitive periods of development, recognizing that children will have high interest and the ability to acquire language during their early years. The planned environment offers experiences for children with great emphasis on learning through senses and movement. "How does a child," she asked, "starting with nothing orient himself in this complicated world? How does he come to distinguish things, and by what marvelous means does he come to learn a language in all its minute details?" (1966, p. 39.)

Debate among theorists regarding how children best learn concepts will continue. Careful observation of the effects of Early Childhood practices on children lead to acceptance and implementation of some theories and rejection of others. Research studies and reaction from those that work directly with children—the teachers—will inspire renewed debate with advice to the teaching professional regarding learning opportunities for young children. Continuation of study and experiences with children increases understanding of child growth and development. Knowing how children learn provides the Early Childhood teacher with the tools for developing appropriate curriculum.

The major ideological bases appear to fall within groups, yet no two educational references agree on the way that the theories are categorized. Dr. Lillian Katz, in *Talks with Teachers* (1977, p. 73), recommends continual review of learning theories because of the strong effect many theories have within the field. A widely accepted understanding, combination, or eclectic approach calls for teachers to take the best for the children in their classroom from theories and to blend them to create an applicable ideology (Figure 1–5).

Types of Programs

The terms *child development center, preschool, child care, nursery school, latchkey,* and *early learning center* are references to programs or schools for young children. The title of a school may provide a clue to identifying the purpose of a program, the **type of program,** and the curriculum. The title can also be misleading. Programs with similar titles may not necessarily have the same purpose nor offer similar benefits and curricula. Some provide child care, some provide opportunities for learning, and some provide both care and learning. Schools and facilities for preschoolers accomplish their purpose in many ways. Some programs offer care and/or learning in homes, some in centers, and some on employee work sites. Some programs offer care and/or learning to infants and toddlers, some to preschoolers, and some to school-age children before and after school. There is a great variety in the types of programs and the ways in which professionals categorize these offerings.

Opportunities in early care and learning of children result from societal needs, creating great variation in program types. Although types of programs are difficult to categorize, some types are readily apparent and offer a foundation for appreciating the variety of ways in which professionals meet the prevailing needs of children (Figure 1–6).

FIGURE 1–6 Eight Types of Programs for Young Children

Child Care	Operated by public agencies, community, and private for-profit businesses. Child care offered to larger groups of children while parents are employed or are in training. Often called day care for children for half or full day. Many center-based programs provide learning opportunities. States vary in licensing and regulation requirements. Federal government sets minimum requirements.
Cooperative	Cooperation and participation of parents is the core component of cooperatives. Some cooperatives are sponsored by school districts. A trained director-teacher is hired to facilitate children's program and parent education. Parents also cooperate in informal play groups where the primary purpose is to have the children and adults interact.
Employer-supported	Companies support child care for young children in a variety of ways: on-site centers, paying for child care costs, reserving spaces in community centers, hiring of a professional in Early Childhood to refer and approve appropriate facilities. Corporations have documented the benefits to employer and employees. The United States military operates the largest network of employer-supported child care.
Enrichment/compensatory	Head Start, the icon in enrichment programs, was established in 1965 by the federal government to provide opportunities for low-income children. This program was established to offer compensatory opportunities to children whose circumstances limited their experiences. There are other enrichment programs. Some focus on language development, especially when English is the second language for children.
Faith-based	Religions support programs for young children in the private sector. Some faith-based programs introduce children early to their religious doctrines. Churches and synagogues also provide day nurseries for children whose parents either work or are unable to care for the children during the day. Day-of-worship child care has been traditionally offered by many religions.
Family child care	More children in the United States receive child care in private homes other than their own than any other form of child care arrangement. The setting can replicate a child's own home and provide individual attention. There is great variation in licensing and regulation requirements.
Preschool/nursery	Accommodates preschoolers ages two-and-a-half to kindergarten age. Still referred to as the traditional nursery school offering a half-day program that zooms in on young children's development in affective areas, especially social development and independent abilities. Curriculum is offered during schedules with open blocks of time for free play with choices of child-initiated and teacher-directed activities.
Training/lab	Campus child care/training facilities have changed with the evolution of Early Childhood Education. Many early nursery schools initiated at universities created the path that programs today follow. Today many colleges offer training laboratories that meet both the college parent-student needs for child care and support courses in Early Childhood Education, observation, and practicum.

ESSENTIAL CONSIDERATIONS

When we look at what is valuable as we develop curriculum for young children we find that programs of quality meet the needs of the enrolled children with standards of quality and appreciation for diversity. The standards for quality are defined within the framework of best and developmentally appropriate practices (Kagan, 1997, p. 56). The apparent alliance growing among educators and parents contributes to the well-being of children and therefore becomes an essential consideration in Early Childhood Education. Teachers know that the connections with families and communities strengthen connections with and enhance appreciation for inclusion of the many cultures, languages, and religions in the daily program planning for children. The probability of strengthening connections increases with increasing recognition for harmony, equity, and respect.

Best Practices for Quality Programs

The movement for developmentally appropriate curriculum and **best practices** spread in response to concerns about elementary school class work that was increasingly thrust upon preschool-age children. This trend accelerated in the 1970s, requiring young children to work at their desks completing endless supplies of dittoed assignments, pressuring them to be ready for kindergarten. The National Association for the Education of Young Children emphasized instead the knowledge of child development and relations between the home and program (Bredekamp & Copple, 1997, p. 17). The concept of **best practices** calls for appropriate environments and appropriate hands-on activities that foster optimal growth of each child enrolled. The notion of **developmentally appropriate practices** (DAP) encourages appropriate ex-

pectations, appropriate environments, and appropriate experiential activities that foster optimum growth. Choice and flexibility are encouraged to accommodate each child's developmental level (Bredekamp, 1987, pp. 2–3). Studies have validated the importance of DAP, noting that hands-on, experiential curriculum reduces stress-related behavior, such as fear and anxiety (Burts, Hart, Charlesworth, & Kirk, 1990, p. 407).

Strengthening Connections: Harmony, Equity, Respect

Another important consideration is the need to strengthen connections among all those who contribute to and participate in programs for children. Each child comes to a setting of care and learning with a foundation influenced by their family and community. The familial influences contribute to the way a child approaches new experiences and people. Family expectations and values further direct perceptions of what is considered to be appropriate child behavior. There may be variation between parental and staff expectations regarding child-rearing practices (Bhavnagri & Gonzalez-Mena, 1997, p. 2). Parents and staff members may differ in their view of when a child should acquire a skill, or when a child should make friends or begin to write.

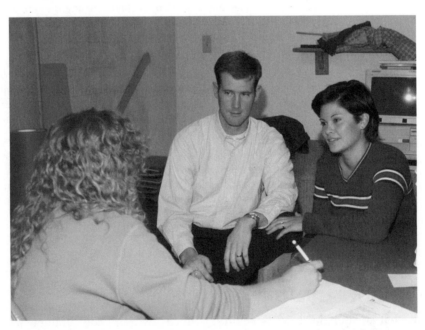

Early Childhood Education teachers need to prepare a curriculum that is responsive to family expectations.

For these reasons, teachers need to prepare curriculum that is responsive to the great diversity of homes and communities. This calls on staff to support **harmony, equity,** and **respect** in their school settings. This also requires that we model peaceful interactions, respect each other's customs, listen to and learn about each other's languages and religions, and appreciate our diverse family customs and situations. There are binding commonalities among families worldwide. Grasp these threads of similarities as you appreciate diversity.

Teachers desiring to strengthen connections will offer sensitive and relevant curriculum to help children enrolled in their programs achieve their full potential. It is beneficial to authentically represent and include all children appropriately. The words *all children* must be understood to accept and include children with abilities and disabilities, from families who identify with a particular race or ethnicity, and those who self-identify with more than one group. There is need to respect the religions and faiths of families. When teachers positively and authentically include "all children" they show high regard for each child because children's identities are formed by gender, capabilities, individuality, and the social circumstances of their families and communities. Acceptance is therefore encapsulated within the concept of **authentic inclusion.** It is authentic inclusion that will promote harmony, equity, and respect by building on the anti-bias and multicultural curriculum to achieve culturally affirming programs for children and families. This approach integrates anti-bias experiences into the whole curriculum rather than adding on activities to achieve bias-free settings. The Network of Educators of the Americas is a nonprofit organization that is promoting peace, justice, and human rights. This nonprofit group promotes equitable relationships among children, families, staff, and community (Boyd, 1998, p. 33). Recognition, representation, and inclusion of children must closely and consistently represent American cultures within this diverse American society (Gollnick & Chinn, 1990, p. 15). Teachers need to fully appreciate the identity of each child—smaller, with a different way of thinking and feeling—and recognize commonalities and welcome differences.

REVIEW

The term *curriculum* refers to all the experiences that affect a child while interacting in a school setting. Skills in curriculum planning increase when teachers complete course work. Planning empowers teachers to offer appropriate, hands-on activities that actively engage the child. Curriculum planning benefits children and teachers and establishes stability and security, balances the types of experiences for children, and increases the interaction between the children and teachers.

Basic ideas about how children learn and think drives the type of curriculum offered, as does the theoretical perspective of the staff. Definitions and terms within the field of Early Childhood Education vary, yet there is wide agreement about the importance of the early years of children's development.

There are essential considerations in Early Childhood that contribute to the quality of programs for children. Both the concept of "best practices" and the encouragement of harmony, equity, and respect contribute to valuable programming for young children.

KEY TERMS

authentic inclusion
best practices
curriculum
developmentally
   appropriate
   practices
Early Childhood
   Education
equity

experiences
fundamentals
harmony
Montessori Method
respect
technology
theoretical
   perspectives
type of program

RESPOND

1. Collect two brochures from Early Childhood programs. Read each brochure to identify the curriculum program offered at each school. List two features of the curriculum described that you would consider using in your own program and explain why.
2. Review the Fundamentals for Early Childhood. Select one and write a one-page essay regarding the concept. Document the essay with at least two references from other books, research studies, or Web sites.
3. Check the list of program types (Figure 1–5) and select one for visitation. Call to arrange an interview with the director or one of the teachers. Develop a list of six questions about curriculum to ask during the interview. Prepare a two-page paper summarizing the responses to the interview questions.

4. Assess one of the following Web sites on the Internet. Describe the information available on this Web site which will contribute to your knowledge about authentic inclusion:

Adoptive Families of America

http://www.adoptivefam.org/

Native American Resources on the Internet

http://hanksville.org/NAresources

March of Dimes

http://www.modimes.org/

REFERENCES

Barnhart, C. L., & Barnhart, R. K. (Eds.). (1990). *The world book dictionary* (Vol. 1). Chicago: World Book.

Berk, L. E. (1994). Vygotsky's theory: The importance of make-believe play. *Young Children, 50*(1), 30–38.

Bhavnagri, N. P., & Gonzalez-Mena, J. (1997). The cultural context of infant caregiving. *Childhood Education, 74*, 2–8.

Bloom, B. (1981). *All our children learning.* New York: McGraw-Hill.

Boyd, B. F. (1998). A guide to multicultural education. *Childhood Education, 75*(1), 33.

Bredekamp, S. (Ed.). (1987). *Developmentally appropriate practice in early childhood programs serving children from birth through age 8.* (Expanded edition). Washington, DC: National Association for the Education of Young Children.

Bredekamp, S., & Copple, C. E. (Eds.). (1997). *Developmentally appropriate practice in early childhood program serving children from birth through age 8* (Rev. ed.). Washington, DC: National Association for the Education of Young Children.

Burts, D. C., Hart, C. H., Charlesworth, R., & Kirk, L. (1990). A comparison of stress behaviors observed in classrooms with developmentally appropriate versus developmentally inappropriate instructional practice. *Early Childhood Research Quarterly, 5,* 407–423.

Cohen, D. H. (1972). *The learning child: Guidelines for parents and teachers.* New York: Pantheon.

Dworetzky, J. P. (1996). *Introduction to child development* (6th ed.). St. Paul, MN: West.

Gollnick, D. M., & Chinn, P. C. (1990). *Multicultural education in a pluralistic society* (3rd ed.). New York: Merrill.

Hanna, L. (1972). Meeting the challenge. In B. C. Mills (Ed.), *Understanding the young child and his curriculum* (pp. 230–239). New York: Macmillan.

Hymes, J. L. (1969). *Early childhood education.* Washington, DC: National Association for the Education of Young Children.

Katz, L. G. (1977). *Talks with teachers: Reflections on early childhood education.* Washington, DC: National Association for the Education of Young Children.

Levin, J. A. (1996). Research summary: Educational electronic networks. *Educational Leadership, 54*(3), 46–50.

Lindsey, G. (1998/99). Brain research and implications. *Childhood Education, 75*(2), 97.

Montessori, M. (1966). *The secret of childhood.* New York: Fides.

National Institute of Child Health and Human Development. (1997, April 3). *Results of NICHD study of early child care reported at Society for Research in Child Development meeting, 1–6* [On-line]. Available http://www.hih.gov/nichd/html/news/rel4top.htm.

Orem, R. C. (Ed.). (1974). *Montessori: Her method and the movement—What you need to know.* New York: Capricorn Books—Putnam's Sons.

Piaget, J. (1955). *The language and thought of the child.* New York: Meridian Books.

Shade, D. D. (1996). Software education. *Young Children, 51*(6), 17–21.

Shore, R. (1997). *Rethinking the brain: New insights into early development.* New York: Families and Work Institute.

CHAPTER 2

Considering Children's Needs: *Skills Developing During Early Childhood*

Curriculum Profile

Three preschoolers run across the grass, past the raised garden beds, to the shaded area under the large tree. You look at the reference album in front of you holding each enrolled child's picture and name. You recheck your assignment for the college observation course. The assignment indicates that you are to record the behavior and language of three children who are engaging in the same activity at the child development center. You are to record behavior for sixty seconds.

Lee, Martin, and Justin participated for sixty seconds in different activities. The written observations indicate different levels of activity, different language expressions, and different physical behaviors. Initially, it appeared that the boys are different ages, that they're at different developmental levels, and that each has achieved different levels of physical skills. One sixty-second observation does not begin to document precise understanding about development. However, there is one comparable attribute about the three

Lee	Martin	Justin
Runs to climbing structure.	Slides down climbing structure slide holding hands on side.	Standing by climbing structure watching Lee.
Leaps up the ladder using every other rung.	Lands on sand with bottom hitting first.	Leans on slide.
Pounds his hands on chest and yells, "I'm here, I'm great."	Leans over, pushes himself up with both hands.	Holds hands over sand before pressing them into sand.
Runs to opposite slide with hands in air.	Rubs hands together, trying to remove sand. Wipes hands on pants.	Raises eyebrows and watches when Lee shouts.
Lands backward.	Walks quickly to just abandoned tricycle. Looks at child who just got off.	Follows Martin to the tricycle path walking side of path.
Stands up, walks backward to end of sanded area surrounding structure.	Mounts tricycle, pushes pedals.	Watches Lee moving toward fence.
Stands up, walks backward to end of sanded area surrounding structure.	Moves rapidly down path to gas station fuel tank.	
Falls backward, legs raised, laughs.		
Looks around, fixes on teacher hanging butcher paper on fence.		
Calls out, "I want to, I want to . . ."		

preschoolers. All three boys are three years and eleven months old. Their behaviors are different even though they are the same age chronologically.

Chapter Outline

Study Guide

As you study the sections in this chapter you should be able to:

- Examine how children's needs are met in an Early Childhood program.
- Become familiar with the ways children develop skills.
- Learn the Developmental Focus areas.
- Compare and evaluate individually appropriate, developmentally appropriate, and age appropriate.
- Identify the importance for ongoing assessment of children's needs and skills.

WHAT YOU NEED TO KNOW TO MEET CHILDREN'S NEEDS

Children of all ages move and behave uniquely. You read about three children, Lee, Martin, and Justin, in the Curriculum Profile. The observer recorded different levels of activity, different language expressions, and different physical behaviors. These preschoolers are the same chronological age, yet they move and act individually. Children grow physically at a rapid pace during early childhood. Beginning with a baby's active **exploration,** acquisition of skills continues throughout the preschool years. The manner and timing of the acquisition of skills follows a distinct pattern unique for each child.

Each Child is an Individual

Have you ever wondered why some children are so different from their parents or their siblings? Four-year-old Jason has blond hair and blue eyes and holds his little sister's hand as they enter the preschool. Emily's big dark brown eyes shine against her black hair and olive skin. Have you ever wondered how your life now would be different if your living arrangements were different while you were growing up? These questions challenge researchers to continue the quest to establish to what degree our heredity influences who we are and to what degree our families and environments continue to influence us.

As a teacher of young children, you will marvel at each child as an individual. You will appreciate that each child's **development**—the sequence of changes and patterns of his growth—is his own. Temperament, reaction, and level of **curiosity** all contribute to the child's own way of participating. The child's rate of growth is also a factor in the child's individuality. Most children who are about the same age follow a similar sequence in development. However, the timing of specific achievements, such as crawling and reading, is highly individual (Cohen, 1972, p. 175). This means that Hector might begin to walk at nine months but Marc might not take his first solo steps until sixteen months. The norm indicates that the majority of children begin to walk at twelve months. Both Hector and Marc are within the normal range for walking but also demonstrate individualized behaviors. Development of specific abilities can occur within a span of two years, from one year preceding the age to one year beyond (Read, Gardner, & Mahler, 1993, p. 61).

The Concept of the Whole Child

Although we look at each child as an individual, each child develops as a whole person. Reference to the concept of the **whole child** by educators and caregivers indicates that there is interest in supporting the development of the child in all areas of growth. There are various ways to divide these areas of growth in order to examine the outcome of research studies related to that particular aspect of development. Information within this textbook is organized into three major areas of development: physical, affective and aesthetic, and cognitive and language. A more thorough examination of these areas of development will be covered in the next section.

DEVELOPMENTAL FOCUS AREAS

Look at photographs from your childhood. They show rapid physical development as you developed skill in rolling over and walking. You became capable of recognizing people, and within a few years you could point to your printed name. You developed your emotional and social skills and thinking abilities.

Early Childhood teachers and child development specialists find that it is easier to understand the behavior of children when the areas of development are categorized into major groups such as physical development, social and emotional development, and cognitive development. The identification of these **Developmental Focus areas** helps to facilitate the study of child growth and behavior in order to study and comprehend a large and increasing volume of knowledge about young children.

Knowledge about child development has modified over time with the continuing influences of current events, findings from interdisciplinary research, and changes in accepted teaching practices. There is a consistent and growing body of knowledge that many child development professionals agree on and incorporate into their teaching practices. However, caution is necessary before we apply the research compiled in references. We should not assume that there is universal acceptance and applicability of child development theory (Bhavnagri & Gonzalez-Mena, 1997, p. 3).

Categorizing areas of development helps Early Childhood teachers and child development specialists gather information about children to more effectively focus on specific behaviors and other needs of children. Focusing on developmental areas allows effective identification of the needs of the whole child. Development does not occur in one area. Children develop physically, affectively and aesthetically, and cognitively with language, with predictable sequences within each domain (Figure 2–1).

Physical Development

Physical development is the dimension of growth that relates to basic physiological changes such as height, weight, and motor capabilities. Biosocial development, another term used to reference this aspect of growth, emphasizes the contributions of the contextual aspects. A child's heredity and environment and the reciprocal interaction of people in that environment work together to influence the outcome of physical development.

Children ages three to five generally are in motion, and that is what makes them so observable. They are developing rapidly during the preschool years, although more slowly than in the first two years of their lives. Young children are capable of many physical activities. They are using their large muscles—walking, running, climbing, pedaling, and throwing. They are developing dexterity by

FIGURE 2–1   Developmental Focus Areas

Area	Description	Also referred to as
Physical	Basic physiological changes such as height, weight, and motor skills.	Biosocial
Affective and aesthetic	Affective: changes in psychological, social, emotional abilities, personality and relationships. Aesthetic: includes artistic and expressive characteristics, sensorial awareness.	Psychological Social Emotional Creative
Cognitive and language	Mental abilities including language; *cognitive* is derived from a Latin word meaning "to know."	Mental Intellectual Thinking

participating in both group and solitary play settings. Coordination, balance, and control matures, increasing a child's movement participation. Inviting children to pour, dig, place, hold, stack, reach, and assemble improves their small motor abilities and helps them develop small muscles. Positive outcomes in large and small motor experiences leads to self-confidence in the mastery of movement.

The sequence of fine motor development will signal readiness for drawing and writing. The children's daily accomplishments are observable: holding the faucet long enough to get a drink of water; finally hooking the bottom of the jacket to begin the zip; holding the hand steady enough for

Young children are capable of many physical activities.

the guinea pig to nibble the feed. Healthy children develop positive attitudes when participation in physical activity is a positive experience. Teachers who are patient and encouraging facilitate children's confidence for approaching physical tasks. Modifications of materials and experiences or alternative activities are necessary for inclusion of children with disabilities that will allow their participation to the greatest degree possible. Modifications will then facilitate their potential to be maximized.

Children need daily opportunities to engage their large and small movement muscles. They need many chances to experience their bodies and senses. Experiences that encourage balance, spatial relations, and directions match well with children's needs. Opportunities to engage the senses, particularly hearing, seeing, and touching, promote perceptual-motor development. For example, when a teacher traces a child's body and names the parts of the body, the child hears the teacher's words, feels her hand, and perceives her own body in a different way (Curriculum Activity Guide 3).

Early care and learning professionals provide optimum activities to support physical health and safety. Programs are arranged for children to develop self-help skills such as washing, toileting, dressing, and eating. Lessons regarding personal and public safety extend learning about physical capabilities.

Affective and Aesthetic Development

Affective development of young children encompasses growth and changes in social and emotional behaviors. **Aesthetic development** refers to awareness and sensorial responsiveness to beauty and

Participation in group settings expose children to different languages, values, and expectations.

the surroundings. Although there is overlap among the characteristics of affective and aesthetic development, each benefits children's development in unique ways.

Affective development is related to the dimensions of sociability, emotions, and feelings. Included within this developmental domain are characteristics such as temperament and personality, attachment and autonomy, trust, self-esteem, and self-confidence. Other behavioral aspects of affective development include interactions and reactions, prosocial abilities, and gender and role identity. Children's emotions and reactions to circumstances provide an indication of their feelings, their likes and dislikes, and their attitudes. Some children readily adjust to new situations and people. Other children may have difficulty separating from their parents or primary caregivers. Contextual experiences—influenced by family, siblings, community, religion, economic level, ethnicity, and gender role expectations—contribute to the child's social and emotional identity. During early childhood, the socialization process expands beyond the home to child-care and education settings, where children encounter adults other than their parents and family members. Participation in group settings exposes children to different expectations, values, and languages. As they spend more time with other children, their peers, they will potentially acquire a variety of social skills that help them to become a group participant. Teachers guide the development

of skills such as listening, waiting, sharing, and problem solving as they nurture children's interaction in an extended group setting, thereby influencing children's social and emotional behaviors.

The basic elements of aesthetic development are sensitivity and responsiveness to beauty in our surroundings, especially of nature and art. The development of aesthetic awareness emerges when children feel pleasure in their expressions, find new ways to enjoy tasks, use their imaginations, and explore new and different objects. The potential for creative appreciation and expression is greatest for children in programs that plan ways for them to express themselves. The word *aesthetics* actually has to do with responding to our environment through our senses. Through contact with the environment there are great possibilities for children to enjoy and wonder (Haskell, 1979, p. 5). Using all or some of the senses allows children to develop preferences for color, form, shape, and sound. As children wonder, explore, and discover they enhance their sensorial skills to discriminate the features in their surroundings.

Program philosophy and guidelines direct the staff to form curriculum to meet the children's affective and aesthetic development needs by planning experiences for preschoolers with emphasis on social, emotional, and sensorial skills. Activities that help the child feel secure and welcomed enable them to separate, adjust, and expand their social interactions. Giving children opportunities to make independent choices increases feelings of trust, confidence, identification, and understanding of inclusion (Curriculum Activity Guide 4 [CAG]). Self-directed activities promote competence and pleasure in self-expression. Using some or all of the senses to participate in art media allows explorative and creative abilities to unfold. An activity about the colors found naturally in the outdoors increases awareness of colors in nature (Curriculum Activity Guide 5 [CAG]). Curriculum encouraging non-bias experiences offers chances for a program to promote experiences that are authentically inclusive.

Cognitive and Language Development

Cognitive development relates to knowledge and how it is acquired. This category of growth includes mental abilities and language acquisition. Other descriptive phases of the cognitive Developmental Focus area include thinking and mental abilities, memory and logic, intellectual growth, conceptualizing, language, creativity and divergent thinking, language, literacy, and communication.

Human infants are born actively seeking information. The inquisitive behavior and the innate reflexes help babies interact with their environment. Babies' senses give them information (sensation) that they then process (perception), acquiring beginning knowledge (cognition). Very young children understand objects in terms of their own action on objects. There is a cumulative advantage to learning associated with well-planned activities that permit the children to go on to something else, sustaining their intrinsic motive for learning (Bruner, 1960, pp. 6–7). There is consensus that appropriate settings filled with experiences that have relevance to children's lives and capabilities, enhance learning. Healthy preschool children are curious and motivated to investigate new experiences.

Focused language skills, a critical part of cognitive development, point to the importance of activities emphasizing abilities to listen (Curriculum Activity Guide 6 [CAG]), express, and verbally communicate. Language and communication skills are the avenue for social contact. Home languages of the children must be recognized to be more than simply a way to talk and communicate. The language of the home and community is the way that children express knowledge about their reality, their communities, and their families (Elkin & Handel, 1989, p. 46). Listening and responding to languages allow us to understand the thinking and feelings of the children.

SKILL DEVELOPMENT: A PROCESS

You have read that each child is an individual developing as a whole person and learned that development can be categorized within three major focus

A drive for independence, exploration, and curiosity motivates this child toward building new skills.

areas. Now, look back at the Curriculum Profile at the beginning of this chapter. You read about three children, Lee, Martin, and Justin. Lee leaped up the ladder. Martin slid down the climbing structure slide holding his hands on the sides. Justin stood by the climbing structure watching Lee. Three different children, the same age, participating at different activity levels in the same outdoor environment. When did Lee learn to leap? How did Martin know to hold his hands on the side of the slide? Why did Justin watch Lee? Review of the children's enrollment information and additional observation could provide answers; however, it is more important that we understand that the behavior of the three boys is appropriate. Each preschooler progresses along a path of his own, acquiring new and more complex skills. Children in a preschool setting, two years through five years of age, gain abilities by watching, listening, imitating, interacting, and playing.

Observation provides records of children's progress, abilities, energy, and needs. A developmental profile, required in some Head Start and state-funded programs by the third month of enrollment, is one method used to evaluate behavior and capabilities of a child. By knowing a child's capabilities staff can plan opportunities to balance experiences that facilitate continued, positive expansion of skills. A child is able to progress in a comfortable environment that offers satisfying, safe, and interesting experiences.

Reasonable Expectations

A child pushes the pedal down on the tricycle with great determination. Another child walks around and around the blanket trying to smooth each corner, while a third stacks the blocks repeatedly to balance the geometric shapes. The longer you interact and observe children, the more you see how common, basic characteristics of childhood are revealed. Healthy children are determined to master the challenges in their environment. Determination encourages children who are curious and eager to explore and strive for independent mobility. There are developmental milestones that children reach in the early childhood stage. For example, Trisha balances on the walking beam. Gilbert pedals the two-wheel bike. Jamal unzips his jacket. Your familiarity with capabilities and patterns of growth that normally occur in certain stages helps you predict and expect behavior. A reasonable **expectation** of children's behavior leads to appropriate curriculum planning.

Descriptions of children's behaviors, illustrating typical traits and patterns of physical growth and development, are available as a result of the early efforts of Arnold Gesell. He focused primarily on the genetically determined developmental sequences of growth (Etaugh & Rathus, 1995, p. 41). The charts provide developmental schedules of motor behavior, adaptive or problem-solving behavior, language, and personal-social behavior considered to be normal for the age, the stage, or transition.

Developing Skills

Curiosity, exploration, and drive for independence motivate the children toward building skills. Children are born with innate biological capacities. As they mature they develop these capacities—physically, socially, emotionally, and cognitively. Children develop particular skills because their abilities develop as they mature and interact in an environment. You were born with the ability to speak a language. You developed the skill to speak Korean, Spanish, English, and so on (Figure 2–2). There are many more languages, and you might be fortunate to have developed skills in more than one language.

Skills are developed abilities in body movement, thinking, and social and emotional behaviors (Figure 2–3). As children mature, they acquire physical skills, affective skills, and cognitive skills and become more independent. They begin to unbutton their own sweaters, recognize their name in print, and gain self-confidence. When Shelly begins pedaling the two-wheel bike she rides with her friends around the path. Her skill in sociability increases along with the motor achievement of pedaling a two-wheel bike.

Children attain new and diversified abilities as they grow and change. Their brains mature and

FIGURE 2–2   An Ability Becomes a Skill

Ability ——▶	Skill
Innate/biological Occurs with maturation	Develops Influenced by environment
You were born with the ability to speak a language.	*You developed the skill to speak Korean, Spanish, English, and so on.*

FIGURE 2–3   Developing Skills

A skill is a developed ability in body movement
A skill is a developed ability in social/emotional behavior
A skill is a developed ability in thinking

their bodies change, causing development of movement, sociability, and thinking. There is great variability among children. Maturational progress takes place, and changes occur in the ability to control the head, torso, legs, feet, arms, hands, and fingers. A healthy body allows a child to participate and interact. Participation, interaction, and practice increase opportunities to develop added proficiency in the development of skills.

Your role is to focus on developing abilities, the innate capacities of children, so that you can enhance their developing skills. The acquisition of skills illustrates a sequence of behaviors. The child has opportunities to master a skill that will open up new options for acquiring additional skills. For example, three-year-old Sun begins to jump after watching other children for several days. She moves her feet up and down throughout the week during snack, sitting, standing, watching the fish bowl, and petting the guinea pig. Sun begins to jump to music while playing in the outside music/movement area. The next week Sun is seen jumping while she is hanging her jacket in the activity room, during a mural-painting activity, and while approaching the snack table (Curriculum Activity Guide 7 [CAG]).

APPROPRIATE: DEVELOPMENTALLY, CULTURALLY, AND LINGUISTICALLY

Teachers who are sensitive to young children plan appropriate experiences to promote their development. The word *appropriate* implies that an activity is suitable for the enrolled children. The suitability of a particular activity is dependent on many factors. Early Childhood educators need to understand the development of children, including the variations that occur during these early years (Bredekamp & Copple, 1997, p. 9). This will be the way we will know how to plan curriculum that is appropriately designed to authentically include all

children coming from diverse backgrounds and with special needs.

A child is an individual with certain abilities and skills. Each child has an age, temperament, pattern of growth, family culture, and language. We build activities that are suitable for early childhood when we consider the child as this individual with many characteristics.

Developmentally Appropriate

Young children are individuals. Some are active, some quiet. You see differences among them in their size, appearance, activity level, and maturity. You can see the differences between three-year-olds and four-year-olds. Five-year-olds are all the same age but demonstrate dissimilar capabilities.

The emphasis on age is significant in our society and is an important part of everyone's identity. "How old are you?" is a frequent inquiry filled with anticipation of expected behaviors. The expectations for specific behaviors are age-related. A child's chronological age is the numerical indicator that marks the child's number of years since birth. The chronological age provides a hint to a broad range of behaviors and skills that may occur during a particular age. However, each child follows a sequential direction of growth that is distinct. Therefore we will not find all three-year-olds or four-year-olds or five-year-olds accomplishing or participating in the same activities. The chronological age can reveal when a child is expected to achieve a certain skill. Most children follow a rate of growth that is sequential and appropriate for their age. Norms are established as standards to assess individual children. Norms, such as the developmental milestones charts, provide a general guide by age. There is much variability within all the developmental areas among children of the same chronological age. Behavioral differences in rate of growth pace children into their own individualized and natural pattern of growth.

This is the reason we need to distinguish between the age of children and their developmental age. **Developmental age,** which is sometimes called developmental level, is influenced by individuality that reflects a child's unique hereditary and life experiences. The developmental age takes shape because it is influenced by many different factors, such as distinctive traits and temperament, rate of growth, emotional responses, activity level, abilities, interests, family, and environment. Children's patterns and pace of development contribute to the developmental age (Figure 2–4).

FIGURE 2–4   Factors Influencing Developmental Age

Temperament	Abilities
Rate of growth	Interests
Emotional responses	Family
Activity level	Environment

Children can approach the same learning opportunity with differentiated behavioral outcomes because of their individual behavioral differences and characteristics.

Knowing a child's age, and more importantly focusing on his developmental age, provides careful clues to matching **individually appropriate** curriculum experiences. The developmental age describes the abilities, capabilities, skills, and readiness for new challenges. Knowing the general capabilities of three- and four-year-olds helps you select a book to read during small-group time. Knowing the specific listening and attention capabilities of the children expected to participate in the small group helps you to more precisely match the book selection to the developmental level of the children (Curriculum Activity Guide 8).

Appropriate practices for early education provide indicators for designing curriculum that assists children in gaining and improving skills. An effective curriculum design supports skill growth in all of the areas and matches activities to the children.

Culturally and Linguistically Appropriate

The child's culture and language are interwoven with their development and identity. Children need to acquire positive views about a multicultural and multilingual society during their early years of schooling. Children need to appreciate that we live in a world where people come from different places and backgrounds, but we are more alike than we are different (Fillmore, 1993, p. 12).

Activities truly are suitable when they respond to the child's cultural and linguistic diversity, when they are **culturally and linguistically appropriate.** (Bredekamp & Copple, 1997, p. 4). Appropriate practices with exposure to many aspects of diversity will promote the child's ability to cope with new and old aspects while exploring his own identity (Hall, 1999, p. 6). Children need to use the non-bias materials on an ongoing basis to avoid artificial, add-on experiences. The materials provided must portray current lifestyles and cultural traditions and be sensitive in presenting historical information (Hall, 1999, p. 11) (Curriculum Activity Guide 9).

Cultural and linguistic relevance extends to all areas of the curriculum. Curricula for children's programs are most appropriate when the experiences satisfy curiosity, build confidence, and challenge young learners in a nurturing and joyful environment. Responding to the children with acceptance encourages tolerance for differences and new ideas: *I see you pasted the wood chips on the styrofoam pieces, that's very interesting. We are going to taste kiwi fruit. It is peeled and cut in many different ways, in half, and in wedges. You piled the sand in an interesting way.* It is ongoing and supportive interactions that encourage developmentally, culturally, and linguistically appropriate experiences.

ONGOING ASSESSMENT OF CHILDREN'S NEEDS AND SKILLS

Ongoing **assessment** is the process that helps you to make important daily decisions related to curriculum planning, implementation, and changes. Information collected through observation and documentation of behavior of enrolled children should be combined with your growing knowledge about best practices.

Taking Cues from Children

Children's needs, interests, and prior experiences direct the initial selection of curriculum activities. Whether or not a child approaches, interacts, or selects particular materials depends on several factors. Children engage in activities that have relevance to them. Children understand what they can see and do. Children are naturally curious, yet their interest level on any particular day may relate more to their present well-being. A hungry child may be more interested in the Cooking Center filled with an aroma of pancakes and syrup. Another child may walk away from firefighter props introduced in the Discovery Center because sirens sounded during his drive to school that morning.

Teachers who listen to children's responses gain insight about the children's level of understanding. Teacher Marisa provided a flannel board experience illustrating apple trees with three children who are four years old. The children experienced various activities throughout the week related to the concept—*an apple can be different colors.* Other activities related to the concept of apple were replaced with additional child-initiated materials. Christina and Jake joined the cooking experience table, where apples were prepared in individual fruit cups. Jake pointed to the golden delicious apple and said, "That's a pear, that's a pear, it's yellow." Teacher Marisa made note to continue offering the cooking experience to add experience and clarification to the concept: *an apple can be different colors.* She also added a new activity to include other round, yellow fruit. When you listen to children as they participate in the activities, as teacher Marisa did, you will gain important insight into their needs. Review the participation of children to understand what they are thinking. Modify curriculum plans to more effectively meet the developmental needs of the enrolled children based on your observations. Keep initial activities focused and simple. Children who have never touched or tasted an apple need to see it, touch it, smell it, and hear the word "apple" as they participate in a cooking activity.

Children can participate in experiences at their own pace, acquiring basic skills before advanced abilities. Three-year-olds have shorter legs, take smaller steps, and have brief attention spans. Plan a leisurely walk to a nearby grocery store. The activity advances capabilities in walking and enjoyment of the outdoors and offers social interchange with the other participants taking the walk. The teacher remains alert to the children's responses and questions. These observations stimulate the planning of curriculum activities to be offered during the following days and weeks. This group's participation in similar excursions during the next few months reveals observable changes in behaviors and physical development. Increasingly, children are observed walking more rapidly, talking to each other more as they walk, and commenting about the sights and sounds of the streets and the grocery store.

Assessing What Children Say and Do

Learning and continuing to take cues from children will prepare you for the more-formalized process of assessment. Assessment may take many forms, including listening to what children say, observing what they do, and appraising and predicting their behavior. Children change and so must the curriculum. Collected data, foundations about child development, and program requirements combine to create curriculum with appropriate expectations for children. Assessment should be conducted on children in their usual and familiar settings (Shepard, Kagan, & Wurtz, 1998, p. 7). In addition, the value of early intervention for children with disabilities has long been recognized as the best way to plan a program to meet individual educational needs (Cook, Tessier, & Klein, 1996, p. 102).

Assessing a child's behavior will contribute to your ability to identify **age-appropriate** activities that will match his range of competence and readiness. The intended use of assessment should be identified because it will determine how the assessment is conducted. The timing of data collection will be most helpful if the collection occurs regularly as children acquire skills and learn content (Shepard, Kagan, & Wurtz, 1998, p. 7). Assessments are meaningful for educational planning; communication with parents; identification of children with special needs; and, program evaluation and accountability (Hills, 1993, p. 21).

Assessment that collects information about children doing what they are doing in the routine of the center is called *performance based.* The intent is not to evaluate children's behaviors to find reason to exclude them, but instead to review the collection of facts to improve and identify more effective ways to engage the children in the experiences. Objective assessments describe the behavior without the observer's personal opinions or inferences. Teachers can reflect on the gathered information and observations as an appraisal of children's strengths and needs. Tasks that children perform and projects in which they engage can become part of an assessment. This method is thought to be "better suited than traditional tests to measure what really counts: whether students can apply their knowledge, skills, and understanding in important, real-world contexts" (McTighe, 1997, p. 7).

Collecting Information— Assessment Methods

Data is collected informally and formally; individually and collaboratively. Casual conversations with families during arrival and pick up balance more formal interviews and conference settings. Jotting down notes during the day continues to be a popular and useful method for teachers. More elaborate strategies include checklists, journals or logs, running records, and time samples. The recorded information creates the ongoing assessment of children that is needed for curriculum development and modification. Teachers gather information about children using different methods (Figure 2–5).

FIGURE 2–5   Assessment Methods

Assessment Method	Example
Checklist	
Assessment using a checklist bases review in part on prior observation of a child and knowledge about child development. Skills and abilities and specific behaviors are observed and checked for presence, absence, or whether the skill is repeated, one or more children may be observed periodically.	The checklist indicates which children have mastered the obstacle course and which need more opportunity for practice.
Casual note	
Brief records are written throughout the day on a small tablet kept in an apron pocket or on clipboards placed in accessible locations throughout the indoor and outdoor area. Notes may include words to help the teacher remember to record more detailed observation at the end of the day. A language sample of a child could be recorded. A casual note may prompt the teacher about an activity or child's participation.	A casual note reminds the teacher that neither Erin nor Beth finished mural painting and need to do so next week.
Conversation	
Informal conversations with the children and their families provide the ideal assessment technique for gathering data about the child.	Monique tells the welcoming teacher about her golden retriever puppy.
Logs	
Records are kept of daily and weekly activity participation interest/activity centers. This can also be a record of certain children who participate often in a particular area. The date is important.	The same eight children participate in the block area. Several children have left the area in tears during the week.
Time sample	
The behavior of a child is recorded for a short, intermittent period. The time interval is set prior to observation and is determined by the particular behavior to be assessed. This tracks the frequency of a behavior.	Five-minute observation of Liu at the climbing structure. Teacher has observed him approaching the structure for several days but not actually attempting the climb.
Portfolio	
Collection and storage of selected samples of children's typical work demonstrating everyday skills and progress.	Documentation can include drawings, dictation of stories, writing, photos of block and sand play, art.

What the assessment tools provide is a more focused view about a particular child, a group, or the interaction between a child and the group. Review of data will help you to make more meaningful decisions about sustaining the children's activities. For example, a closer look at the Block Interest Center log assessment might reveal that most of the children who left the block area in tears did so at 11:45 AM. Teachers need to review the daily schedule and the log and consider whether an earlier lunch time might be more beneficial for the children.

The methods by which teachers gather information about children has changed and so have the materials used to document behavior and actions.

The conventional cumulative folder, with records and testing results, has been replaced with portfolios. "Many have wholeheartedly embraced the idea that student work samples in a portfolio are valuable documentation of children's learning and progress" (Gronlund, 1998, p. 4). Portfolios, added at all educational levels, document progress and identify levels in order to guide behavior. Portfolios, to be considered a method of assessment, must be more than an expandable folder holding random observations and examples of a child's work (Pierson & Beck, 1993, p. 30). Staff need to identify the reasons and methods for collecting the material and data for a portfolio. A portfolio provides a

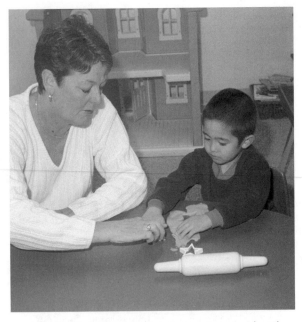

By assessing a child's behavior, the teacher can identify age-appropriate activities that will match the child's range of competence and readiness.

systematic and appropriate method for assessment of young children. Samples of the children's work, tape recordings, checklists, videos, observations, photographs, records of parent conferences and interviews, parent evaluations, developmental profiles, and health evaluations can become part of the authentic record of a child during the period of attendance.

A record of a child's progress in different areas of development is referred to as a *developmental profile*. A developmental profile is a record of a child's physical, cognitive, social, and emotional development. Some programs that contract with funding agencies must complete a developmental profile of each child on enrollment and at least once every twelve months. This application connects the needs of children to the curriculum. The intent of the developmental profile is that it be used to plan and implement age and developmentally appropriate activities (California State Department of Education, Child Development Programs, 1995).

Assessment and review contribute to more appropriate planning and also help parents understand whether their children are developing well. Parents want to know if their children are behaving and learning normally. Does the child need extra support and possible intervention? Parents' insight into the daily behavior of their children may contribute significant data for teachers (Wolfendale,

1998, p. 355). Parents can gather information about behavior to pinpoint periods when their children's actions may be out of adjustment with their emerging needs (Katz, 1994, EDO-PS-94-15).

Documentation of the experiences in which children participate regularly places assessment within the domain of the teacher. The work sampling assessment method can be used to observe and record the actions of children in different educational areas and at different times. The Work Sampling System was developed by Samuel Meisels to "assess and document skills, knowledge, behavior, and accomplishments" of children. This performance assessment system looks at the children's work completed in the different areas of the curriculum with checklists, portfolios, and summary reports (Meisels, 1993, p. 36). The actions of children are observed and recorded in different education areas and at different times, causing work sampling to be a curriculum-embedded assessment (Meisels, 1996/1997, p. 60).

Professionally reliable interpretation rests primarily on objective data. Observations made over time allow teachers to see patterns of behavior that will drive curriculum modification.

REVIEW

Remembering that each child is an individual who develops as a whole person is important for Early Childhood educators. The study of children is divided into major categories, making it easier to understand the behavior of children. Children develop physically, affectively and aesthetically, and cognitively with language. Predictable sequences occur within each of these developmental focus areas. Three children might be the same age but will not behave in the same manner. Knowing the Developmental Focus areas helps teachers to set reasonable expectations for the children as they grow and develop. A teacher's role is to focus on children's developing abilities to facilitate the development of physical skills, affective skills, and cognitive skills.

Understanding the concept of developmental age contributes to the design of appropriate curriculum with emphasis on the individual needs of the enrolled children. Children will benefit the most when experiences satisfy their curiosity, build their confidence, and challenge them in nurturing and joyful environments.

Collecting information about children will contribute to your ability to identify age-appropriate activities. Assessment is done in many different ways, providing a more focused view about a particular child, a group, or the interaction between a child and the group. Watching and listening to children over time will give you clues into their patterns of behaviors. This insight will drive the curriculum planning and modifications necessary for meeting children's needs and for supporting their developing skills.

KEY TERMS

aesthetic development
affective development
age-appropriate
assessment
cognitive development
culturally and
   linguistically
   appropriate
curiosity
development

developmental age
Developmental Focus
   areas
expectation
exploration
individually
   appropriate
physical development
skills
whole child

RESPOND

1. The director of your center has asked you to present a five-minute presentation at the monthly parent meeting. The purpose of this meeting is to help the parents of the enrolled children to understand that children develop individually. Prepare a typed or word-processed outline for this presentation, including discussion about developmental age.

2. If you are a parent, review the photographs and records of your child or children. What age did your child or children roll over, walk, talk, attend a birthday party? If you are not a parent, call your own parent and ask when you and your siblings accomplished certain skills. Write a summary describing the similarities and differences among your children or you and your siblings. Note the age with year and month; for example, 2.3 would be two years and three months.

3. Locate a current professional journal article about assessment. Examples include the articles cited in the references by Gaye Gronlund and Sheila Wolfendale. Write a one-page paper summarizing the article.

4. How does an organization like the Children's Defense Fund support authentic inclusion? You can access the Children's Defense Fund on the Internet at http://www.childrensdefense.org/.

REFERENCES

Bhavnagri, N. P., & Gonzalez-Mena, J. (1997). The cultural context of infant caregiving. *Childhood Education, 74*, 2–8.

Bredekamp, S., & Copple, C. D. (Eds.). (1997). *Developmentally appropriate practice in early childhood programs serving children from birth through age 8* (Rev. ed.). Washington, DC: National Association for the Education of Young Children.

Bruner, J. S. (1960). *The Process of Education*. New York: Vintage.

California State Department of Education. (1995). *Funding terms and conditions and program requirements, Fiscal Year 1995–1996 for child development programs.* Sacramento, CA: CSDE.

Cohen, D. H. (1972). *The learning child.* New York: Pantheon.

Cook, R. E., Tessier, A., & Klein, M. D. (1996). *Adapting childhood curricula for children in inclusive settings* (4th ed.). Englewood Cliffs, NJ: Merrill.

Elkin, F., & Handel, G. (1989). *The child & society* (5th ed.). New York: Random House.

Etaugh, C., & Rathus, S. (1995). *The world of children.* Orlando, FL: Harcourt Brace.

Fillmore, L. W. (1993). Educating citizens for a multicultural 21st century. *Multicultural Education,* Summer, 1993.

Gronlund, G. (1998). Portfolios as an assessment tool: Is collection of work enough? *Young Children, 53*(3), 4–10.

Hall, N. S. (1999). *Creative resources for the anti-bias classroom.* Albany, NY: Delmar.

Haskell, L. L. (1979). *Art in the early childhood years.* Columbus, OH: Charles E. Merrill.

Hills, T. W. (1993). Assessment in context—Teachers and children at work. *Young Children, 48*(5), 20–28.

Katz, L. G. (1994). *Assessing the development of preschoolers.* Urbana, IL: ERIC Clearinghouse on Elementary and Early Childhood Education.

McTighe, J. (1997). What happens between assessments. *Educational Leadership, 54*(4), 6–12.

Meisels, S. J. (1993). Remaking Classroom Assessment with the work sampling system. *Young Children, 48*(5), 34–40.

Meisels, S. J. (1996/97). Using work sampling in authentic assessments. *Educational Leadership, 54*(4), 60–65.

Pierson, C. A. & Beck, S. (1993). Performance assessment: The realities that will influence rewards. *Childhood Education, 70*(1), 30.

Read, K., Gardner, P., & Mahler, B. (1993). *Early childhood programs: Human relationships and learning* (9th ed.). Chicago: Harcourt Brace.

Shepard, L., Kagan, S. L., Wurtz, E. (Eds.). (1998). *Principles and recommendations for early childhood assessments.* Washington, DC: National Education Goals Panel.

Wolfendale, S. (1998). Involving parents in child assessments in the United Kingdom. *Childhood Education, 74*(6), 355–358.

CHAPTER 3

Early Curriculum Basics:
Play, Discovery, Creativity

Curriculum Profile

A small head appeared in the cloud formation, and then arms, trunk, and short legs stretched through the opening. The wooden, hinged panels, painted with fluffy clouds, created an encircled area with crawl tunnels leaving just enough room for the climber to move in and out. The carpeted area reduced sounds while protecting the explorer. To the left a three-year-old turned plastic knobs, adjusted a set of oversized head phones, and pulled on a metal steering wheel. The more she pulled on the steering wheel the more her body seemed to lift up. The two boys in the rounded structure at the far end of this indoor area took turns changing seats, carefully bending and placing trays. Periodically they viewed the scenes outside the small porthole windows. The busy activity continued until a loud announcement turned the children's attention toward the adults occupying surrounding seating.

The activities described did not occur in a school setting or any other Early Childhood program. The children were not observed in any home or park. The four children were different ages, from different families, and waiting to travel to different destinations at an airport terminal area created just for children. Their spontaneous activity was similar because they were allowed to truly play.

Chapter Outline

Study Guide

As you study the sections in this chapter, you should be able to:

- Appreciate the significance of play in the lives of young children.
- Define the values of play experiences during early childhood.
- Understand how to support creativity.
- Examine the ways children think and learn.
- Identify active questioning methods.
- Review the introduction of technology for early childhood.
- Recognize how parents contribute to the early childhood curriculum.
- Review ways to link parents with technology.

PLAY

In its most basic form, **play** is a child's spontaneous, unrestricted, joyful response to the environment. To some adults it can appear random, undisciplined, unproductive, and even something to hold in check. If a child is to become a socialized member of society, we as parents and educators must understand and guide the child's play. Depending on our approach to child development, we can either regard the child's natural instinct to play as a positive tool for learning or an obstacle. Early Childhood professionals are constantly called upon to look at play.

Play is a word that we use and hear throughout the day, particularly in early care and education. The word generates mixed responses despite the quantity of data substantiating the benefit and value of play for young children. We know that play helps children learn about their world and acquire the competencies they will need for the rest of their lives. Children resolve challenges and conflicts in all of their developmental areas (Cohen, 1972, p. 338). A baby plays with a rattle, the toddler plays with the ball, and the preschooler plays with the tricycle, all developing important physical skills. Playing peek-a-boo, pointing to people and saying their names, and sitting with friends at preschool while a story is read all help children develop their affective and aesthetic skills, as well as cognitive and language skills.

Play Experiences During Early Childhood

Activity time for play provides opportunities for children to gain confidence, which in turn affects their interpersonal skills. Play provides children occasions to observe, to discover, and to understand their world. When activities are self-chosen, playing can be therapeutic, satisfying, and fun.

During play children interact with others, acquire prosocial skills, try out roles, test behaviors, and begin to understand their surroundings. When children play, their activity is real to them. A common misconception of adults is not accepting or validating children's play. Kirk announces upon his arrival at preschool that he is the bus driver, Allie tells Rafael that he must get off the swing, and Stacia asks if she can turn on the garden hose (Curriculum Activity Guide 10 [CAG]).

Children naturally progress through play stages. There are many theories about play, with those of Mildred B. Parten and Sara Smilansky maintaining strong acceptance in the Early Childhood research literature. Parten classified social participation among preschool children in free-choice play (Figure 3–1).

Children will imitate the adult world, trying to recreate behaviors of their parents and other adults that they observe. This happens especially when the setting allows them to engage in what is called Dramatic or Sociodramatic Play (Smilansky, 1968, p. 7). Sara Smilansky described the stages of

FIGURE 3–1   Categories of Social Participation

Unoccupied behavior	The child is occupied watching anything happening, glancing, following teacher, sitting in one place.
Onlooker	The child watches certain children play, often talking to other children being observed. Remains close to group but does not enter the play situation.
Solitary independent	The child plays independently, making no effort to contact or get close to other children.
Parallel activity	The child selects activity near other children but plays independently with toys similar to those used by the other children; in close proximity but not with other children.
Associative	The child engages in conversation and common activity with other children. Each child follows own desires because associative play lacks organization and task assignments.
Cooperative	Children play in an organized group activity, whether constructing a product, achieving a goal, dramatizing, or playing formal games. One or two members of the group control play activity.

Parten, M. B. (1996). Social participation among pre-school children. In K. M. Paciorek & J. H. Munro (Eds.). *Sources: Notable selections in early childhood education.* Guildford, CT: Dushkin. (pp. 116–118).

play development in her 1968 book, *The Effects of Sociodramatic Play on Disadvantaged Preschool Children* (pp. 6–7). She documented that Dramatic Play is valuable in developing children's social skills and imagination. Dramatic Play occurs when children voluntarily engage in social activity using imaginary objects and imitating people and surroundings. Sociodramatic Play is the most developed form of play because children engage in play related to a theme and in cooperation with at least one other child (Curriculum Activity Guide 11 [CAG]).

Valuing Children's Play

The rush of today's society forces an extra challenge before Early Childhood teachers who believe that play is essential for total development of young children. Has society stopped listening to the statement by Lawrence Frank? "Play is the way a child learns what no one can teach." The contribution play makes to children's learning and thinking skills is significant. The values gained translate to courage, curiosity, commitment without reserve, self-acceptance, optimism, gaiety, cooperation, and emotional maturity (Hartley, 1973, p. 315).

Children need to become totally involved and focused when they play. Play is the way they learn and understand. In play, children practice, pretend, and participate, and in doing so, they acquire skills. Play engages children actively so that they learn by doing, manipulating, and moving. As children develop their abilities they begin to master their world because play allows them to gain con-

trol of their bodies, experience the objects in their surroundings, and become aware of their emotions. Play is truly play when children choose the activities from available selections in an appropriately prepared environment where choices are available.

The significance of play is rationalized by professionals who have stated that children naturally learn through their play because it is play that helps them learn about the world. "As a child begins to move around and develop motor coordination, his play—which is really his work throughout his childhood—enables him to exercise his muscles as well as his imagination" (Salk, 1983, p. 152). The notion that play is a child's work remains as strong as it was when stated by Dr. Maria Montessori in 1966 in her book, *The Secret of Childhood* (p. 196). She wrote about the child's work (Figure 3–2) to emphasize that there were fundamental differences between the work of children and adults.

Author-educator John Holt stated that the child "wants to make sense of things, find out how things work, gain competence and control over himself and his environment, do what he can see other people doing" (1969, p. 184).

However, total agreement regarding the reference of play to be a child's work does not exist. It is feared that if we consider a child's play to be work, then there is the risk that we may "miseducate," according to David Elkind, by using conventional elementary school lesson plans for preschool children. This, he believes, will discourage the sense of

FIGURE 3–2   Excerpt from Maria Montessori's
The Secret of Childhood

It is important for us to know the nature of a child's work. When a child works, he does not do so to attain some further goal. His objective in working is the work itself, and when he has repeated an exercise and brought his own activities to an end, this end is independent of external factors. As far as the child's personal reactions are concerned, his cessation from work is not connected with weariness since it is characteristic of a child to leave his work completely refreshed and full of energy.

Montessori, M. (1966). *The secret of childhood.* New York: Fides.

competence and creativity that play should generate during the early childhood years (Elkind, 1992, p. 156).

Promoting Playful Experiences

The teachers' attitudes about play will influence whether or not parents of enrolled children accept the curriculum with a foundation of play. This is why it is essential for teachers of young children to understand and appreciate the benefits that play generates for children and to support play in the classroom. Teachers understand **value of play** and the relationship of play to the skills and concepts valued by parents and schools in the community (Nourot & Van Hoorn, 1991, p. 40).

Programs for young children must provide time for the children to play. Children need uninterrupted time to become absorbed in an activity; they stay with an activity longer when they are engrossed. During longer play segments, preschoolers participate in more total play activity, including group play, constructive play, and group-dramatic play (Christie & Wardle, 1992, p. 29). Some programs allow time for what is called free play, which indicates that children are able to choose what they do, how they do it, how long they do it, and with whom they do it. During free play children are allowed to choose activities of interest and to pursue them at their own ability levels. Teachers must be ready to develop the educational content of any activity in a way that does not deny a child the chance for discovery during their free play (Landreth, 1972, pp. 186–187) (Curriculum Activity Guides 10 and 11 CAG).

"Free play is 'play' because the activity strikes so deep a chord of pleasure within them. But free play is learning" (Hymes, 1981, p. 92) and considered to be educationally productive as the hallmark of the early childhood. Some professionals believe that teachers of young children will promote playful experiences by setting the stage for play (ample time, materials, and choices); guiding with play-coaching strategies (modeling and verbal interactions); and observing children to understand the development of play and children's levels of participation (Nourot & Van Hoorn, 1991, pp. 46–47).

During play, children acquire skills by practicing, pretending, and participating.

We all need to remember the joyful experiences of childhood play. A beginning student with exceptional insight used the example from the movie *Hook* to emphasize the importance of "getting inside the child, remembering what it was like to pretend and to play." She explained that "the Lost Boys were trying to tell Peter Pan that to be like them, he needed to believe in what they did. He needed to believe in pretending. He needed to be able to play" (Curriculum Activity Guide 12 [CAG]).

DISCOVERY, CURIOSITY, AND EXPLORATION

With problem-solving skills paramount, a review of children's natural way of learning is essential. Children are naturally curious about people and their surroundings. When curiosity is supported, children begin to become self-motivated to gather information, inquire, and experiment. You might see a bell and know that you can cause it to make a ringing sound. You might demonstrate this to children. But, if you allow children to try and figure out that moving the bell causes it to make a sound, you facilitate discovery for them. Children want to find out what happens when they hold brushes with yellow paint and brushes with blue paint and move the brushes across paper. They may discover that the two brushes create a different color. They are able to discover because they are allowed to follow their curiosity.

Discovery occurs when children's natural interests lead them to try out the unstructured and flexible materials and arrive at a new understanding. "From the very beginning of his education, the child should experience the joy of discovery." These words, written by Alfred North Whitehead in 1929 (p. 14), are still valid today and fit the current recommendations for learning experiences for young children. Teachers need to allow children to discover by tailoring experiences to their interests and capacities. Teachers need to be patient, honest, and offer activities that are "exciting, correct, and rewardingly comprehensible" (Bruner, 1960, p. 22). In his publications *The Process of Education* (1960) and *Toward a Theory of Instruction* (1965), Jerome Bruner detailed the essence of curiosity and the natural motivation to learn. "Observe a child," Bruner explained, "or group of children building a pile of blocks as high as they can get them. Their attention will be sustained to the flashing point until they reach the climax when the pile comes crashing down. They will

return to build still higher" (1965, p. 116). It is apparent that children's curiosity drives their motive to learn as well as their desire to achieve competence. The key contributions that teachers are able to make include guiding children, rather than giving out information, providing hands-on material, and assisting them to discover answers for themselves.

Interactive Questioning

Polly Greenberg (1998, p. 32) recommends, in a statement about language and literacy, that "Children need to become alert to, and interested in, language, and the sounds in words, which can be accomplished through meaningful activities and in playful ways." One way that we can encourage interest in language is to appropriately practice **interactive questioning.** Interactive questioning adds an important aspect to teacher-questioning skills. Using interactive questioning purposefully grants respect to children's linguistic abilities and to the languages and cultures of the children's homes. Interactive questioning implies that we accept the eye movements from children who might be acquiring English as their second language and from children who may not verbally reply but who communicate with a clear rise of their eyebrows.

Teachers will expand children's language by avoiding crowding them, talking over them, or over-questioning them. Teachers should encourage and exchange language maintaining cultural and linguistic respect. Rosalind Charlesworth lists ways to invite communication, starting with demonstration of our interest as listeners and observers. This is accomplished by smiling, nodding, and reflecting back on the children's comments. Use indirect questions, allowing children to make choices: *What makes you do that? I was wondering if the bird would jump down?* Use questions that permit children to be silent: *Can or do you want to describe what you did? I don't know that I have a choice, do you?* Once you observe that the children are ready, ask open-ended, or interactive, questions, such as: *Can you tell me why? Would you show me how? What do you think about the end of the story?* Help children discuss and describe, as Charlesworth describes, talking to think, by commenting: *Tell me what is happening in the sand. What do you think will happen next? Let's think about what will change when you put the juice in the gelatin* (Charlesworth, 1987, pp. 331–332).

Preschoolers will be encouraged when asked what happened after the reading of a story. Personal

Early Childhood Education teachers can encourage interest in language by practicing interactive questioning.

responses are also encouraging, for example, *What would you say goodnight to in your bedroom?* (Howard, Shaughnessy, Sanger, & Hux, 1998, p. 39). Older preschoolers and primary-age children will benefit from recognizing that new ideas and different creative activity can be confusing. Go beyond giving instructions, describing, and giving examples. Help children become aware of the thinking that they are using by asking questions such as *What are you trying to do now? Do you have a long enough hose to reach?* Assist children in developing reflective attitudes so that they can learn to ask themselves questions: *Which brush should I use to create that pattern? What button should I click on to close the screen?* (Antonietti, 1997, p. 74).

Blending Technology into the Curriculum

Changes occur everywhere and influence our daily and future lives. Changing family patterns, the urbanization of society, and technological advances also affect children. Urbanization and **technology** (Curriculum Activity Guide 13 [CAG]) are altering the way children's routine needs are met, including approaches for care and learning. It is time for educators to determine how to best use technology to affect positive outcomes for children (Arce, 1999, p. 168).

As the information age increasingly influences education, children will be faced with more choices

and knowledge rather than just receiving what a system requires them to learn. Teachers will have access to greater knowledge bases (Turner, 1996, p. 23), which create additional educational challenges to determine the types of information that should be accessible.

The teacher of young children will continue to evaluate the appropriateness of technology to enhance children's abilities to learn and socialize. The National Association for the Education of Young Children (NAEYC) Position Statement related to technology suggests that technology is appropriate when it is integrated into the setting as an additional tool to support children's activities and maintain equitable access (1996, p. 12).

Teachers need to consider acceptable elements of software programs for young children. The term *software* refers to the packaged applications you will use to run teaching and learning programs on a computer. First, consider the content and match it to the developmental age of the children enrolled in your program. The content should be presented for a variety of levels. Secondly, the software for young children should hold their attention by attracting and sustaining their involvement for about ten minutes per session. Ask if the software program gives the children feedback indicating progress and completion of goals for the computer activities. Does the software avoid bias and violence and ensure safeguards for appropriate Internet sites? Consider these suggestions and the ease of use and value for the price before adopting and purchasing software programs for children enrolled in your program (Hohmann, 1998, pp. 60–62).

Learning with the help of technological tools provides a supplement for education but will not replace the teacher (Pool, 1997, p. 6) because "digital literacy" requires the ability to understand and evaluate information found with the technological tools available. We will have greater access to a larger amount of information that we can adapt for young children. The feasibility of multimedia projects will increase with technological advances, but it will still be the teachers who must avoid misinterpreting the children's abilities to manipulate the computer as an indication that they have the cognitive abilities to understand what flashes on the screen (Elkind, 1996, p. 23). Educators support discovery and children's creative abilities when they select software that offers children the most opportunities to interact with the computers. Children need to have as much control as possible so that they can cause changes on the screen. They need to have the power to move graphics on the screen and then observe the consequences of their actions (Shade, 1996, p. 20).

CREATIVITY

You hear the word **creativity** often if you spend any time in a program for preschoolers or in Early Childhood Education preparation classes. The word *creativity* holds a certain status in many programs generally describing planned activities for the children. The word *creativity* actually means the quality and the ability to create. *Creative* is defined as inventive, productive, and having the ability to make a thing that has not been made before (Barnhart, 1990, p. 486). Children who show creative abilities notice differences, see the unusual, want to complete tasks by themselves, are confident, and are able to solve problems (Todd & Heffernan, 1977, p. 63). All the behaviors related to creativity involve thinking, acting, making to solve a problem or to make something new (Mayesky, 1998, p. 4). "Do you think that the creative experiences provided for children in most settings allow them to be original and make something new? Do the activities help them find their own creative abilities and problem solve? Do the settings allow them to bring forth something new? (Haskell, 1979, p. 3)

Applying the ideas about creativity to young children requires that teachers highlight their developing abilities with an emphasis on the process of experiencing creative expression. Equally important is the recognition that the prime years for creative development are between the ages of three to five years (Pica, 2000, p. 36). The creative development of young children will occur within all areas of growth, including physical, affective, and cognitive. For example, young children will move rhythmically to music, express feelings as they role play, and discover a new way to park the tricycle.

Many Ways to Think and Learn

There are many ways to think about an object and to learn about that object. Theories regarding multiple ways to think have been widely accepted. Howard Gardner's presentation of **multiple intelligence theory** suggests that there are at least seven different capacities of intelligence combining several independent abilities. The theory of multiple intelligence (MI) initially outlined seven distinct categories of intelligence, including: linguistic, musical, logical-mathematical, spatial, kinesthetic, interpersonal, and intrapersonal (Craig, 1996, p. 355). An eighth intelligence focusing on nature has been added since the initial list of seven. Adults and children display different strengths of intelligences. One may have strength in language ability, and another in interpersonal ability (Fogarty, 1999, p. 77).

It is not necessary to determine how many intelligences children display; rather, teachers need to be sensitive to the types of activities in which children may participate. This calls for teachers to also look at the many factors that influence how a child thinks and learns, including interests and family context (Hatch, 1997, p. 26).

Supporting Creativity

Teachers who keep in mind the true meaning of creativity allow children to do their own work by exploring the materials with their developing skills. Children need to make choices and to try out materials. They need to figure out how objects work and what certain materials will do in order to make sense of their world. This implies that we unlock creativity by using materials from real-life and by appreciating the different ways that children approach the materials (Antonietti, 1997, p. 73). The theories of both Jean Piaget and Maria Montessori validate the notion that young children are naturally curious about their surroundings and try to understand. Curiosity during the early years of development is displayed by the children's active manipulation of objects. As children mature, curiosity becomes apparent in their questions. The early education program will help to gratify children's curiosity by providing activities matching their developmental level (Ault, 1977, p. 177). "Creativity is the result of an individual using certain personality traits to bring something productive into existence." The natural spontaneity and creative spirit of children may develop when these attributes are valued by supportive adults. When adults impose their "standards and demands it can actually block further development" (Elkind, 1976, p. 216).

Accept each question and enjoy all the "why teacher" questions, giving interaction and questioning responses as appropriate. You will encourage creativity by offering opportunities for children to come up with new questions, solutions, and novel ideas. This takes patience, time, and appreciation for the process of doing rather than concentrating on an end product. The participation in the experience is important to young children.

Teachers need to allow children to establish their own creativity by working with different materials.

That creativity is "regarded as a higher mental process is important because it causes learning to be exciting and playful" (Bloom, 1981, p. 145). You can also outfit the classroom with actual materials, with the children's own work in a setting that is a continuation of the natural environment and of the home environment (Elkind, 1976, p. 221).

PARTNERING WITH PARENTS FOR QUALITY CURRICULUM

Studies report that children benefit from well-designed and well-implemented partnerships between the school, family, and community. Partnerships result when teachers consistently inform parents about the curriculum and about their children's progress and needs, thus utilizing **parents as resources.** Partnerships result in higher achievement levels of the children, benefiting the children, the schools, and the families (Sanders & Epstein, 1998, p. 341). Greater parent involvement has a positive effect on the entire program. This was demonstrated in a study of accredited schools by the National Association for the Education of Young Children (Bredekamp & Berby, 1987, p. 15).

There are many ways that educators can help establish a program of partnership with parents. Parents will need suggestions for establishing a home environment that supports their children and regularly provide input to teachers to modify and improve the curriculum. In addition, we need to work continuously at refining our methods of communication and welcoming parents as volunteers.

What Do Parents Want for Their Children?

Parents turn to early childhood professionals, who provide the care and education for their children, for answers about how their children learn, behave, and progress. Parents are concerned about how to be effective in their parenting roles. Parenting education programs are increasing in popularity because parents want help on parenting issues (Martinez Gonzalez, 1998, p. 351). As educators we need to focus on the common needs of parents everywhere. Parents care about their children, and educators need to accept that parents are the most important factor in their children's success. The school, family, and community program that promotes partnerships will determine how parents become involved in their children's education (Epstein & Sanders, 1998, p. 392). The message directs us to build communication skills and trust and let parents know that they do make the difference.

Professionals may be eager to share what they consider to be suitable program practices, but studies have indicated that parents select child care, for example, differently than the professionals recommend. Many parents choose childcare situations in which the set of cultural values and beliefs are similar to their own (Daniel, 1998, p. 11). Maintaining cultural values and the language of the home appear to be, in part, the reasons for this difference and should alert teachers to the importance of cultural and linguistic awareness.

One way that we can help parents is to prepare them and their children for beginning the school and child care experience. Encourage the parent to come to school before the child's first day. Suggest that the parent bring a camera and tape recorder to help the child become more familiar with the staff. Recommend books that will help the child and parent make the transition to school, such as *Don't Forget to Come Back* by R. Harris (Blecher-Sass, 1997, pp. 12–14). Guide the parent and child in establishing a familiar good-bye routine at school. Suggest that both the parent and child sign-in, greet the teacher who is welcoming the children, and then together review the discovery table or the new bulletin board before saying good-bye.

FIGURE 3–3   Children's program newsletters can provide ongoing communication with families.

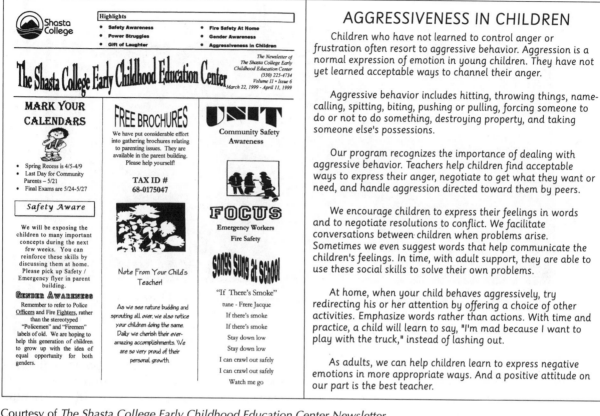

Courtesy of *The Shasta College Early Childhood Education Center Newsletter.*

Families as Resources for Learning

As a teacher of young children you will become the bridge between the school and the child's home. You will connect parents with resources and services and invite the parents to participate in the school's programs and activities. There are greater chances for the children to develop competence where links between the home and school are strong (Garbarino, 1992, p. 80). The Early Childhood Environmental Rating Scale (ECERS) is an evaluation tool that identifies indicators of quality in children's programs. The ECERS identifies provisions for parents, including information sheets, parent involvement and input, as an indicator of the rating scale (Harms & Clifford, 1980, p. 35). It has been demonstrated that, at all income and education levels, parents become partners in their children's education when schools reach out (Epstein & Sanders, 1998, p. 393).

Staff members recognize the benefit of family involvement to children and the program because the family expands learning opportunities to the children in the school. This expanded opportunity occurs particularly when the children's program provides ongoing communication with the family through, for example, a newsletter (Figure 3–3).

Receptive teachers enhance family partnership opportunities by surveying the interests and talents of parents of enrolled children. The informal surveys are followed with encouragement to parents to share their time and abilities in their child's classroom.

The family also benefits from classroom involvement because a child enjoys opportunities to participate in activities directly with the parent or parents, grandparents, or other family members such as aunts and older siblings. Classroom participation, both indoor and outdoor, creates many shared experiences for the child to discuss with family members at a later time. Parent-child interactions can be observed by teaching staff, who gather additional insight into the child's individual characteristics (Curriculum Activity Guide 14 [CAG]).

Parent participation in a program seems to be related to a parent's perception of his or her own parenting role and whether there will be a positive effect on the child's education. Consistent participation in

Outdoor classroom participation creates many shared experiences for the child to talk with family members at a later time.

meetings is often related to basic support such as child care (Powell, 1998, p. 66).

Another way to increase partnerships is to help families to create settings for learning in the home. In this way, parents are recognized as the child's first teachers (Barbour, 1998/99, p. 71). Encouraging children to bring books and manipulatives home and "care for a pet for the weekend" contributes to the home-school partnership. Parents' contribution to the school comfortably begins when common items from home contribute to the curriculum needs. This exchange can expand the families' and children's concept of family pride. Although it may be difficult for one teacher to obtain enough empty paper towel rolls or plastic containers for the entire group, families that bring in requested items feel good about contributing needed supplies. The parent and child who drag in the walnut branch that broke from their backyard tree contribute to the curriculum. A teacher's appreciation is magnified when children begin to explore the tree branch and ask questions such as: *Who brought the tree branch? What are those round things on the tree? I have a tree that has nuts, too.* The children's questions and responses suggest ideas for new curriculum planning. Their interest may lead to a classroom filled with tree branches from many homes and places. Continued questions and interest lead to a project about fruit trees, all initiated by the support-

ive involvement of a family. Supporting families, the most important resource in a program, will contribute ongoing benefits to the curriculum (Figure 3–4).

Linking Parents with Technology

Teachers of young children find that they are a resource for parents in most areas that affect the development of their children, and a link between **parents and technology.** Providing information about technology creates another connection between the school and home. Computers, software questions, and especially Internet-access concerns face teachers and parents alike. Teachers need to apply the same principles recognized to ensure healthy growth of development of young children when commenting on the selection of appropriate software programs and access to the Internet.

Parents need to participate in policy setting meetings concerning technology use and practices at the school. Experienced parents will contribute to the teachers' knowledge, and parents just arriving into the computer age will benefit from the discussion and decisions. The position statement in *Technology and Young Children—Ages Three through Eight* issued by NAEYC in 1996 (pp. 11–16) outlines recommendations to assist professionals in making decisions about appropriate technology and learning

FIGURE 3–4   Families as Resources for the Curriculum

Parent works in hospital	Parent has access to old x-rays	Children exmaine x-rays
Family cultivates a vegetable garden	Child brings extra cherry tomatoes to school	Grandfather visits and plants tomato vines
Family travels to mountains	Family collected pine cones and small river rocks	Child brings pine cones and river rocks to school
Family creates piñata (decorated paper maché hollow figurine that is filled with candy)	Family gives piñata to school for celebration	Piñata displayed Paper bags decorated with colorful crepe paper

tools. This document reminds Early Childhood educators that professional judgment is needed to ensure that specific use of technology is age, individually, and culturally appropriate; that technology can enhance children's cognitive and social abilities; that technology is integrated into the everyday classroom; that equal access is available for all children with increased access for special needs if access meets their needs; that stereotyping and exposure to violence are avoided; that teachers act as advocates for suitable applications for children; and that professional development opportunities exist.

There are suitable and helpful Internet Web sites, some more well known than others, that can provide parents with information about their children, such as the American Academy of Pediatrics Web site (http://www.aap.org/). There are also unique and specialized Web sites such as New Beginnings that provide a guide for refugee and immigrant parents (http://eric-web.tc.columbia.edu/families/refugees/). A workshop for parents to introduce the basic procedures and guidelines to the computer and access to the Internet can be beneficial, particularly in helping parents to evaluate credible Web sites sponsored by reputable organizations. One more link with parents and the children's home environment involves building relationships that will positively affect the children's curriculum.

REVIEW

Basic concepts that contribute to suitable curriculum for young children include play, discovery, and creativity. Teachers who keep in mind the meaning of creativity will support discovery as the natural way for children to learn. Technological changes also affect the way teachers gain access to and provide an increasing volume of information for young learners.

The rationale for play in programs for young children is clearly documented with specific values in all Developmental Focus areas. When play dominates activity time, there are significant opportunities for children to attain motor skills, interact with others, observe their surroundings, and understand their world.

Quality programs for young children identify family involvement as a necessary component. Family involvement in programs benefits the children, family, and staff because parents contribute their time and resources, which positively connect the school and home.

KEY TERMS

creativity
discovery
interactive questioning
multiple intelligence
   theory
parents as resources

parents and
   technology
play
technology
value of play

RESPOND

1. Read and present a review about a book written by an influential early leader in Early Childhood Education, such as James L. Hymes' *Teaching the Child Under Six*, John Holt's *How Children Learn*, or Maria Montessori's *The Secret of Childhood*. If these classics are unavailable, read David Elkind's *Miseducation*.
2. Access CYFERNET at http://www.cyfernet.mes.umn.edu/ Describe how CYFERNET Web resources can help teachers and families.
3. Describe five reasons why play is valuable for young children.
4. Prepare an article for a parent newsletter about the many ways that parents can contribute their time and home resources to the school program. Include the commitment that the school dedicates to the home-school partnership.

REFERENCES

Antonietti, A. (1997). Unlocking creativity. *Educational Leadership, 54*(6), 73–75.

Arce, E. M. (Ed.). (1999). *Perspectives: Early childhood education.* Boulder, CO: Coursewise.

Ault, R. L. (1977). *Children's cognitive development.* New York: Oxford University Press.

Barbour, A. C. (1998/99). Home literacy bags promote family involvement. *Childhood Education, 75*(2), 71–75.

Barnhart, C. L., & Barnhart, R. K. (Eds.). (1990). *The world book dictionary.* Chicago: World Book.

Blecher-Sass, H. (1997). Good-byes can build trust. *Young Children, 52*(7), 12–14.

Bloom, B. (1981). *All our children learning.* New York: McGraw-Hill.

Bredekamp, S., & Berby, J. (1987). Maintaining quality: Accredited programs one year later. *Young Children, 43*(1), 13–15.

Bruner, J. S. (1960). *The process of education.* New York: Vintage.

Bruner, J. S. (1965). *Toward a theory of instruction.* New York: W. W. Norton.

Charlesworth, R. (1987). *Understanding child development* (2nd ed.). Albany, NY: Delmar.

Cohen, D. H. (1972). *The learning child.* New York: Pantheon.

Christie, J. F., & Wardle, F. (1992). How much time is needed for play? *Young Children, 47*(3), 28–31.

Craig, G. J. (1996). *Human development.* (8th ed.). Upper Saddle River, NJ: Prentice Hall.

Daniel, J. E. (1998). A modern mother's place is wherever her children are: Facilitating infant and toddler mothers' transitions in child care. *Young Children, 53*(6), 4–12.

Elkind, D. (1976). *Child development and education: A Piagetian perspective.* New York: Oxford University Press.

Elkind, D. (1992). *Miseducation: Preschoolers at risk.* New York: Alfred A. Knopf.

Elkind, D. (1996). Young children and technology: A cautionary note. *Young Children, 5*(51), 22–23.

Epstein, J. L., & Sanders, M. G. (1998). What we learn from international studies of school-family-community partnerships. *Childhood Education, 74*(6), 392–394.

Fogarty, R. (1999). Architects of the intellect. *Educational Leadership, 57*(3), 76–78.

Garbarino, J. (1992). *Children and families in the social environment.* (2nd ed.). New York: Walter de Gruyter.

Greenberg, P. (1998). Thinking about goals for grownups and young children while we teach writing, reading, and spelling and a few thoughts about the "J" word. *Young Children, 53*(6), 31–42.

Harms, T., & Clifford, R. M. (1980). *Early childhood environmental rating scale.* New York: Teachers College Press.

Haskell, L. L. (1979). *Art in early childhood years.* Columbus, OH: Charles E. Merrill.

Hartley, R. E. (1973). Play, the essential ingredient. In J. K. Frost, *Revisiting early childhood education—Readings.* New York: Holt, Rinehart & Winston.

Hatch, T. (1997). Getting specific about multiple intelligences. *Educational Leadership, 54*(6), 26–29.

Hohmann, C. (1998). Evaluating and selecting software for children. *Child Care Information Exchange, 123,* 60–62.

Holt, J. (1967). *How children learn.* New York: Pitman.

Howard, S., Shaughnessy, A., Sanger, D., & Hux, K. (1998). Let's talk! Facilitating language in early elementary classrooms. *Young Children, 53*(3), 34–39.

Hymes, J. L. (1981). *Teaching the child under six* (3rd ed.). Columbus, OH: Charles E. Merrill.

Landreth, C. (1972). *Preschool learning and teaching.* New York: Harper & Row.

Martinez Gonzalez, R. A. (1998). The challenge of parenting education: New demands for schools in Spain. *Childhood Education, 74*(6), 351–354.

Mayesky, M. (1998). *Creative activities for young children* (6th ed.). Albany, NY: Delmar.

Montessori, M. (1966). *The secret of childhood.* New York: Fides.

National Association for the Education of Young Children. (1996). NAEYC position statement: Technology and young children—ages three through eight. *Young Children, 51*(6), 11–16.

Nourot, P. J., & Van Hoorn, J. L. (1991). Symbolic play in preschool and primary settings. *Young Children, 46*(6), 40–50.

Parten, M. B. (1996). Social participation among preschool children. In K. M. Paciorek & J. H. Munro (Eds.). *Sources: Notable selections in early childhood education.* Guildford, CT: Dushkin.

Pica, R. (2000). *Experiences in movement with music, activities and theory* (2nd ed.). Albany, NY: Delmar.

Pool, C. R. (1997). A new digital literacy: A conversation with Paul Gilster. *Education Leadership, 55*(3), 6–11.

Powell, D. R. (1998). Reweaving parents into the fabric of early childhood programs. *Young Children, 53*(5), 60–67.

Salk, L. (1983). *The complete Dr. Salk: An a-to-z guide to raising your child.* New York: World Almanac.

Sanders, M. G., & Epstein, T. L. (Guest eds.). (1998). International perspectives on school-family community partnerships. *Childhood Education, 74*(6), 340–341.

Shade, D. D. (1996). Software evaluation. *Young Children, 51*(6), 17–21.

Smilansky, S. (1968). *The effects of sociodramatic play on disadvantaged preschool children.* New York: John Wiley & Sons.

Todd, V. E., & Heffernan, H. (1977). *The years before school: Guiding preschool children* (3rd ed.). New York: Macmillan.

Turner, J. (1996). Technology and change of mind: An interview with Robert Ornstein. *Montessori Life.* Winter, 22–24.

Whitehead, A. N. (1929). *The aims of education.* New York: Mentor.

CHAPTER 4

Environments for Young Children: *Places for Curriculum*

Curriculum Profile

What do you remember about your school experiences? Did you attend a preschool or a child-care program? What happened in kindergarten? What do you remember that made you feel happy or sad? These questions are asked of students in an introductory Early Childhood Education class at the beginning of each semester. The students are asked for one-sentence responses on newsprint with specific grade identifiers. Students do not put their names next to any of the recorded remarks. They are then asked to join small groups to discuss the types of experiences listed as happy and those listed as sad. Comments collected from previous years are distributed to the groups. Students express relief when they find that there are many similarities between their comments and those made by students five, ten, and fifteen years earlier. After analyzing the comments, each group presents suggestions for positive Early Childhood programming and environments that will generate happy responses from young children.

Level	Most Common Positive Remarks	Most Negative Remarks
Preschool	Playing	Napping (most mentioned)
	Painting	Leaving mother
	Liking teacher	Missing mother
	Stacking blocks	Having a mean teacher
	Singing and music	Not allowed to use bathroom
Kindergarten	Liking the teacher	Taking naps
	Loving recess	Having different teachers
	Making friends	Spanking
	Cutting and pasting	Feeling bad/not recognizing name

An informal tally for remarks about preschool and kindergarten experiences collected over an eight-year period reveals commonalities and suggestions for curriculum.

Chapter Outline

Environments That Strengthen Curriculum
  Places for Young Children
  Standards for Early Childhood Programs

Indoor and Outdoor Classrooms
  Indoor Places
  Outdoor Places
  Storage for Curriculum Supplies

Interest Centers
  What to Call the Interest Center?
  How to Set Up Interest Centers

Environments for Inclusive Curricula

Study Guide

As you study the sections in this chapter, you should be able to:

- Understand the description of environment for young children.
- Identify the conditions of settings that create quality Early Childhood programs.
- Become familiar with standards for quality settings.
- Explain how to adapt a facility where appropriate Early Childhood curriculum could be offered.
- Appreciate the importance of the indoor and outdoor arrangements.
- Understand the value of outdoor activities and what type of setting should be arranged outside.

- Know about Interest Centers.
- Examine the ways to create inclusive settings.

ENVIRONMENTS THAT STRENGTHEN CURRICULUM

In Early Childhood Education we use **environment** to describe the surroundings, the conditions, and the locations of places where care and education take place. The reference to the word *environment* also describes the buildings and play spaces. The implication is that the environment influences growth and development of children. It is in the environment that children interact with each other, with their teachers, and with their parents and other adults. The type and amount of space, arrangement of the furnishings, and materials provided all affect the interaction among children and adults that occurs in all settings for young children. Environments for early care and education are places where people interact with a common goal to nurture and educate young children (Hildebrand & Hearon, 1997, p. 254). The way the facility is designed and arranged tells even the casual visitor about the program guidelines, revealing the types of experiences that will be offered to children and their expected behavior. For example, if the classroom for four-year-olds is filled with tables and chairs, there is an expectation that the children will spend time doing "desk work" rather than moving around the center in free play activity. When the shelves are arranged with materials for children to choose, they become more actively involved with the material, taking initiative and having greater potentiality for developing feelings of initiative and independence (Gestwicki, 1999, p. 101). Providing choices in a planned environment is more fitting to preschoolers' needs.

Places for Young Children

The child-centered facility is right for the child who sees, hears, and fits into spaces differently than you do as an adult (Greenman, 1988, p. 20). The spaces we arrange for young children must, in addition to being safe, offer sufficient number and variety of age-appropriate materials and equipment to create a stimulating learning environment (Bredekamp & Copple, 1997, p. 25). Child-size furniture and equipment will contribute to creating nurturing, home-like **settings.** The addition of soft and cozy items such as sofas and pillows and gentle lighting help to establish a comfortable environment. Flexibility for teachers should also be maintained with the provision of both permanent and mobile equipment and furniture. Flexible furnishings will make it easier for children who use adaptive equipment to use the facility. Provision of extra space may increase interaction among all of the enrolled children. The classroom environment will support movement and independence when children are able to "determine their own behavior and manage some of their own materials" (Cook, Tessier, Klein, 1996, p. 297). Young children need a lot of space to try out the curriculum activities, and the space needs to be divided in such a way that the children feel secure and are able to explore (Caples, 1996, p. 15). Organization of the available space affects the behavior of children no matter what curriculum experiences are offered. The environment determines how children respond and play. The building design, including the ceiling height, door placement, and lighting within the facility, influences decisions about the type, time, and length of curriculum activities. Materials that are open-ended give children choices and facilitate their creativity, decision making, and different ways of thinking (Gestwicki, 1999, p. 102). The placement of materials, such as blocks, into well-organized, low, and inviting storage can be open to a centralized activity area or "like a successful music nook or a quiet reading corner or writing center, need to be spatially and acoustically well defined with partial partitions, bookcases, and the other ways of subdividing space and creating resource-rich activity pockets" (Moore, 1997, pp. 19–20).

Decisions about the environment should place safety first, with accessibility to the building, classrooms, restrooms, and exits also given significant priority. The group size, ages, and needs of the children, number of adults who will participate, and balance between areas of active and quiet play are all factors that staff need to consider when design-

Child-size furniture contributes to creating a nurturing, home-like setting.

ing or arranging the environment. The placement of activity areas and the movement of children and adults (traffic pattern or pathways) are further aspects to be reviewed because they affect the functionality of the environment.

The weather poses another challenge to teachers who determine how the indoor and outdoor spaces are used. Some regions of the country have specific seasons that directly affect the children's program and therefore the curriculum. Extremely hot temperatures in areas such as the Southwest limit outdoor activities, just as cold winters do in the northern states and the Midwest. Pollution levels also affect participation in outdoor activity. In areas where agricultural burning or crop spraying are routine, staff members must take these environmental hazards into account when planning outdoor curriculum activities for young children.

Sharing facility space with another program or group poses yet another challenge. Some programs for young children regularly close the program down at the end of each week so that a weekend program for children can be arranged. Common examples of shared spaces are facilities used by faith-based schools that need the classrooms for weekend services or religious school. These arrangements tap the creativity of teachers who want to offer opportunities for children to sustain projects into multiple weeks. Teachers become most innovative when successfully dealing with situations in which older school-age children share common rooms and outdoor areas with the preschool-age children.

Standards for Early Childhood Programs

Early Childhood Education programs are governed by licensing regulations established within each state. State regulations usually address only the safety of the children. Program standards improve as increasing numbers of programs participate in voluntary accreditation programs. However, setting standards poses challenges to Early Childhood professionals, who must first establish the definition of "quality." "Quality results from the relationships among the standards and the factors they comprise," rather than listing its components separately (Bredekamp, 1999, p. 59).

A widely subscribed voluntary accreditation process that was initiated in 1984 is a commendable approach for evaluating your program by the National Academy of Early Childhood Programs (division of the National Association for the Education of Young Children [NAEYC]) (Bellm, Whitebook, & Hnatiuk, 1997, p. 98). NAEYC-accredited programs were found to be six times more likely to be considered high in quality than those programs that were not accredited (Bredekamp, 1999, p. 61). The characteristics of high-quality facilities are based on the criteria developed by the Academy and include staff–child and staff–parent interaction, administration, staffing and staff qualifications, physical environments, curricula, health and safety, nutrition and food service, and program evaluation. Criteria call for developmentally appropriate practices with suitable expectations, activities, and materials. The accreditation review process involves the staff as they participate in the evaluation of their program in terms of developmentally appropriate practices (NAEYC, 1986, p. 34). The Family Child Care Accreditation Project, at Wheelock College in Boston, has been working with family child-care providers, trainers, and advocates across the nation to develop a system that sets high standards for quality in family childcare. "Child care licensing standards strive to protect children from harm by setting a 'floor' for minimally adequate quality. Achieving accreditation raises child care quality from adequate to beneficial. Sustaining accreditation requires continuous quality improvement and ongoing professional development" (Lutton, 1998, p. 2).

Preparation and training programs also commit to standards and quality. The Child Development Associate Credential (CDA) is sponsored by the Council for Early Childhood Professional Recognition. CDA endorsement is available to candidates working with young children, infants, toddlers, and preschoolers, in center-based care, family child-care, and as a home visitor. Competency goals include the ability to establish and maintain a safe, healthy learning environment (Puckett & Diffily, 1999, p. 358).

Centers that earn high scores when evaluated with the Early Childhood Environment Rating Scale (ECERS) (Harms & Clifford, 1980) excel in features such as safety, organization, and variety of equipment and materials in the activity areas. This evaluation tool, developed by Richard Clifford and Thelma Harms, is used by some projects to screen candidates participating in Early Childhood Mentoring (Nattinger, 1997, p. 4-A-6).

INDOOR AND OUTDOOR CLASSROOMS

Indoor and outdoor environments will enhance children's positive growth and development when the teachers coordinate curriculum planning and resources. You will be able to meet your program guidelines as you create and maintain an environment leading to curriculum with best practices.

Jim Greenman, in his book entitled *Caring Spaces, Learning Places: Children's Environments That Work*, suggests a list of ten innovative ideas. The dimensions of children's settings that he outlines request that we include comfort and security, softness, safety and health, privacy and social space, order, autonomy, and mobility in the environments (1988, p. 73).

Indoor Places

The child-centered learning environment, including the space and equipment, is age-level appropriate when it is kept simple for the youngest learners. The spatial organization of materials in **indoor places** must be inviting and accessible. "The key is *access*—access to a range of working spaces, access to materials, access to other children and other adults; in short, the ability to access their own creative process" (Hubbard, 1998, p. 29).

Your creative and efficient use of the available space will be an ongoing challenge. Keep in mind your program guidelines and needs of the enrolled children you are serving and you will keep the curriculum alive. "Children and adults tell us how the room should be by their behavior" (Greenman, 1988, p. 136).

There are some features in the environment that will help you avoid limiting the curriculum. For example, cooking activities proceed more smoothly when the children can conveniently wash their hands. The placement of the bathrooms in the environment also affects the schedule. When bathrooms are located to allow easy access, there will be fewer interruptions to the children's flow of activities.

Teachers can adapt the space in facilities by enhancing the physical design with light or with room dividers, lower **shelving,** fabric safely draped to lower ceilings, and improved pathways. The flow of traffic is important for all children but is especially valuable for children with disabilities, who will benefit from wider spaces that are clearly defined. The floor space needs to be free of islands and equipment that is fixed permanently (Caples, 1996, p. 15). Teachers are challenged to renovate buildings by removing walls to facilitate mobility, provide large activity areas, improve traffic flow, and enhance supervision.

The use of movable shelving allows the greatest flexibility in room arrangement. The child-size, sturdy shelves create zones for activities. Organized shelves encourage children to select materials themselves and return these materials to the same places. Labeling the shelves with pictures and words to identify the places where the items are to be returned contributes to each child's independent participation in the environment. Organized shelves and cabinets should be height-appropriate for young children, and shelves need to be large enough to store containers. Materials and supplies stored in mesh baskets, plastic tubs with handles, and trays need to be attractively arranged on shelves to invite a child to experience the activity fully. Materials placed on a shelf can be stored in containers made of different tactile materials to assist visually impaired children to select a particular manipulative or material.

Outdoor Places

When teachers invest as much time planning learning experiences in **outdoor places** as they do indoor experiences, young children gain appreciation and responsibility for their natural surround-

ings. Most people think of standard features in outdoor settings: safe and approved fencing and ground cover under climbing structures, sand area, path for wheel toys, swings, and climbing structures. The outdoor environment should also feature innovative activity areas while maintaining safety; however, maintenance and security considerations outdoors cause some limitations. Tables for manipulatives and art might need to be permanently secured, sand covered, and wheel toys stored each night.

Outdoor equipment should be scaled to different physical abilities and activity levels of the children. Areas also need to be sheltered to create shade during sunny weather and protection from rain. Outdoor activities are especially beneficial for children who attend extended day programs. Children who spend the full day in school need programs that schedule outside time for longer periods, even in extreme temperatures. Outdoor experiences can include gardening, winter picnicking, spring snack and walks, and bird and wildflower watching (Hosfield, 1998, p. 26).

Studies have shown that children who engage in positive outdoor experiences with nature during early childhood do not develop negative or distrustful perspectives about nature (Curriculum Activity Guide 15 [CAG]). Positive exposure to the outdoors helps children form lasting behaviors of respect and care for the environment (Wilson, Kilmer, & Knauerhase, 1996, p. 56).

Outdoor equipment should be scaled to different physical abilities and activity levels of the children.

Permanent sites provide outdoor garden areas supplied with running water. An outdoor area adjacent to the indoor area encourages a free-flow curriculum. Planning and tending a garden help children to appreciate the natural process of growing; gardens with raised beds are easiest to tend (Clemens, 1996, p. 22).

Arranging movable equipment to create an obstacle course can challenge the children's skills and imagination. Popular materials for obstacle courses include tires, boxes, hoops, pillows, plastic stepping tiles, and tunnels. "The possibilities for course ideas are limited only by safety and imagination" (Griffin & Rinn, 1998, p. 18). Obstacle courses contribute to the outdoor environment because they extend the available outdoor equipment and provide large motor activity.

Storage for Curriculum Supplies

A common remark resounds from teachers of young children when asked to indicate "what they really need most in their classrooms." The greatest need appears to be **storage.** The storage of materials is important to the operation of programs for young children, both indoors and outdoors. If adequate storage and retrieval methods are not organized, supplies are scattered and materials lost. Storage spaces for specific equipment should be located close to activity areas intended for the use of that equipment. Wheel toys need to be stored daily

Storage of materials and supplies is critical.

to be protected from weather and vandalism (Sciarra & Dorsey, 1998, p. 174). Storage is indispensable for materials frequently used in outdoor Interest Centers, including easels, paint, sand buckets, dramatic play items, manipulatives, and gardening and construction tools. Long-term storage is needed for supplies purchased in quantities, seasonal provisions, and prop boxes that relate to thematic and project curriculum activities.

INTEREST CENTERS

The Creative Curriculum (Dodge, 1992), recommends that an environment include space for the following activities: blocks, house corner, table toys, art, sand and water, library, music and movement, and the outdoors. Additional spaces for cooking and computers are suggested for older preschoolers and kindergartners. Each space can be regarded as an **Interest Center.** Interest Centers are the core of the curriculum because the curriculum activities are organized around them. They allow children to learn from the environment. "The teacher's role is to create an environment that invites children to observe, to be active, to make choices, and to experiment" (Dodge & Colker, 1992, p. 67).

Early Childhood professionals also refer to Interest Centers as activity areas, centers of learning, discovery stations, learning areas, and learning stations. These delineated areas within the program environment invite children to participate in different types of activities. Specialized areas also allow teachers to plan activities for children to engage in small groups and in individualized experiences. Interest Centers support a flexible curriculum that matches the needs of young children. Teachers plan experiences within the Interest Centers to meet the guidelines of the program and the children's needs. The manner in which the center is arranged and the nature of the materials provided influence the direction of play and exploration.

Each Interest Center, as defined by the program guidelines, should have a clear purpose and description; however, that purpose and description can change with review of the curriculum and the observation and assessment of the children. A Dramatic Play center may change with the seasons or, based on the interests of children, become a post office or a medical clinic. A description of each Interest Center delineates activities in specific areas, both indoors and outdoors, and informs educators and parents informally about the curricular guidelines. Interest Centers often replicate the curriculum areas that are designated by the school; for example, an Art Interest Center replicates the content area of Art. Curriculum areas are discussed in more detail in Chapter 5.

What to Call the Interest Center?

The teaching staff enjoy a degree of freedom in labeling Interest Centers. The possibilities for naming Interest Centers are open to teachers' imaginations. There may or may not be a requirement for standardizing the names of Interest Centers where you work. However, it is reasonable for teachers to decide on a name for each Interest Center to establish consistency for the children and adult participants. The ability to specifically locate an activity is an aid in planning and balancing the activity offerings to children. The Art area may be called the creative area, the art activity area, or the arts and crafts area. The Science area may be called, as appropriate, the science center or the discovery zone. The block area may be referred to as the building area. An area that displays indoor plants and vegetables, a fish aquarium, and a rabbit cage may be referred to as the center for living things. As new ideas become prevalent in society, centers begin to incorporate related items into the Interest Centers. A new addition to the list of Interest Centers in many programs is a technology area, or computer center, where children use microcomputers alone and in small groups (Figure 4–1).

Temporary Interest Centers may be formed as a follow-up to special events and excursions. A trip to the neighborhood bakery may stimulate a new Interest Center about baking. A visit to the hair salon may create an Interest Center about care of nails and hair. Often these follow-up activities relate to a project and fill the Interest Center with Sociodramatic Play.

FIGURE 4–2   Areas for Interest Centers

Indoor	Outdoor
Manipulatives	Sand and water
Sensory	Sensory
Dramatic Play	Dramatic Play
Block	Construction
Music	Music and movement
Quiet reading loft	Quiet reading pillows
Discovery	Discovery
Art	Art
Technology	Trike path, climbing
Science	Science
Cooking/Nutrition	Gardening
Pets	Pets

Interest Centers can be further categorized as indoor and outdoor areas to help the teacher in planning. Interest Centers with a wide variety of names (Figure 4–2) meet program requirements when they evolve from the needs of the children and keep program guidelines in clear focus.

Replicating similar and related spaces outdoors improves chances that children will participate in situations within each of the developmental domains. There may be more opportunities for small muscle development indoor and large movement outdoors. Therefore, manipulation will more likely be found indoors, and a wooden bridge for wheel toys and dramatic play outdoors.

How to Set Up Interest Centers

Interest Centers are arranged to facilitate activities that provide either child-directed experiences or teacher-guided experiences. The materials and

FIGURE 4–1   What to Call the Interest Center?

Art	Exploratory	Creative	Media
Literacy	Language	Library	Quiet
Music	Listening	Rhythm	Movement
Dramatic	Housekeeping	Social play	Imaginary
Science	Experiment	Cooking	Exploration
Block	Building	Construction	Unit block
Gardening	Living things	Pets	Plants
Computer	Technology	Telecommunications	

arrangements of materials are signals to the children of the way in which the material can be used. The abilities of the children and knowledge and skills required to engage in the activities determine the degree of teacher supervision. For example, an Interest Center equipped with a magnifying glass and seeds placed on trays encourages a child to view the seeds with the magnifying glass with little teacher interaction. A tracing of the magnifying glass, taped on the table or on a tray, signals that the lens is to be placed back there when the viewing is complete. This same station may display photographs and books. A visual with drawings of seeds might also be provided to encourage children to match and place on the task card the seeds that have been viewed. Varied magnifying strengths can be added later in the week once the children have become engaged with the activity. A sign hung or placed near the center, visually displaying the number of children that the activity will accommodate, positively directs children as they respond to the prepared environment.

There is no formula or defining requirement regarding how you set up the areas for activities. You will find similarities among programs that individualize curriculum and arrange Interest Centers for child-initiated play. For example, the Manipulative Center provides children with opportunities to engage in fine motor experiences. Children use their small muscles to place and manipulate small pieces. Activities in this center offer children opportunities to match, organize, fit, cut, place, and move objects. Besides development of motor skills, there are opportunities to develop skills with mathematical concepts (such as classifying), critical thinking, verbalization, and problem solving (Curriculum Activity Guide 16 CAG).

A Block Center, with unit and hollow blocks, provides opportunities to stretch and use large muscles while exploring mathematical concepts. The block area remains a standard area of learning for young children. The organization of blocks is important because the arrangement enhances children's exploration and discovery, securing blocks as an integral part of the curriculum. Block play builds friendships and enhances self-esteem as children share, communicate, and problem solve. Children building with blocks often role-play events and work through their feelings (Mayesky, 1998, pp. 360–361). When teachers add props and accessories to the Block Center the children's play expands.

No matter how you organize the areas or what you name them, Interest Centers certainly offer benefits for the entire program (Figure 4–3).

Activities in this Interest Center offer children opportunities to match, organize, and move objects.

FIGURE 4–3   Interest Centers Benefit Children

Help achieve program goals	Engage individual children
Encourage exploration	Engage small groups of children
Introduce concepts	Initiate child-directed experiences
Expand projects	Create follow-up neighborhood trips
Expand themes	Organize space for discovery and play

ENVIRONMENTS FOR INCLUSIVE CURRICULA

Movable equipment with open areas provides the greatest opportunity to modify the environment to satisfy the special, individualized needs of all young children. **Inclusive settings** adapt the environment with modifications to welcome children with disabilities. The environment should remain culturally and linguistically sensitive through each day, week, and month with respect for the children and their families to achieve an authentically inclusive program. Generally, the physical setting and environmental arrangements that are effective for all preschoolers are also suitable for children with varying abilities and children from culturally and ethnically diverse families. A flexible setting, accomplishing best practices for all children, can be modified to help children with special needs function more comfortably once individual needs have been identified (Loughlin & Suina, 1982, p. 216).

Environments will best meet children's needs when the staff practices authentic inclusion with appropriate and daily representation of all children. This requires teachers to display photographs, drawings, and artifacts representative of all children, families, and communities. We are a multicultural, multiracial, multiethnic, multilingual, multieconomic, and multireligious society with a common goal to support the positive growth and development of children and families. Check your environment with the recommendations issued by the position statement prepared by NAEYC, *Responding to Linguistic and Cultural Diversity: Recommendations for Effective Early Childhood Education* (Chang, Muckelroy, & Pulido-Tobiassen, 1996, p. 188):

- Does your environment foster positive racial identity?
- Does your environment build on the cultures of the families and promote cross cultural respect?

- Does your environment preserve the children's home languages and encourage all children to learn a second language?
- Does your environment allow reflection about race, language, and culture?

Does your environment provide for children who are new to the community or country or on the move? Children move with their families because of work transfers, seasonal and agricultural work, military placement, homelessness, and changes in the structure of the family unit. Does your center welcome and reflect where they have been and may go? (Gillies, 1998, p. 36).

Program facilities will need to comply with the American Disabilities Act (ADA). Public Law 94–142 became effective in 1975, authorizing children with disabilities to be mainstreamed as early as possible into the regular setting. Removal of barriers opens the environment to include children with disabilities; thus all children are allowed to explore materials, to experiment, and create (Udell, Peters, & Templeman, 1998, p. 46). Teachers will meet needs of children with disabilities by adapting the environment. One way would be to clearly display materials. For example, teacher Sven ensures that paste and paper are within Maya's reach and that other jars are not in the path of her arm movement. Clear placement and display of materials helps children with perceptual problems to focus on the meaningful components. Children with limited mobility can be aided by placing collections of materials in many varied locations in the indoor and outdoor classroom environment. Multiple accessible art shelves with paper, crayons, markers, and scissors facilitate more immediate and active participation (Cook, Tessier, & Klein, 1996, p. 296).

Utilizing varied shelf levels provides adaptable access to children with limitations of reach. Modification of carriers, with flexible handles and straps, assists young learners with limited balance or mobility (Loughlin & Suina, 1982, p. 215).

Children with visual limitations benefit from classroom arrangements that are consistent and that have direct pathways free of obstacles. Auditory and tactile cues enhance the environment as a means of designating specific areas. The use of both carpeted and uncarpeted zones encourages independence because the change in floor surface physically tells the child that she is in a specific activity area. Modified easels, magnetic boards, tables with rims, easily grasped objects, and portable work spaces increase accessibility and help children to participate in activities applying their capabilities (Loughlin & Suina, 1982, p. 216).

Technology is transforming education, increasing opportunities for children with disabilities. Technological tools such as computers modified with larger screens and voice-activated modifications open up successful school experiences for children with disabilities. Boundaries are reduced when the world becomes accessible on screen. Teacher-guided, on-line communication through Internet links introduces young children to interaction previously inaccessible to them. "By giving students access to and training in the Internet, we empower them to become active learners" (Doyle, 1999, p. 13). New Web site links for children with disabilities appear each day, such as http://www.irsc.org/disability.htm. It is particularly beneficial to provide skills for teachers and parents about finding resources on the Internet because Web sites may not remain active.

REVIEW

Early Childhood environments influence the development of young children and the way that teachers and caregivers nurture and educate. Settings that are child-centered need to be predictable and encourage spontaneity in responding to the needs of the children.

Indoor places need to be age-level appropriate with accessible materials stored on sturdy, child-size shelving. The organization of the environment will depend on guidelines based on the program, the age of the children, and the facility layout.

The outdoor environment offers activity areas and opportunities with nature that have lifelong benefits for children. Besides the common outdoor features such as sand and paths for wheel toys, the outdoor areas give children opportunities to garden or to challenge obstacle courses.

Interest Centers create areas or zones for specific learning and activities. What an Interest Center is called is a decision that is made by the program staff. Interest Centers provide both child-directed and teacher-guided experiences by creating spaces so that children learn from the arranged environment.

Generally, a flexible physical setting that is individualized for all young children also benefits children with special needs.

KEY TERMS

environment	outdoor places
inclusive settings	settings
indoor places	shelving
Interest Centers	storage

RESPOND

1. Select Interest Centers for an Early Childhood program. Label each center as you lay out a floor plan and outdoor area. Decide the general placement of the Interest Centers in both the indoor and outdoor environments.

2. Participate in an outdoor adventure with children, either with a school program or as a personal experience, such as a walk in a park, a snack picnic in the snow, or a visit to a garden. Observe the children's reactions during the adventure. Summarize and write a one-page paper about what you believe to be the benefits to the participating children.

3. Connect with a Web site to gather information about environments for young children. Identify the Web site and list five recommendations suggested. Possible Web sites include:

Teaching Strategies

http://wwwteachingstrategies.com/

Montessori Foundation

http://www.montessori.org/

High Scope Education Research Foundation

http://www.highscope.org/

4. Visit a center that enrolls children with special needs. Observe how the environment allows inclusion of children with special needs. List five modifications to the outdoor environment and five to the indoor environment that allow children with varying capabilities to participate in the curriculum.

REFERENCES

Bellm, D., Whitebook, M., & Hnatiuk, P. (1997). *The early childhood mentoring curriculum: A handbook for mentors.* Washington, DC: Center for the Child Care Workforce.

Bredekamp, S. (1999). When new solutions create new problems: Lessons learned from NAEYC accreditation. *Young Children, 54*(1), 58–63.

Bredekamp, S., & Copple, C. (Eds.). (1997). *Developmentally appropriate practices in early childhood programs* (Rev.). Washington, DC: National Association for the Education of Young Children.

Caples, S. E. (1996). Some guidelines for preschool designs. *Young Children, 51*(4), 14–21.

Chang, H. N. L., Muckelroy, A., & Pulido-Tobiassen, D. (1996). *Looking in, looking out: Redefining child care and early education in a diverse society.* San Francisco: California Tomorrow.

Clemens, J. B. (1996). Gardening with children. *Young Children, 51*(4), 22–27.

Cook, R. E., Tessier, A., Klein, M. D. (1996). *Adapting early childhood curriculum for children in inclusive settings* (4th ed.). Englewood Cliffs, NJ: Merrill.

Dodge, D. T. and Colker, L. J. (1992). *The creative curriculum.* (3rd ed.). Washington, DC: Teaching Strategies.

Doyle, A. (1999). A practitioner's guide to snaring the net. *Educational Leadership, 56*(5), 12–15.

Gestwicki, C. (1999). *Developmentally appropriate practice: Curriculum and development in early education* (2nd ed.). Albany, NY: Delmar.

Gillies, W. D. (1998). Third culture kids: Children on the move. *Childhood Education, 75*(1), 36–38.

Greenman, J. (1988). *Caring spaces, learning places.* Redmond, WA: Exchange Press.

Griffin, C., & Rinn, B. (1998). Enhancing outdoor play with an obstacle course. *Young Children. 53*(3), 18–23.

Harms, T., & Clifford, R. M. (1980). *Early childhood environment rating scale.* New York: Teachers College Press.

Hildebrand, V., & Hearon, P. F. (1997). *Management of child development centers* (4th ed.). Upper Saddle River, NJ: Merrill.

Hosfield, D. (1998). A long day in care need not seem long. *Young Children, 53*(3), 24–28.

Hubbard, R. S. (1998). Creating a classroom where children can think. *Young Children, 53*(5), 26–31.

Loughlin, C. E., & Suina, J. H. (1982). *The learning environment: An instructional strategy.* New York: Teachers College Press.

Lutton, A. (1998). Sixteen states use tiered reimbursement rates to support accreditation. *Accreditation works for states and communities.* Boston, MA: The Family Child Care Accreditation Project.

Mayesky, M. (1998). *Creative activities for young children* (6th ed.). Albany, NY: Delmar.

Moore, G. T. (1997). Houses and their resource-rich activity pockets. *Child Care Information Exchange, 113,* 15–20.

NAEYC (1986). Child care centers, preschools now being accredited. *Young Children, 41*(2), 34–35. Washington, DC: National Association for the Education of Young Children.

Nattinger, P. (1997). *California early childhood mentor program handbook.* Unpublished.

Puckett, M. B., & Diffily, D. (1999). *Teaching young children: An introduction to the early childhood profession.* Orlando, FL: Harcourt Brace.

Sciarra, D. J. & Dorsey, A. G. (1998). *Developing and administering a child care center* (4th ed.). Albany, NY: Delmar.

Udell, T., Peters, J., & Templeman, T. P. (1998, Jan/Feb). From philosophy to practice in inclusive early childhood programs. *Teaching Exceptional Children 30*(3), 44–49.

Wilson, R. A., Kilmer, S. J., & Knauerhase, V. (1996). Developing an environmental outdoor play space. *Young Children, 51*(1), 56–61.

CHAPTER 5

Designing a Managed Curriculum: *Beginning with Review and a Plan*

Curriculum Profile

What do you want to know about Early Childhood curriculum? Both entry level and experienced students have responded to this question in a brainstorming session and offered many interesting answers. Check the responses that match questions you have about Early Childhood curriculum.

How do you make curriculum fun and keep the children's interest?

Are there regulations that must be followed related to curriculum?

How can I provide meaningful activities for children with disabilities?

How can I convey to the children that they might not always have choices?

I think that I have been doing the right activity, I just don't know why I plan the activities that I do.

What is the right way to teach children in a class who are different ages?

Chapter Outline

Curriculum That Is Good for Young Children
Curriculum Linked to Assessment
Individualizing Curriculum: Observe/Review/Plan
Child-Initiated Activities
Inclusive and Sensitive
Multi-Age Grouping
Teacher-Guided Experiences

Identifying Curricular Guidelines
Guidelines for Children, Families, and Programs
Developing Practical and Meaningful Guidelines

Approaches to Planning
Developmental Focus Approach
Curriculum Area Approach
Thematic Approach
Project Approach

Creating an Emergent and Integrated Curriculum
Emergent Experiences
Integrated Experiences

Establishing and Recording a Curriculum Plan and Schedule
Getting Started: What Is Happening Now?
Flexibility within a Framework

Framing a Schedule
Recording Long- and Short-Term Curriculum Plans
Adapting Plans for Extended-Day Activities

Maximizing Curriculum Resources
Parents and Community Guests
Trips in the Neighborhood

Study Guide

As you study the sections in this chapter, you should be able to:

- Consider how regular observation of children influences the curriculum.
- Describe "observe/review/plan."
- Review examples of child-initiated, inclusive, and sensitive activities.
- Understand multi-age grouping of children.
- Know about Grouptime as a teacher-guided experience.
- Establish curricular guidelines.
- Examine the Developmental Focus Approach, Curriculum Area Approach, Thematic Approach, and the Project Approach for creating curriculum for young children.

- Describe curriculum areas.
- Identify appropriate themes.
- Become familiar with the process of webbing to identify relevant experiences.
- Understand the concepts *emergent* and *integrated*.
- Analyze the building blocks for creating a curriculum plan.
- Consider how the daily schedule influences the curriculum.
- Compare written curriculum plans.
- Review ways to expand curriculum resources.

CURRICULUM THAT IS GOOD FOR YOUNG CHILDREN

Curriculum Linked to Assessment

In Chapter 2 you learned that when centers conduct ongoing assessments of the enrolled children it helps teachers make decisions related to curriculum planning and implementation. As you observe and listen to children you will gather important data about their needs, skills, and interests. Most of the information will be collected as you interact with them during the course of the **daily schedule**. You or other staff may also record what you hear and see using the various assessment methods (see Figure 2–6), which include casual note taking, checklists, logs, and time samples. Assessments provide teachers with language samples that reveal a child's feelings and degree of understanding (Figure 5–1).

The assessment information that is collected on an ongoing basis will help you to plan many different learning experiences. You will be more efficient in matching the plans with the ability differences among the enrolled children and at altering curriculum plans to accommodate their progress and needs (Wortham, 1996, p. 108).

Individualizing Curriculum: Observe/Review/Plan

Since the children's needs change rapidly, so must the curriculum. Teachers review the health, the feelings, the comfort, and the security needs of children and adjust schedules and planned experiences as needed. The daily events, interactions, and health of children affect their behavior at home and at school. In addition, changes at school, such as absent or new staff members, may also alter the children's behaviors. Young children may be able to act out their feelings of stress, anxiety, or discomfort, but will be unable to relate the causes. Most often teachers need to rely on their observational skills to interpret the actions of children to determine the cause of behavioral changes. There are some apparent reasons for behavior changes. Children are more likely to be ill during the winter months. Children who are in the early stages of the flu or a cold may become irritable and sleepy, requiring some changes to curriculum plans. Children who have been absent due to an illness may need adjustment time when reentering into group activities. Children may need to adjust to substitute teachers who have replaced the regular staff absence due to illness. The teacher must **observe** the children, **review** the observation to identify behavioral changes, then **plan** the curriculum accordingly.

The observations of Bradley (Figure 5–1) provided a language sample: "I can't get those to work" and a glimpse of behavior. An observation of Laila (Figure 5–2), reveals another language sample. Let us now look more carefully at the comment that Laila made at 3:20 PM to determine if the **curriculum plan** could be modified to better meet Laila's needs (Figure 5–2). The teacher's comments, or review, indicated that Laila was delivered to school by her grandmother because Laila's mother is out of town for two weeks. If you

FIGURE 5–1　Assessment Reveals Feelings and Understanding

Anecdotal Assessment

Child's Name *Bradley*　　　　　**Age** *4.2*　　　**Date** *0/0/00*　　　**Time** *9:05AM*

Observer *Teacher Brett*　　　**Location** *Outside Manipulative Table*

Observation of Behavior

Bradley throws scissors down on table. "I can't get those to work." Picks up piece of paper and tear it into pieces. Lifts scissors with his left hand, places it in his right hand, throws it down again.

Comments

Bradley is interested in the scissors. He is not successful but tries again. Plan specific small motor activities.

FIGURE 5–2   Assessment Reveals Feelings and Understanding

Anecdotal Assessment

Child's Name   *Laila*   Age *3.8*   Date *0/0/00*   Time *3:20PM*

Observer   *Teacher Brett*   Location   *Block Interest Center*

Observation of Behavior	**Comments**
Laila returns the last blocks she was using to the shelf. She walks to the window, looks out, turns and looks at the clock. She comments as she walks away from the window, glancing back, "My mama's never gonna pick me up."	*Laila's careful watch of clock and window shows that she is anxious for her mother's arrival. Laila has been sucking her thumb and watching the clock. She was delivered to school by her grandmother.*

---

respond to Laila's immediate needs, you might invite her to join a small group of children who are waiting in the comfortable book area for a story to be read. Laila may need individual attention and direction until her grandmother arrives to pick her up. At the end of the day, you would collaborate with other teachers and assistants to individualize the curriculum plans for the next week. Individualizing the curriculum, simple review, and modification of plans (Figure 5–3) takes a little time, but the potential benefit for Laila is great.

Child-Initiated Activities

As you begin to look more precisely at the methods for organizing the children's activities, you need to pause and appreciate the many ways that children's programs effectively meet their needs with generous backing for **child-initiated** activities. Child-initiated activities are set up in both the indoor and outdoor environments with encouragement and support for the child to select and engage in that particular activity for the amount of time desired. Child-initiated activities can be realized by allowing blocks of open or free time during the daily schedule.

The profession offers considerable validation for including child-initiated experiences with planned activities. One of the country's most famous educators, John Dewey, encouraged educators to apply theories to remain in harmony with principles of growth. He did not believe that one extreme idea was necessarily better than another. Instead he promoted quality experiences that were worthwhile and meaningful to the children (Frost, 1973, p. 426). Dewey also stressed that freedom of intelligence was attained with freedom of physical

FIGURE 5–3   Assessment: Observe/Review/Plan

Anecdotal Assessment

Child's Name   *Laila*   Age *3.8*   Date *0/0/00*   Time *3:20PM*

Observer   *Teacher Brett*   Location   *Block Interest Center*

Observation of Behavior	**Comments**
Laila returns the last blocks she was using to the shelf. She walks to the window, looks out, turns and looks at the clock. She comments as she walks away from the window, glancing back, "My mama's never gonna pick me up."	*Laila's careful watch of clock and window shows that she is anxious for her mother's arrival. Laila has been sucking her thumb and watching the clock. She was delivered to school by her grandmother.*

Curriculum Modification:

1. Request grandmother to arrive earlier if possible and join afternoon snack time.
2. Add book about parent taking trips.
3. Add suitcases to dramatic play area.
4. Place lotto game about departing and returning in manipulative area.

movement. Dewey emphasized that the children's participation is central in the learning process and that the teacher is not just a passive observer without a plan (Frost, 1973, p. 429). These ideas give purpose and justification for activities that are initiated by the child. Other well-known educators, such as Benjamin Bloom, have also validated child-initiated experiences, speaking about the need to allow the child to "find pleasure in learning . . . with opportunities to make new discoveries" (1981, pp. 79, 81). In the Montessori environments children choose to work individually, with another child, or in small groups (Humphryes, 1998, p. 9). Children who are encouraged to choose their own experiences are seen as active learners (Weikart, 1988, p. 65) who make meaningful choices through active involvement (Bredekamp & Copple, 1997, p. 18). The curriculum activities *Let's Look it Up!* and *What Kind of Muffin?* allow children to make choices in a prepared environment (Curriculum Activity Guides 17 and 18).

You will discover the best practices for the children in your program when you offer children meaningful choices within boundaries (Bredekamp & Copple, 1997, p. 23). Your growing knowledge about child development and cultural sensitivity to your school's community will also contribute to the establishment of best practices for young children. A word of warning, however; teachers must remain sensitive to differences in regard to giving children choices. Some communi-

ties prefer that their children adapt to the values and practices as they exist in their community, and may not necessarily value giving choices to children (Gonzalez-Mena, 1997, p. 68).

Inclusive and Sensitive

Inclusive and **sensitive** curricula prepared to respond to the great diversity of families and communities will model positive interactions and values for children and prepare them for an increasingly diverse and international society. Authentic inclusion, as previously explained in Chapter 1, encourages programs to provide experiences for children that recognize and represent all of the children's identities with respect. Identity is formed by our family, our culture, our language, our race, our religion, our social circumstances, our gender, and our capabilities. Communication, bulletin boards, and activities validating respectful representation promote understanding and non-biased behaviors. The program should have clear guidelines to share cultures, holidays, foods, and traditions throughout the year. Inclusive and sensitive programs create settings in which children with disabilities learn "what they can do."

A number of different strategies can help create inclusive and sensitive settings. Place dolls in the dramatic play center, representing as many different races and ethnicities as possible (try to remember the bi-racial and multi-racial children) as well as dolls with walkers, braces, eyeglasses, and

Curricula should be prepared to respond to the great diversity present in the classroom.

hearing aids. Place cushions from different cultures displaying traditional patterns, colors, and designs. Provide food containers from a variety of cultures with labels in different languages. Add culturally relevant clothing, eating utensils, bedding, and infant carriers (Hall, 1999, p. 11) (Curriculum Activity Guide 19).

Multi-Age Grouping

When you visit a center, notice whether the children are in same-age groupings or in **multi-age groupings** and the size of the groupings. Centers tend to be same-age grouped. The placement of young children in groups is determined by many considerations, including the developmental needs of the children, program guidelines, licensing and funding regulations, availability of staff, and facility resources. There is much justification in the literature for keeping the number in the group small for children throughout the early childhood years (Bloom, 1981, p. 109). Two to three very young children (three years old) might form a small group, whereas a group of six could be considered small for five-year-olds. The age and development of children might affect how groups form, whether children group themselves or whether the group is directed by the teacher.

Single-age grouping establishes a setting, or group, for children who are about the same chronological age. Chronological age is the numerical indicator that marks the child's number of years since birth. Children are provided opportunities in a physical setting that is arranged to accommodate children who are within a specified range. Multi-age grouping places children of different ages in settings in which they will participate in the program for either partial or full-day scheduling.

Studies have indicated that teachers are more likely to attend to differences among the children in multi-age grouping. When there is a wider age span within a group, there is a wider range of behavior and abilities. The wider range of behavior and performance is more likely to be accepted and tolerated by the adults within multi-age groups (Katz, 1995, EDO-PS-95-8).

Teacher-Guided Experiences

An early educator's teaching commitment, including ideas about how children learn and his or her theoretical perspective, influences how the experiences are presented. As a teacher of young children you are always guiding experiences because you

Children need guidance during many Art projects.

set up the environment, plan initial activities, and watch for cues from children that will help you modify or validate your plans. Most teachers strive to provide child-initiated experiences in their curriculum. However, there are two occasions in the Early Childhood setting when **teacher-guided** experiences commonly occur. The first occasion is when the materials for the activity are complex and unknown to the children. This implies that the teacher directs the activity for the child or children. The teacher is there to pose interactive questioning that will stimulate children's thinking. The teacher is also there to clarify childrens' participation in the activity and offer resources and materials. Children need supervision and guidance in many Cooking, Science, and Art projects. But the teacher must still allow children to explore, discover, and create as they play with the materials. A second primary occasion for a teacher-guided experience is the **Grouptime** or circle time, that is prevalent in Early Childhood programs. Whether or not you require all children to participate in a Grouptime, the activity is more suitable to young children when the size of the group is small, so that they can see and touch the materials you are introducing. Grouptime can assume many different formats. In an open schedule, children spontaneously gather around the teacher to read a book, to meet a visitor, or to sing and enjoy fingerplays. Grouptime can be scheduled for different times throughout the day. Some teachers offer Grouptime more than once during the morning and afternoon, allowing children to choose the time when they will join in. Grouptimes provide chances for teachers to introduce new ideas and materials and enjoy collaborating with young participants in planning and reviewing the day (Figure 5–4).

FIGURE 5–4   Mentoring Early Childhood Students for Successful Grouptimes

New Early Childhood Education students are frequently intimidated by the prospect of leading Grouptime, yet veteran teachers often view it as one of their favorite daily activities. The journey from anxiety to enjoyment can be facilitated by adherence to the motto, "Planning is the key."

Successful Grouptime planning is based on a logical sequence of components, regardless of the topic or focus. Ideally, all Grouptime elements should be related to the topic or theme for optimum continuity.

I. *Arrival to Grouptime/Settle Down*
Familiar songs with large motor movement to 'get the wiggles out.' (Depending on the children's readiness to settle down, additional large motor songs can be added.)

II. *Focusing/Fingerplay*
From large motor actions, the teacher now focuses the children's attention with a fine motor fingerplay or two.

III. *Main Focus/Body of Grouptime*
Now that the children are settled down and attentive, you can read a story, enact a flannelboard story, or introduce a 'surprise bag.' While this component is typically teacher-directed, it should also be interactive to engage the children and sustain their interest. (Beginning Grouptimes limit this component, and increase over time and as children develop their attention spans.)

IV. *Dismissal*
Children are usually dismissed individually to the next activity with a song or departing activity.

Anxious students are always advised to 'Relax and Enjoy,' and reminded that young children are not nearly so critical as the students are on themselves!

—Kathy Barry, MA
Shasta College

IDENTIFYING CURRICULAR GUIDELINES

The goals of a center will affect the curriculum choices you make. If you are employed, or plan to be employed, by an agency such as a department of education or Head Start program, you will find that a school philosophy or set of goals has already been established. If you work for a private program or faith-based center, the board of directors of the program will establish the school's philosophy and goals (Sciarra & Dorsey, 1998, p. 52).

The educational beliefs held by the school administration and teaching staff also influence a school or program's philosophy. Does the staff believe that a child learns best in a free-choice environment? Does the staff believe that children should self-pace their day? Does the staff believe that achievement of independence is the ultimate goal during early childhood? Does the staff believe that parental input promotes the best educational practices for children? These and other philosophical questions should be addressed by the staff.

Guidelines for Children, Families, and Programs

A **curricular guideline** can be an idea or a plan that defines an intended direction that a program has for the children, program, staff, and parents. The perceptions about children are different because people think differently about development, behavior, and learning. Conceptions about young children, and how they develop, behave, and learn will affect the design of program guidelines. Guidelines then become part of what we need to accomplish, what opportunities we want to facilitate for children, what skills we want them to develop and refine, and what content we want for the curriculum.

Developing Practical and Meaningful Guidelines

Practical guidelines will fit your program needs. Look back at the fundamentals, the comments, and quotes from educational scholars that have been referenced in previous chapters. Decide what you

FIGURE 5–5   Establishing Curricular Guidelines—Ask Yourself These Questions

> What do you want for children and their families?
>
> What outcome do you have in mind?
>
> What types of experiences do you want to offer to children?
>
> Do the goals you are describing define your school program?
>
> Do the goals you are describing provide guidelines to reach specific expectations?

FIGURE 5–6   First Semester ECE Students' Curricular Guidelines

> To treat each child as an individual.
>
> To create a curriculum that meets every child's needs.
>
> To introduce curriculum in a new, exciting way.
>
> To help each child feel good about where he or she may be developmentally.
>
> To offer a program that is always evolving to meet the needs of the child.
>
> To develop and encourage social play.
>
> To create a safe learning environment.
>
> To create an environment that is pleasing and child-friendly.
>
> To encourage discovery and imagination.
>
> (Appreciation is extended to all the Fall 1998 ECE 20 Shasta College students.)

think and value about the fundamentals, theoretical perspectives, types of programs, quality components, harmony, equity, respect, and play. As you begin to develop guidelines that will describe your teaching philosophy, ask yourself these questions: "What are we trying to accomplish?" "Are we sure that is what we really want to do?" "What goal are we trying to achieve?" (Arends, 1991, p. 424) (Figure 5–5). Staff working together to achieve meaningful goals find that the preparation of guidelines identifies a commitment with common agreement and purpose. Early Childhood Education students learn that the process produces worthwhile statements (Figure 5–6).

APPROACHES TO PLANNING

Now that you have thought about meaningful guidelines for your program, how will you begin to plan the activities to match those curricular guidelines? It may be that you adapt your commitment to the curriculum structure that now exists at a school where you are employed. Or, your new ideas may influence the staff to revise their philosophy and goals. You can repeatedly glimpse back at the rationale, fundamentals, and benefits of curriculum (Chapter 1) and the Early Childhood basics (Chapter 3) to acknowledge that a definitive formula does not exist for planning and managing curriculum. There are complementary approaches for organizing experiences for young children, and you may use ideas from some or many programs. There are strong commendations for quality programming and agreement between professional organizations (NAEYC & NAECS/SDE, 1991, p. 21). There are centers that follow a particular curricular procedure, such as the many Head Start programs that use High Scope, which emphasizes key experiences and a decision-making framework (Gestwicki, 1997, p. 45). Your interest in a particular method or approach may relate to your personal experiences, your place of employment, or the curricular guidelines you have defined.

A curriculum plan can designate a specific method or approach. A school's curriculum can combine one or more approaches, each allowing for unexpected and spontaneous learning opportunities. Four general approaches to planning the curriculum will be reviewed. Each approach considers the needs of young children, their individual differences, and the relevancy of activities to the children's cultural and linguistic needs and interests.

Developmental Focus Approach

The **Developmental Focus Approach** focuses on development of the whole child with special consideration of developing skills. The Developmental Focus Approach primarily organizes activities that help children acquire competence in the different areas of development. The experiences are suitable for young children and compatible with their developing abilities. This approach encourages opportunities for children to explore, to discover, and to build on their own interests. The total learning concept (Hendricks, 1980, p. 4) emphasizes real-life orientation within five categories, including the physical self, emotional self, social self, creative self, and cognitive self. Dr. Maria Montessori's educational approach encourages self-development within a prepared environment and uses a three-part sequence of materials and activities, including motor, sensory, and intellectual. She believed that teachers need first to discover the true nature of children, then proceed to assist them in their normal development (Orem, 1974, p. 50).

The developmental approach to planning the curriculum is a framework that encourages teachers to provide challenging yet age-appropriate experiences. Although you may plan an activity to focus on one developmental area, there will be effects on the children's other developmental areas. This is why this approach is considered to be holistic, or meeting the needs of the "whole child." Visualize three-year-olds and four-year-olds painting on a large stretch of butcher paper hung on the outdoor fence. They use large painting brushes and make large strokes (physical development—large movement). Once the butcher paper dries, the children and teacher together decide to hang the colorfully painted butcher paper to provide a shaded shelter (affective development—social). Some of the children bring picture books to this outside shaded area (cognitive development—literacy).

The Developmental Focus areas used throughout this textbook are physical, affective and aesthetic, and cognitive and language. A more detailed discussion of the Developmental Focus areas was provided in Chapter 2.

Physical

The Physical Developmental Focus area relates to the dimension of physiological growth and changes. This area is immensely critical for Early Childhood programs because all children need to move their bodies, within the capabilities that each child has, to engage their senses and challenge their muscles. As you begin to consider specific experiences for children, expand the Physical Developmental Focus area to include **sensorial** experiences. Sensorial experiences invite the children to use their senses. Sensory Education, a major aspect of the Montessori Method, introduces materials sequentially, with emphasis on sensory growth. Qualities of color, form, dimension, sound, and texture are presented with concrete experiences to educate the senses (Orem, 1974, p. 75) (Curriculum Activity Guide 20 [CAG]).

Affective and Aesthetic

The Affective and Aesthetic Developmental Focus area encompasses growth and change in social and emotional behaviors as well as a growing sensitivity to beauty in nature and art. The affective domain looks at children's sociability, feelings, personality, reactions, and interactions. The aesthetic aspect of this Developmental Focus area covers creativity and expressiveness (Curriculum Activity Guide 21 [CAG]).

Cognitive and Language

The Cognitive and Language Developmental Focus area is the category that includes mental abilities and the acquisition of language, communication, and literacy. Studies validate the relationship between early experiences and cognitive development. Practices need to promote acceptance of the home language and culture to effectively promote growth in this Developmental Focus area for all children.

Now consider how children's behaviors and changes within each Developmental Focus area can be translated into appropriate and relevant experiences (Figure 5–7).

Alfred North Whitehead, 1929

Let the main ideas which are introduced into a child's education be few and important, and let them be thrown into every combination possible. The child should make them his own, and should understand their application here and now in the circumstances of his actual life (1929, p. 14).

Curriculum Area Approach

An Early Childhood curriculum can be managed by organizing the children's activities by subject areas. Subject areas are also referred to as content areas and curriculum areas. The term **curriculum area** is used throughout this textbook and provides the rationale for calling this method to preparing curriculum for young children the Curriculum Area Approach.

The Curriculum Area Approach is organized by disciplines or subject areas such as Art, Language, Mathematics, Music, Physical Education, Science, and Social Studies. There is a long tradition favoring curriculum that is divided into subjects. Continued support for this approach is evident particularly in elementary and high schools, where subject-matter curriculum is most common. You may work in a program that calls the curriculum area the subject or content area. Remember, there is a great deal of variability in Early Childhood terminology (Figure 5–8).

During the beginning stages of the Early Childhood Education movement (late 1960s), the

FIGURE 5–7   Developmental Focus Areas (Related Developing Abilities)

Areas of Development	Children's Related Developing Abilities	
Physical	physiological changes growth, height, and weight large muscle movement small muscle movement motor abilities perceptual/motor abilities health/safety/nutrition/wellness awareness movement responses to music and rhythm	
Affective and Aesthetic	sociability emotions and feelings temperament and personality self-awareness trust self-confidence interactions and reactions	prosocial gender role identity creative expression discovery making choices artistic expression dramatic expression
Cognitive and Language	thinking and mental abilities memory and logic intellectual growth conceptualizing grouping, matching, ordering creativity communication seeing cause/effect	literacy listening comprehension inquiry intuition imagination verbal fluency problem-solving

FIGURE 5–8   Common Curriculum Areas

What Curriculum Areas Are Commonly Called	What Curriculum Areas Are Most Often Included
Curriculum areas, Subject areas, Content areas	Art Language Mathematics Music Physical Education Science Social studies

curriculum for pre-kindergarten children was influenced by the elementary school format. Some professionals advocated for activities that suited the younger children. The framework that evolved reflected the traditional curriculum with a strong foundation in subject areas (Hymes, 1981, pp. 25–35, Hildebrand, 1971, p. 22).

The curriculum areas generally include recognizable categories and/or combinations. The selection of the curriculum areas will also reflect the preferences of the center administration, board of directors, and teaching staff. Patterns do appear that reflect popular trends, research outcomes, and national needs. Extensions and combinations of basic subject areas continue to increase, creating a wide variety of curriculum areas. Individual programs tailor the curriculum by adding and deleting areas to more effectively meet the needs of their children. Science, literacy, mathematics, and technology have gained importance. The addition of a curriculum area for computers is an example of the evolving nature of the Curriculum Area Approach. Which options would you choose if you needed to set up the children's program using the Curriculum Area Approach? Would you use the word *Science,* or *Science and Nutrition,* or would you have a separate curriculum area for nutrition? What would you call the art area—*Art or Arts and Crafts?* Topics are generally categorized within related curriculum areas, giving the teachers liberty to organize in ways that suit their program guidelines (Figure 5–9).

Art

Art provides opportunities for children to explore and create in a natural setting that encourages creative and spontaneous pleasure with the materials. Basic art expression materials include clay, crayons, chalk, pencils, markers, glue, paint, paper, pasta, prints, modeling dough, and scissors.

Creative Dramatics

Children are given the chance to express themselves through movement, gestures, language, and nonverbal communication. Creative Dramatics (Curriculum Activity Guide 22 CAG) encourages children to improvise drama given suggestions, stories, or events. The children imagine and respond naturally, using their own actions and verbal responses. Materials can be used to stimulate children's imaginations and expressions (Edwards, 1990, p. 92).

Health, Safety, Nutrition

Concepts about healthy living habits for the entire life span can be introduced in the Curriculum Area Approach of Health, Safety, and Nutrition. Children will benefit by developing meaningful experiences to understand their own development and safety and wellness behaviors.

Communication and Literacy

Communication includes listening and verbal fluency. Literacy opportunities occur daily in an early learning program with a print-rich setting filled with books, bulletin boards, word labels, and nurturing teachers to respond to children's questions and requests for stories.

Mathematics

The curriculum area of Mathematics allows exploration and discovery. Numbers are everywhere for children to use to discover mathematical concepts

FIGURE 5–9   Topics Categorized within Curriculum Areas

Art	**Communication and Literacy**	**Science**
art media	literature	sciencing
artistic experiences	communication	physical science
arts and crafts	literacy	biological science
creative activities	reading	science
shape and form	linguistics	discovery
	reading readiness	plants
	language arts	animals
		technology
Mathematics	**Social Understanding**	**Music and Rhythm**
math and technology	social world	music and rhythm
time, space, numbers	community helpers	music experiences
size and shape	people in the world	songs and fingerplays
math experiences	sociodramatics	musical sounds
pre math	learning culture	
Movement	**Creative Dramatics**	**Health, Safety, Nutrition**
movement	dramatic expression	health
perceptual motor	puppetry	safety
sensorimotor	Sociodramatics	nutrition
sensorial		cooking
health and safety		

by manipulating real materials in child-initiated activities. Mathematics is integrated throughout the children's setting and curriculum. Children learn to analyze, arrange, compare, graph, measure, order, pair, pattern, and reverse in mathematical activities.

Movement

Children acquire specific motor skills through physical movement, feeling their bodies move, and by understanding the changes in body movements. Children develop their large motor skills and small motor skills in an environment that allows them to participate in active experiences. Coordination, balance, and control mature as children participate in appropriate movement activities.

Music and Rhythm

Children will hum, repeat parts of songs, listen to tapes, move to the rhythm of music, participate in fingerplays, and enjoy instruments in programs in which experiences respect their need for creative movement. Teachers will guide children in the curriculum area of Music and Rhythm when they maintain small groups, provide adequate space, and appropriately address the attention span and interests of the participating children.

Science

Concepts expand when children become aware of their world. Both biological and physical science concepts are included within most science curricula for young children. Children also engage in manipulation of objects to discover, cook, care for pets, and garden while observing the cause and effect phenomenon of matter, energy, and space.

Social Understanding

Planned activities contribute to young children's self-awareness, helping them to accept, comfort, express, initiate, motivate, and nurture. Children's emotional well-being will emerge as they interact with adults and other children in the center. Thoughtful curriculum (Curriculum Activity Guide 23 [CAG]) incorporates bias-free experiences into planning and implementation of the curriculum with encouragement for children to reach their full potential.

Thematic Approach

The **Thematic Approach** in Early Childhood organizes the curriculum around an idea or a topic. This approach allows children to explore a topic in depth by participating in a collection of related activities. Some identify this approach as an **integrated** curriculum because teachers can connect the planned experiences from different curriculum areas to the selected **theme.** This method allows you to arrange opportunities to expose children to new ideas and to develop their skills within many subject areas, including Science, Mathematics, and Art.

The words *unit* and *resource unit* are used interchangeably with the word *theme.* A unit connects several themes or topics. Regardless of the word used to describe your curriculum approach, coordinate activities to reinforce your curricular goals and maintain flexibility in the daily, weekly, and monthly plan (Eliason & Jenkins, 1981, p. 28).

A theme sets a broad, general framework that allows children to plan, explore, and construct their own learning. Goals for young children in the design of the Thematic Approach leads to learning during the early years when teachers accept that children need to be active, curious, and confident and to think creatively (Kamii, 1973, p. 150). When emphasizing active learning, teachers need to practice caution to avoid overprogramming precise objectives about the concepts that children are to acquire from the specific preplanned activities (Katz, 1994, EDO-ps-94–6).

The Thematic Approach to planning the curriculum continues to be popular in Early Childhood programs. Children can contribute to the planning, explore topics thoroughly, and enjoy the challenges of the experiences. Teachers will be able to establish long-term goals while continuing to adjust the plans to meet the interests and needs of the children. They can use themes to guide and organize the activities and experiences. Themes integrate curriculum areas to avoid teaching children isolated information by subject areas. They also provide numerous ways to balance activities among the curriculum areas.

If your school plans to use primarily the Thematic Approach, the staff should collaboratively select themes that are most familiar to the children in your program. The activities related to each theme will have more relevance to the children as the activities are offered. Avoid emphasis on prepared holiday units because these tend to interfere with a developmental curriculum (Derman-Sparks & A.B.C. Task Force, 1989, p. 86).

Frequently scheduled themes include those that relate directly to the child, such as Me and My

Family. Expand to topics such as Pets, Friends, and Neighbors. Ask teachers about the themes they use at their centers and why those were selected, and review the numerous books about Early Childhood curriculum. You will find a great variety of unique theme ideas. Hilda L. Jackman suggests that teachers remain responsive to the children and adaptable to their different developmental stages. She shares her favorite suggestions, which can be adapted to any age group (Jackman, 1997, p. 33) (Figure 5–10).

Theme-based curriculum units developed by the authors of *Curriculum in Early Childhood: A Resource Guide for Preschool and Kindergarten Teachers* (Schickedanz, Pergantis, Kanosky, Blaney, & Ottinger, 1997, p. vi) identify major units with related themes. Figure 5–11 lists the major units and the related themes for the unit Animal Baby World.

The Self-Concept Curriculum Model, (Essa and Rogers, 1992, pp. 4, 132) is divided into four major areas, which include the child, home and family, friends and school, and community and community helpers. This curriculum keeps the child as the focus, with the major curriculum topics further sectioned to include identity, roles and relationships, environment, movement, safety, health, food, and communications.

The selection and time frame for themes depends on the center's schedule and the enrollment pattern of the children. A center that is open all day enrolls some children for full day, some for half day, and for both full and partial weeks. Children's enrollment may replicate their parent's work or training sched-

FIGURE 5–11   Units with Related Themes

Themes

Familiar Things in Our World
The Physical World
The Animal World
The Plant World
The World of Communication
The World of Vehicles and Transportation

Units for the theme *The Animal World*

There Are Many Different Kinds of Animals
Baby Animals
Domesticated Animals
Animals in Their Climates
What's inside Animals' Bodies?

—Judith A. Schickedanz, Mary Lynn Pergantis, Jan
    Kanosky, Annmarie Blaney, and Joan Ottinger

Resource: *Curriculum in early childhood* (1977).
Needham Heights, MA: Allyn & Bacon.

ule. Some children may attend only Tuesday and Thursday, some only afternoons. The variation of enrollment patterns challenges staff to offer themes that overlap, and remain flexible, yet are exciting for young children. A list of possible or recommended themes does not imply that they are all planned and implemented each year (Figure 5–12). Once again, the emphasis is on the developing abilities of the children, the life experiences of their families, and events and circumstances in the communities.

Teachers who use themes to organize their curriculum can plan and prepare activities of common interest to the children in their group. Long-term planning gives teachers time to gather information about the topic and to collect the related materials to implement the activities. The related materials are called props. Teachers, volunteers, and parents collect and replenish props over time. Some of the props, and small equipment that is difficult to locate in a short period, can be stored in labeled boxes called "prop boxes." Prop boxes are then ready when the theme calls for specific materials (Figure 5–13).

Project Approach

The **Project Approach** to organizing curriculum is considered to be an integrated curriculum method. With this approach, children explore an idea about real

FIGURE 5–10   Favorite Themes—A Child's Connection to the World

Magnificent Me	My Five Senses
I Am Special	Textures
All About Me	Things That Grow
My Family and I	Things That Fly
Families	The Environment
Friendship	Plants and Gardening
Caring and Sharing	Day and Night
Getting to Know You	Animals
Seasons	Opposites
Weather	

—Hilda L. Jackman

Resource: *Early childhood education curriculum: A child's connection to the world* (1977). Albany, NY: Delmar.

FIGURE 5–12   Early Childhood Education Center Theme Options

Fall: Our New School	**Spring: Our New Friends**
I'm Me, I'm Special	I'm Growing
My Senses: Taste, Smell, and Touch	Pets
My Senses: Sight and Sound	Community Helpers: Medical
Zoo Animals	Letter Carrier: Love
Dinosaurs	Five Senses: Taste, Smell, Touch
Woodland Animals	Five Senses: Sight and Sound
Day and Night	Transportation: Land
Farm Life	Community Helpers: Police
Make Believe	Community Helpers: Fire
We Pretend	Birds
Tools and Small Machines	Ecology and Plants
Food in My World	Reptiles and Amphibians
Family Gathering	Fine Arts/Music/Drama
Family	Small Creatures: Insects/Spiders
Love and Winter Season	Rodeo and Farm
Love and Family	

Resource: Shasta College Early Childhood Education Center (1996). Redding, California.

FIGURE 5–13   Prop Boxes Related to Themes

Theme: Picnic	**Theme: Market**
picnic basket	cash register
paper plates	bags
napkins	signs
table cloth	coupons
Theme: Gas Station	**Theme: Emergency Room**
gas hose	clip boards
window cleaner	uniforms
tire pump	stethoscopes
credit card register	scale
signs	X-ray images
maps	medical supplies

topics thoroughly. Children work together in small groups with the goal of finding out more about a topic of interest to them. Children are able to apply their skills creatively and meaningfully to a project through drawing, writing, designing charts, block construction, and Dramatic Play. Project work is viewed as complementary to the elementary level curriculum and to the more informal aspects of the curriculum for the young children (Katz, 1994, EDO-PS-94–6).

Children can explore a project within a theme or unit for an extended time depending on the ages, interests, and skills of the children. Organiz-ing curriculum around projects moves curriculum away from instruction that seems to only satisfy the requirement to provide activities in each subject area. This, some believe, only distributes unrelated arbitrary facts about that content area. A good project meets many developmental needs and provides opportunities to work in many curriculum areas (Booth, 1997, p. 84). With the Project Approach, the teacher may initially select topics of study related to the children's interests and everyday experiences, the availability of local resources, and the personal experiences and knowledge about the project topic (Kats, 1994, EDO-PS-94–6). As children help plan activities, they become more experienced in planning activities.

The Project Approach uses a **webbing** structure to record children's ideas, interests, and responses about a topic. Webbing is the creating and recording of the ideas suggested by children during "brain-storming" sessions. The teacher encourages participation by asking the children questions and recording their ideas. The procedure works well with older preschoolers and primary-age children because they have a greater foundation of knowledge and experiences. The webbing process graphs ideas for activities that emerge from the children's knowledge and interests with guidance and input from the teachers. Younger children may simply indicate what they know about a topic, which can provide the basis for planning (Figure 5–14).

FIGURE 5–14   Webbing Young Children's Comments: Beginning Ideas for a Project

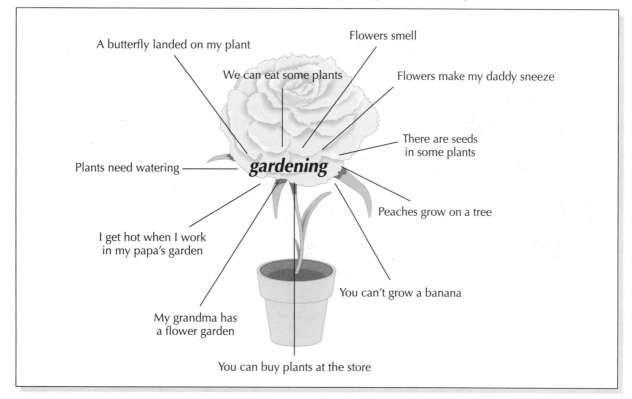

A butterfly landed on my plant

Flowers smell

We can eat some plants

Flowers make my daddy sneeze

There are seeds in some plants

Plants need watering

gardening

Peaches grow on a tree

I get hot when I work in my papa's garden

You can't grow a banana

My grandma has a flower garden

You can buy plants at the store

CREATING AN EMERGENT AND INTEGRATED CURRICULUM

In the section on child-initiated activities earlier in this chapter you read about the ideas of John Dewey, Benjamin Bloom, and Maria Montessori—all advocates for curriculum that provides choices for children. Child-initiated activities, choices, and assessment form the basis for **emergent** and integrated curriculum.

Emergent Experiences

When curricular activities flow from the children's interests they are considered to be emergent. The concepts of following the child and knowing the child is well documented in the work of Dewey and Montessori. The use of the word *emergent* in relation to Early Childhood curriculum gained acceptance in the early 1970s with Betty Jones' article *Curriculum Is What Happens* (Taylor, 1999, p. 103).

Curriculum is considered emergent when teachers document general goals that propose directions for the activities and projects. In the Reggio Emilia Schools in Italy, curriculum emerges

with each activity or project. Teachers adjust to the reactions and needs of children but do not establish the curriculum in advance (Gandini, 1993, p. 7). There is respect and regard for the children's ideas.

Integrated Experiences

Integrated means that the activities and experiences that are offered in a program are balanced among the Developmental Focus areas and across the curriculum areas. The goal is to achieve balance and to avoid providing activities separated into the distinct subject areas such as Art, Mathematics, Music, Science, and Social Studies (Seefeldt & Galper, 1998, p. 147).

Whoever the author or whatever the terminology, curriculum can be described and organized in many ways. The children's growth and development in all the domains are continuous, as is the need to meet their changing developmental needs. You will facilitate meaningful choices for participation throughout the day with careful observation. Your observation will allow you to combine a continuum of experiences while balancing the Developmental Focus areas and curriculum areas.

Washing hands may be just one activity that integrates many curriculum areas.

The addition of themes and projects may also match your curricular guidelines to help you achieve an emergent and integrated curriculum. When four-year-old Mathew shows enthusiasm for the obstacle course, you can incorporate an-other area of the curriculum that is challenging and interesting to him. When Matthew asks "What is square?" you can expand his enthusiastic participation with the obstacle course by adding square boxes and round tires. These additions to the obstacle course may further challenge his large muscles (curriculum area of Movement), and the square boxes and round tires add concepts of mathematics (curriculum area of Mathematics) to an activity that Matthew enjoys and in which he has sustained interest.

One activity will often integrate many curriculum areas. When children prepare cream cheese, celery, and raisins to make "bumps on a log" for a snack they interact (curriculum area of Social Understanding); wash their hands (curriculum area of Health); listen and answer and ask questions (curriculum area of Communication); and cut the celery into three pieces (curriculum area of Mathematics).

Curriculum planning will also support emergent and developmentally appropriate practices when activities are integrated and related to a theme. The theme may vary by regional location and interest and events in the children's lives. The transportation theme has relevancy to children whose homes may be located near an interstate highway (Figure 5–15).

FIGURE 5–15   Theme: Transportation—Selected Activities in Curriculum Areas

Art	small toy tire track art fence painting with toy vehicles color rubbing, transportation vehicle	**Social Studies**	vehicles in block area roadway in sand table travel props
Language	color assessment of vehicle vehicle guessing game word choices: *car, bike, train*	**Movement**	red/green light, trike path wheels on the bus follow directions
Science	tools/machines magnet activities auto parts	**Grouptime**	truck sizes what trucks do safety signs public transportation
Mathematics	size sequence/vehicles cars/garages—counting vehicle sorting size progression cards (dump truck)	**Visitor**	parking officer bus driver bike repair service
Health and Safety	safety street signs cross street safely safety lotto game	**Bulletin Boards**	"Be safe, buckle up" safety signs trucks and cars

Resource: Shasta College Early Childhood Education Center (1996), Redding, California.

ESTABLISHING AND RECORDING A CURRICULUM PLAN AND SCHEDULE

Collaboration among the staff members will establish program consistency and maintain a natural flow of activities for all the children. Planning and implementing a balanced program consistent with a responsive schedule encourages feelings of security and safety for the children (Read, 1976, p. 91). Continuity, consistency, security, and safety are critical considerations in the establishment of curriculum plans and schedules for Early Childhood programs.

Getting Started: What Is Happening Now?

How do you start and how can you avoid "false starts" in development of curriculum? Packaged, prescribed activities for children generate "false start" curricula. Activities that are "canned" ignore the needs of the enrolled children, the program guidelines, and the merged ideas of the staff. A school curriculum can "false start" when the staff makes "best guesses" in the activity selection. Staff who together plan experiences grounded on the assessed needs of the enrolled children can avoid the false start problem in program curriculum. "Watered down" elementary school activities forced on young children also result in false start curriculum with inappropriate experiences that will not meet the children's developmental needs. Young children do not benefit from false start curricula caused by the random selection of activities and experiences. Approaches such as "what shall we do today with the children" and "they seem to be interested this week in bugs" cause staff to set up random, unrelated activities. Children's needs are met when their interests and perspectives are integrated into purposeful curriculum planning.

Start by looking at your program. What experiences do you plan and offer now, and in which of these experiences do the children engage and seem to enjoy? Look at your program guidelines, the environment, and the activities you are now offering. Take inventory during a two-week period, listing all the "experiences that happen to the children." This is your current curriculum as it exists. Review the list with other staff members. Do these activities meet your curricular guidelines? Invite parents to participate in the review process, and then review the guidelines. Do the listed experiences meet the guidelines? This preliminary preparation readies you for the next step, identifying an overall framework.

Flexibility within a Framework

You want to prepare a curriculum plan for your program that works well for the children, their families, and your staff. Remain flexible and establish strategies for ongoing review of activities and experiences, both planned and spontaneous. You need to routinely examine the overall weekly and monthly curriculum to confirm that there is a balance of individual, small-group, and large-group activities. There should also be a balance of child-directed activities to assist the children in learning to make choices and decisions and teacher-guided activities that allow the children to develop abilities to understand instructions and follow directions. The balance should address both the individual needs of the children enrolled and the composite needs of the group.

There is much variability in curriculum planning. It is not uncommon for the administration and staff of a program to first suggest long-term plans to use as a broad guide for the curricular direction. Making long-range plans allows a school the necessary lead time to schedule staff, to order equipment and supplies, and to invite guests and volunteers.

The type and purpose of a facility influences program goals. The purpose, philosophy, and guidelines influence the nature and design of a curriculum framework. The procedure for planning takes numerous forms, with an initial review of the program guidelines. Next, the children's needs and interests need to be initially assessed, although assessment will be an ongoing procedure. Selection of the curriculum design (approach or combination of approaches) should also occur. A yearly or multi-yearly calendar will help you to determine days of attendance and special occasions. The daily and weekly schedule format for staff and children should be confirmed as well. Building a beneficial curriculum plan encompasses sequential steps (Figure 5–16) that lead you to the concrete aspect of curriculum—Children's Activities.

FIGURE 5–16   Building Blocks of Curriculum Planning

Curricular Guidelines
Children's Interests and Needs
Curriculum Approach
Curriculum Plan and Schedules
Curriculum Activities

Framing a Schedule

Schedules are designed to focus on the children's needs. Special occasions, staffing considerations, and the children's behavioral changes cause modifications to the suggested schedule. Staff members who are afforded preparation time for shaping curriculum activities, other than the time spent directly with children, will be in a position to exemplify the curriculum planning considerations. It is important to also establish contingency plans. What meaningful experience can you substitute for the carpentry activity specifically scheduled with the expected participation of two volunteers who, at the last minute, could not attend? How will activities be arranged to help children cope on the day a fire occurred in the neighborhood? Scheduled activities must be rotated in response to interests and changing needs. For example, staff members remove the dinosaurs from the water and sand table the week after regional mudslides and flooding. Toy cars, trees, houses, and people figures are added, allowing children to express their emotions about the crisis through play.

Activities can be organized within a framework of suggested time or within a spontaneous schedule. Both of the frameworks can offer many curriculum choices. Some programs schedule free-choice blocks of time within the overall daily schedule. Free-choice blocks of time provide children with spontaneous curriculum opportunities within a framework. Identify the blocks of time for child-initiated activities and for Grouptime. Activities within these blocks of time provide children with choices in a framework offering appropriate experiences. Transition time allows additional flexibility for routine toileting, handwashing, and cleanup. Arrival and departure times vary with each program and for individual children and their families. Routine experiences, such as meals and rest, influence the schedule. The environment, especially the proximity of the outdoor area, will also affect the schedule and determine if a free-flow indoor and outdoor setting is allowed.

Daily planning schedules provide a guide for what happens from arrival to departure during the course of a day. Child-initiated experiences and teacher-guided activities occur during the time blocks, allowing the children to explore, discover, and develop. Some programs provide breakfast, and some provide lunch and snacks. Some teachers schedule more frequent Grouptimes to maintain small numbers of children during the teacher-directed circle activity. The time allotted for activities will overlap because children need varying amounts of time to enjoy a snack, participate in Grouptime, wash their hands, and prepare for departure. Children also need long stretches of uninterrupted time to sustain their play, and the schedule needs to support this validated position (Ward, 1996, p. 22).

Curriculum planners consider the impact of related service schedules such as those created with bus service and mealtime. Inclusion of these and other necessary services may affect how and when curriculum activities are offered. The program duration and school hours also control the schedule outcome. Unforeseen circumstances will necessitate modifications to short-term and long-term schedules, as when an electrical power outage shifts the planned activities to another day.

School demands vary. Children's needs vary. Guidelines for schools vary. In many Montessori schools the daily schedules offer larger blocks of time than other preschools. The long activity periods allow children to engage in activities for as long as three hours without interruption. Children snack when they are hungry, eating individually or with a friend. This pace for routine activities accommodates young children (Humphryes, 1998, p. 12).

Differences in school goals and children's needs direct schools to offer many different scheduling approaches for full-day and half-day programs to achieve the best curriculum practices (Figure 5–17 and Figure 5–18). You will achieve best practices by arranging a schedule that meets the varied energy levels of children, equalizes child-initiated and teacher-guided experiences, and balances time and frequency of experiences. The quality and occurrence of experiences initiated by the children are driven by program philosophy and goals.

Recording Long- and Short-Term Curriculum Plans

You probably are ready to decide on a plan or layout for your curriculum. You have already considered curricular guidelines, the plans that you create to provide a written guide of the children's activities and experiences. The plan can be both a documented proposal and a record. Written plans help teachers and directors maintain accountability to the children, their families, the program, the community, and the profession. Accountability means that you are able to look at and report how the curriculum is satisfying the center's purpose

FIGURE 5–17   Program Schedule

Early Childhood Education Center
Full Day—Multi-Age (3–5 Year Olds)

7:30–8:30	Arrival/Activity centers
8:30–8:45	Grouptime to plan day
8:45–10:00	Activity centers
10:00–10:15	Transition: clean up, toileting, hand washing
10:15–10:30	Snack
10:30–10:40	Grouptime
10:45–11:45	Activity centers (indoor and outdoors)
11:45–12:00	Transition: cleanup, toileting, handwashing
12:00–12:30	Lunch
12:30–2:00	Rest/nap/quiet-time activity centers
2:00–3:15	Activity centers (indoor and outdoor)
3:15–3:30	Transition: cleanup, toileting, handwashing
3:30–3:45	Snack
3:45–4:00	Grouptime
4:00–5:30	Activity centers (indoor and outdoor)
5:30–6:00	Transition: cleanup, juice, prepare to depart

FIGURE 5–18   Program Schedule

Early Childhood Education Center
Half-Day—Multi-Age (3–5 Year Olds)

8:30–9:00	Arrival: greeting, quiet time activities
9:00–9:15	Grouptime to plan day
9:15–10:00	Activity centers
10:00–10:15	Transition: cleanup, toileting, handwashing
10:15–10:30	Snack
10:30–10:45	Grouptime
10:45–11:45	Activity centers (indoor and outdoor)
11:45–12:00	Transition: cleanup, prepare for departure

and goals. By documenting your curriculum plan in some written form you may be meeting agency and licensing requirements. In addition, written curriculum plans, which are readily available and displayed, help the parents and volunteers to un-

derstand the way that children learn and the way teachers guide them. When programs reveal what they do, a sense of trust grows among the school staff, parents, and community.

The layout of a curriculum plan depends on the curriculum approach and the schedule adopted by your school. The conventional method for tracking classroom information has been the use of a lesson plan book that generally has designated boxes or places to write in the planned activities. Whatever written method is used, the recommendations for appropriate curriculum for young children suggest that we offer activities in all developmental areas, that we integrate across curriculum areas, that we support children culturally and linguistically, and that technology is integrated into the teaching (Bredekamp & Copple, 1997, p. 20).

There are as many different written curriculum plans as there are centers. Some plans list the suggested activities next to the time slots on the schedule. Other plans list activities for the Interest Centers and identify a particular experience for Grouptime. Others combine the schedule, listing the day of the week and the time, with activities by filling in square boxes to document the experiences in writing. Basic identifying information, which is helpful to all teachers, should appear on the curriculum plans. This basic identifying information ideally lists the date, name of teacher(s), classroom or grouping of children, and goals for the week or day. A section for review or comment is also beneficial. Programs organized with the Thematic Approach list a theme and activities related to that theme.

There are four curriculum plans detailed to assist you in creating your own document. The designs offer suggestions for managing the four different approaches to curriculum for young children. Each allows the curriculum planner to fill in basic information with additional spaces for information specific to a curriculum approach. The sample curriculum plans present activities suitable for the children who were enrolled in the Shasta College Early Childhood Education Center, which is located in Redding, California, during the 1998–1999 academic year. The center serves as a teacher preparation facility and as a program of learning and care for children of college students and the community. The listed activities demonstrate how the forms can be used without any intention of recommendation for a structure of fixed experiences.

FIGURE 5–19 Curriculum Plan

Developmental Focus Area Approach

Date: xx/xx/xx   Teacher: *Millie*   Group/Classroom: *3- to 5-year-olds*

Curricular Guidelines: *to expose children to ecology.*

	Physical	Affective and Aesthetic	Cognitive and Language
Monday	*Little body bowling*	*Begin junk art group structure*	*Make "Keep Our School Clean" signs*
Tuesday	*Bath scrubber toss*	*Continue junk art with*	*Plastic, wood, metal sort gluing*
Wednesday	*Stringing Cheerios for birds*	*Continue junk art*	*Make bird feeders with toilet paper rolls*
Thursday	*Digging up raised bed for planting*	*Paint junk Art sculpture Hang bird feeders*	*Six-pack holder bubble blowing*
Friday	*Clean Earth parade on park path*	*Litter patrol in neighborhood Wrap junk art to take home*	*Planting lettuce and radish seeds in raised beds.*

Plan for Developmental Focus Areas

The first design creates a form to use with the Developmental Focus Area Approach (Figure 5–19). You can list activities that will contribute to children's growing abilities within three developmental domains. Curriculum should be balanced throughout a week, offering some activities to facilitate physical development, some for affective and aesthetic development, and some for cognitive and language development. Continue your commitment to create a plan that meets the needs of the children enrolled in your school.

Plan for Curriculum Areas

A plan for managing the Curriculum Area Approach is provided with the second design (Figure 5–20). Activities may be planned for each curriculum area to fulfill your curricular guidelines. Check to ensure that the children's play will direct spontaneous discovery throughout the week's experiences. Maintaining balance among the subjects and curriculum areas is important. Look at the week's plan to determine whether children have been given opportunities to participate in the different curriculum areas and that the experiences have meaning to their lives.

Plan for Interest Centers

The third design provides a method for acknowledging the value and materials designated within an Interest Center. This form may be displayed on a bulletin board, filed in a teacher notebook, and placed within the Interest Center (Figure 5–21). Mount a plastic document display to the top of one of the children's shelves. The Interest Center Plan can be placed there for review by teachers, parents, and volunteers. The form describes the materials that remain constant in the Interest Center and the activity or activities that are featured. The featured materials may relate to a current theme or project. Replace these Interest Center Plan forms as new materials or added activities need to be documented.

FIGURE 5–20 Curriculum Plan

Curriculum Area Approach

Week: xx/xx/xx   **Teacher:** *Janet*   **Group/Classroom:** *3- to 5-year-olds*

Curricular Guidelines: *To introduce children to common farm animals. To introduce children to farmers and the work that they do.*

Art
Group farm mural
"It looked like spilt milk"
Watercolor farm animals

Creative Dramatics
Set up horse corral
   outside with stick
   horses, tack, straw
   bales, other props

Health, Safety, Nutrition
Milk & yogurt tasting
Cooking Activity: butter
Cooking Activity: bread

Communication and Literacy
Farm stencil books
Farm sticker dictation
Farm animal books
Farm word cards

Mathematics
Farm animal sort
Matching mothers/babies
Sensorial table: measuring
   bird seed, grain.

Movement
Riding stick horses
Plowing
Climbing on hay bales

Music and Rhythm
Old MacDonald
Square dance
Western music with
   scarves

Science
Eggs—incubator
Sheep/Wool
Computer: reference farm

Social Understanding
Farmers and Tools
Add tractors to block area
Farm animals and fences
Farms helping (co-op, bureau)

Grouptime *Books: <u>Little Red Hen,</u> <u>Life on the Farm,</u> <u>I Want to be a Farmer</u>*
Guest brings chicken, set up egg incubator.

Theme *Farm Life*

Date: **Review:**

Curriculum Planning Form for Integrating Activities

The fourth curriculum plan suggests a design for integration of the curriculum approaches presented: Developmental Focus Area, Curriculum Area, Thematic, and Project (Figure 5–22). It is a challenge to fit the desired information on an eight and one-half by eleven page. You may want to create a large plan for display, which will demonstrate how your curriculum integrates the Developmental Focus areas, the curriculum areas, a theme, and projects. Again, the balance among the Developmental Focus areas should be the primary consideration. Mark a *P* for physical, *A* for affective and aesthetic, and *C* for cognitive and language to identify how an activity satisfies a Developmental Focus area. Look for a balance of activities by reviewing these letters and the distribution of activities among the curriculum areas. When you identify a theme or project, more activities may occur in one area than another. Think about the activities you want to propose, as a guide, for one week. Keep alert to spontaneous learning and stay flexible.

The page-size design will allow only a listing of the activity titles. However, titles alone do not always indicate the value and direction of the activity. The design should be validated with observations of the children to clarify the relevance of experiences. The curriculum plan will be further clarified with forms detailing each activity (to be discussed in Chapter 6) and with the **Interest Center Guide** forms that will demonstrate the experiences arranged for children throughout the indoor and outdoor environment.

FIGURE 5–21

Interest Center Guide

Interest Center *Science*   **Theme** *spring*

Art	Cooking	Literacy	Quiet Reading	Outside Art	Outside Large Motor
Block	Computer	Manipulatives	*Science*	Outside Circle	Outside Sand/Water
Circle	Dramatic Play	Music/Rhythm	Sensorial	Outside Garden	Trike Path

Interest Center Guidelines   **Approximate Age Range** *3–5*

Children and families will be invited to contribute signs of spring such as flowers, tree blossoms. Special requests will be made for mulberry leaves for the silk worms.

Developmental Focus   **Physical**   **Affective and Aesthetic**   **Cognitive and Language**

Curriculum Area *Science*

Interest Center Materials

    Constant *Reference books, plants, flowers, spring flower lotto activity tray, window thermometer and chart, magnifying glasses.*

    Featured *Silk worms*
                Worm farm
                "Signs of spring" flowers and branches

Preparation/Set Up

1. *Set up silk worm farm for viewing (plexiglass)—label.*
2. *Prepare signs inviting parent contributions.*

Teaching Strategies

1. *Teacher will invite children's questions as they observe the worms during a Grouptime.*
2. *Children will feed and monitor worms.*
3. *Teacher and children will check and record temperature.*

Possible Outcomes for the Child or Children

    Concepts *Flowers bloom in spring.*
               Birds build nests in spring.
               The weather warms up during spring.
               Silk worms eat mulberry leaves.

    Skills *Observation and prediction*

    Vocabulary *spring, blossom, silk worm, temperature, mulberry leaves*

Child Participation   **Date**

FIGURE 5–22 Curriculum Planning Form

Curriculum Planning Form

Week: xx/xx/xx   Teacher: *Regina*   Group/Classroom: *3- to 5-year-olds*

Curricular Guidelines: *To provide experiences for children to feel special about themselves and their families with positive emphasis on cultural identity.*

Theme/Unit/Project: *I'm Me, I'm Special*

Developmental Focus

Physical   (P)   Affective and Aesthetic   (A)   Cognitive and Language   (C)

Activities in Curriculum Areas

Art
Body tracing   (A)
Pasting magazine   (A)
   pictures of houses
Mural of copied baby
   photographs   (A)

Creative Dramatics
Domestic play   (A)
Dramatizing   (A)
   Are You My Mother?

Health, Safety, Nutrition
Cooking individual snack   (P)
Family holiday food   (P)
Cooking: Puree fruits   (P)

Communication & Literacy
Dictation "I like"   (C)
Book about Me   (C)
Recording/listening   (C)

Mathematics
Baby to adult sequence   (C)
Height strips   (C)
Weighing   (C)

Movement
Shadow dancing   (P)
Following footprints   (P)
Digging a hole   (P)

Music & Rhythm
"I'm very special"   (P & C)
Instrument guessing
   game   (C)

Science
Listening to heartbeat   (P)
Thumbprints and
   magnifying glass   (C)
Different smells   (C)

Social Understanding
Mirror—Alike/different   (A)
What my parents do   (A)
The sound of names   (C)

Group time   *Parent and an infant introduced during Grouptime. Share photos of infant as a newborn.*

Date: Review:

Adapting Plans for Extended-Day Activities

Schoolchildren attending your **extended-day activities** will also benefit from a managed curriculum. Consider the behaviors and characteristics of school-age children as you adapt curriculum plans. School-age children, particularly primary age, (kindergarten through third grade) are closer developmentally to preschool children than to older elementary school students. Early Childhood programs with flexible and individualized experiences

FIGURE 5–23   Extended-Day Planning Form

Week: xx/xx/xx   **Group/Classroom**: *4th, 5th, 6th* **Staff:**   *Ricardo*

Curricular Guidelines: *to recognize and adapt to the seasonal changes that cause allergies.*

Homework Help:

Review correspondence from classroom, grade level teachers.

Post weekly assignments and due dates.

Schedule computer time.

Project: *Blossoms and Allergies*

Activities: **Physical**

   Healthy sneezing (tissues, elbow)

   Indoor exercise

   Healthy snack planning and preparation (noting food allergies)

   Affective and Aesthetic

   The allergist

   Soothing and relaxing poems

   Helping friends with allergies

   Cognitive and Language

   Search the Internet for causes of allergies

   Blossoms beware

   Charting allergies by person and season

Date: **Review:**

---

are therefore particularly beneficial to primary-age children who attend extended day programs.

School-age children have more refined motor skills but still need chances to move and actively engage in experiences. School-age children are more independent but still are interested in inter-action with peers. They have increased attention spans but need relevant and meaningful opportu-nities to maintain their interest in learning. Your primary role will be to create a nurturing environ-ment for the extended day participants who have already spent six hours in a classroom. It is valu-able for you to know the elementary school curric-ula from many different schools to support continuity and the transition from the school to the extended-day program (Figure 5–23).

The curriculum plan may be completed with appropriate extended-day experiences to meet the needs of the group. Projects are particularly valu-able for school-age children. Projects may evolve from their assigned class homework or emerge from the students' interests. Homework Help may be the time given for the school-age children's own assignments or for mentoring the younger children.

MAXIMIZING CURRICULUM RESOURCES

Curriculum for children expands when parents and guests participate in the program. The Early Childhood teacher should learn early about these

curriculum resources, especially the parents, grandparents, and siblings of students. What occupations, careers, interests, and hobbies relate to the overall curriculum plan? This is the first level of resources and also the most valuable.

Parents and Community Guests

Family participation contributes to the child's and parents' sense of satisfaction. Visits from families contribute to a more meaningful experience for all the children. When Robin's mother, a telephone company representative, visits she brings equipment and a known relationship with the children—she is Robin's mother.

Guests whose occupation relates to the curriculum theme or project will stimulate more involvement because the children are introduced to information about the jobs featured in thematic activities. Uniforms, products, and other types of work-related items encourage more active participation from the children. There are many hands-on items a baker or a florist can bring to the program to share with the children in the surroundings of their familiar facility.

Businesses that adopt a school or early care program connect with the children on a continuing basis and provide them with another link to the community and to jobs.

Trips in the Neighborhood

There will be opportunities for planned and spontaneous walks within the neighborhood of your center. Walks with the children need to occur as often as possible, with the same degree of preparation about safety and consideration for routine scheduling needs. Trips in the neighborhood allow children to experience real-life situations firsthand. Visits to places and with people in their community may help the children to understand and clarify what they see in books and what they hear about in Grouptimes.

All trips and visits should be suitable developmentally for the children enrolled in your program. Consider the length of the visit, including the time to travel and/or walk there and back. What will the children actually see, hear, and feel? Will the experience be meaningful to them?

Trips require preparation and follow-up. Your visit to the location prior to taking the children will allow you to check for safety, evaluate the value of the visit, determine the needed time, and speak to the person or persons responsible for the location. This preparation will help to ensure that the presentation is suitable for young children. The children need to acquaint with the trip location and the

Trips within the neighborhood allow children to experience real-life situations first-hand.

people they will meet. Children can be introduced to these concepts over several days and weeks prior to the trip. Follow-up promotes good relations with the community. A greeting from the children, a thank-you note from the director, and a photo of the children taken on the visit all contribute to positive and cordial follow-up practices. Follow-up activities can also be integrated into the curriculum plan.

Trips to the neighborhood may be done in stages. The first walk to the post office might be to pick up the mail. The next few walks might be to mail letters and buy postage. After several brief visits, the children may be ready to go inside the post office. The same guidelines for quality curriculum apply to the neighborhood trips you plan for your group (Curriculum Activity Guide 24).

REVIEW

Before implementing curriculum, teachers need to observe the children, review observations to identify behavioral changes, and then plan the curriculum. Children benefit from curricula with activities that allow them to make choices that are meaningful and from having boundaries within those choices. One type of activity choice is Grouptime, which is considered a teacher-guided experience.

The variety of experiences a program chooses to offer to the children should be guided by stated purposes. The curricular guidelines describe and define the program and what is wanted for children and their families. The guidelines also affect the selected curriculum approach: Developmental Focus, Curriculum Area, Thematic, or Project. Teachers who balance activities and experiences across the curriculum areas and among the curriculum approaches are exemplifying an integrated curriculum. Curriculum is considered emergent when activities, which flow from observation of the children, determine their interests and needs.

Curriculum plans need to be documented, flexible, and established as guides for implementation of the activities. The steps for developing a plan include designing a schedule with consideration of the needs of the children, families, and staff. The layout of a documented curriculum plan depends on the curriculum approach and the schedule adopted by the program. A program will maximize curriculum resources by inviting parental and community participation.

KEY TERMS

child-initiated	integrated
curricular guideline	Interest Center Guide
curriculum area	multi-age grouping
curriculum plan	observe/review/plan
curriculum resources	Project Approach
daily schedule	sensitive
Developmental Focus	sensorial
Approach	teacher-guided
emergent	Thematic Approach
extended-day activities	theme
Grouptime	webbing
inclusive	

RESPOND

1. Identify three curricular guidelines for young children. Review these with another person either in the course or at a center. Write three additional guidelines with this individual, agreeing on the description of the commitment to children.
2. What approach to curriculum best matches the curricular guidelines identified in item 1 above? Explain the reason for the selection and describe how the curriculum approach will be documented.
3. Become familiar with three different Early Childhood programs in the community. Review the school brochure and/or speak to the center director or a teacher. Describe the curriculum of each program in relation to the major curriculum approaches discussed in this chapter.
4. Call up one of the Web sites on the Internet. Provide two curriculum ideas presented:

Using Ideas from Reggio Emilia in America
http://ericeece.org/reggio/nlspr95a.html

KIDPROJ's Multi-Cultural Calendar
http://www.kidlink.org/KIDPROJ/MCC/

National 4-H Council
http://www.fourhcouncil.edu/

REFERENCES

Arends, R. I. (1991). *Learning to teach* (2nd ed.). New York: McGraw-Hill.

Bloom, B. S. (1981). *All our children learning: A primer for parents, teachers, and other educators.* New York: McGraw-Hill.

Booth, C. (1997). The fiber project: One teacher's adventure toward emergent curriculum. *Young Children, 53*(5), 79–85.

Bredekamp, S., & Copple, C. (Eds.). (1997). *Developmentally appropriate practice in early childhood programs* (Rev. ed.). Washington, DC: NAEYC.

Derman-Sparks, L., & A.B.C. Task Force. (1989). *Anti-bias curriculum: Tools for empowering young children.* Washington, DC: National Association for the Education of Young Children.

Edwards, L. C. (1990). *Affective development and the creative arts.* Columbus, OH: Merrill.

Eliason, C. F. & Jenkins, L. T. (1981). *A practical guide to early childhood education.* St. Louis, MO: Mosby.

Essa, E. L., & Rogers, P. R. (1992). *An early childhood curriculum: From developmental model to application.* Albany, NY: Delmar.

Frost, J. L. (Ed.). (1973). *Revisiting early childhood education: Readings.* New York: Holt, Rinehardt & Winston.

Gandini, L. (1993). Fundamentals of the Reggio Emilia approach to early childhood education. *Young Children, 49*(1), 4–8.

Gestwicki, C. (1997). *The essentials of early education.* Albany, NY: Delmar.

Gonzalez-Mena, J. (1997). *Multicultural issues in child care.* Mountain View, CA: Mayfield.

Hall, S. H. (1999). *Creative resources for the anti-bias classroom.* Albany, NY: Delmar.

Hendricks, J. (1980). *Total learning for the whole child: Holistic curriculum for children ages 2 to 5.* St. Louis, MO: Mosby.

Hildebrand, V. (1971). *Introduction to early childhood education* (16th ed.). New York: Macmillan.

Humphryes, J. (1998). The developmental appropriateness of high-quality Montessori programs. *Young Children, 53*(4), 4–16.

Hymes, J. L. (1981). *Teaching the child under six* (3rd ed.). Columbus, OH: Merrill.

Jackman, H. L. (1997). *Early childhood education curriculum: A child's connection to the world.* Albany, NY: Delmar.

Kamii, C. (1973). A sketch of the Piaget-derived preschool curriculum developed by the Ypsilanti early education program. In Frost, J. L. (Ed.), *Revisiting early childhood education.* New York: Holt, Rinehardt & Winston.

Katz, L. G. (1994). The project approach. *ERIC DIGEST* (EDO-PS-94–6). Urbana, IL: ERIC Clearinghouse on Elementary and Early Childhood Education.

Katz, L. G. (1995). The benefits of mixed-age grouping. *ERIC DIGEST* (EDO-PS-95–8). Urbana, IL: ERIC Clearinghouse on Elementary and Early Childhood Education.

Montessori, M. (1966). *The secret of childhood.* New York: Fides.

National Association for the Education of Young Children & National Association of Early Childhood Specialist in State Departments of Education. (1991). Guidelines for appropriate curriculum content and assessment in programs serving children age 3 through 8. *Young Children, 46*(3), 21–38.

Orem, R. C. (1974). *Montessori: Her method and the movement, what you need to know.* New York: Capricorn.

Read, K. H. (1976). *The nursery school: Human relationships and learning.* Philadelphia: W. B. Saunders.

Schickedanz, J. A., Pergantis, M. L., Kanosky, J., Blaney, A., & Ottinger, J. (1997). *Curriculum in early childhood.* Needham Heights, MA: Allyn & Bacon.

Sciarra, D. J. & Dorsey, A. G. (1998). *Developing and administering a child care center* (4th ed.). Albany, NY: Delmar.

Seefeldt, C., & Galper, A. (1998). *Continuing issues in early childhood education* (2nd ed.). Upper Saddle River, NJ: Merrill.

Taylor, B. J. (1999). *A child goes forth: A curriculum guide for preschool children* (9th ed.). Upper Saddle River, NJ: Merrill.

Ward, C. D. (1996). Adult intervention: Appropriate strategies for enriching the quality of children's play. *Young Children, 51*(3), 20–24.

Weikart, D. P. (1988). Quality in early childhood education. In Warger, C. (Ed.), *A resource guide to public school early childhood programs.* Alexandria, VA: Association for Supervision and Curriculum Development.

Whitehead, A. N. (1929). *The aims of education and other essays.* New York: Mentor.

Wortham, S. C. (1996). The integrated classroom: The *assessment-curriculum link in early childhood education.* Englewood Cliffs, NJ: Merrill.

CHAPTER 6

Activities for Young Children:
Managing Good Ideas

Curriculum Profile

The vendor halls at conferences for professionals in early care and education attract attendees at all times of the day, whether the meeting is scheduled for one day, two days, or three days. It's no wonder: the vendors display new and interesting supplies, materials, equipment, and "freebies," so as conference participants we leave the vendor halls with at least one new book bag, badges, stickers, bubble wands, and ideas for new activities. The workshops and sessions additionally fill our bags with handouts and songs and more ideas for activities. When the conference ends, we are noticed because we board buses with extra luggage, load our vehicles with extra Science and Math manipulatives, and cram overstuffed carry-ons into the overhead compartments on airplanes. We are the ones with the new puppets, new sand forms, and lots and lots of books with ideas for new activities. Songs and movements and ideas for new activities repeat in our heads as we look forward to returning to school to share ideas for new activities with our staff, the children, and our students.

The demands of daily schedules too often set back our great intentions to organize and use that song with the children or that new recipe for modeling dough. By the way, what happened to that recipe for the modeling dough? What book described harvest celebrations? Where is the handout about literacy? And the description of the activity about weather? Early care and education professionals need an efficient way to translate the ideas for new activities into practical use in their classroom. We need a way to manage our ideas for new activities.

Chapter Outline

Study Guide

As you study the sections in this chapter, you should be able to:

- Appreciate that children's questions generate curriculum ideas.
- Understand that activities need to be planned to introduce ideas, encourage exploration, stimulate questioning, and ensure spontaneous learning.
- Identify the curriculum elements: activity title, goal, materials, approach, outcomes, and teaching strategies.
- Use the Curriculum Activity Guide as a tool for documenting the curriculum experience in writing.
- Recognize how activities can be sequenced to support child-centered learning.
- Consider ongoing assessment as a vital step for revising activities.
- Recognize that Curriculum Plans and Curriculum Activity Guides assist teachers in setting up activities.

CURRICULUM ACTIVITIES— WHAT TO CONSIDER

As a practical matter, it is not realistic to expect that you will be able to find enough relevant activities to match the changing needs of the children in your program. This means that you and the rest of the staff will need to adapt, create, and modify the majority of the activities for your center.

By now you are well aware that activities are the core of the curriculum. As you consider each activity, remember that both the experiences you plan and those that occur spontaneously as a result of the environment that you create contribute to the learning experience of the child. The way you plan and organize activities is influenced by what you know about children and your organizing approach. You will need to call on your understanding of the importance of the early years, developmentally suitable experiences, authentically inclusive programs, and involvement of families in your planning.

How Ideas Become Activities

"Teacher look." "Teacher see my rock." "Teacher watch, I can reach the clouds." "I brought my special book." "I have a Band-Aid on my knee today." "That's not a cat, I know it's a rabbit!" Children's questions and statements are not only wonderful to hear but also generate curriculum ideas. The experiences you plan will stimulate more questions and responses and are golden opportunities to enhance and reinforce learning by responding with interactive questioning. Your responses to questions will trigger additional opportunities for spontaneous learning. So, when Trevor asks you why the sand is heavy today, you reply by first asking him what he thinks. He may give answers for a while and then suggest that he feel the sand again and think about how it would become wet. Together you will explore ideas about the sand being wet and heavier. You will also make note to plan additional activities to invite Trevor and other interested children to experience dry and wet materials by touching and manipulating dry and wet objects such as sponges and popped corn. Teachers should plan activities for young children that introduce new ideas that allow continuing exploration and discovery.

More formal assessment methods will help you identify topics of children's interests and note their abilities. We want to ensure that the experiences present fundamental knowledge in terms of the

FIGURE 6–1   What to Consider When Planning an Activity

> Plan to meet curricular guidelines.
> Plan based on children's assessed needs.
> Plan for the individual child.
> Plan modifications for children with disabilities.
> Plan for small groups of children.
> Plan to introduce ideas.
> Plan to encourage exploration.
> Plan to stimulate questioning.
> Plan to ensure spontaneous learning.

child's way of viewing yet are challenging in a way that will hold his curiosity (Bruner, 1960, p. 39).

Defining an Activity

An **activity** is generally defined as an action using movement or mental activity (Barnhart & Barnhart, 1990, p. 22). In early childhood, an activity is an experience planned for young children that is developmentally appropriate and meets the school's curricular guidelines. An activity is an experience that provides opportunities for children to actively participate. Early Childhood professionals also refer to activities as learning opportunities that actively engage children. The spectrum of experiences include large and small movement activities as well as social and solitary time, allowing children to work alone or in small groups. Experiences also involve cognitive and language development and affective and aesthetic development. Activities should meet both the guidelines of the program and needs of the children.

Planning activities that are appropriate for young children calls for teachers to shape activities that will invite children to participate in experiences by encouraging them to question and to respond (Figure 6–1).

WHAT IT TAKES TO CREATE AN ACTIVITY

A starting point when you begin to shape curriculum activities for young children is to be familiar with the common Early Childhood procedures and requirements related to activity planning. Just as with every other aspect of Early Childhood curriculum, there is great variation in the way activi-

ties are organized and labeled. Some programs will ask that teachers simply identify, in writing, the title and purpose of each activity. Other programs require teachers to write down the goals and materials for each activity (Figure 6–2). Understanding a specific method for planning curriculum activities will allow you to adapt the technique to a variety of school settings.

Goals for Guiding Activities

The **Curriculum Activity Guide,** which is used as a template to document activities throughout the text, is designed to guide the direction of a particular experience for young children. Emphasis is placed on the role of the teacher to design experiences that invite children to participate in ways that best suit their interests and stages of development. Using the Curriculum Activity Guide format, teachers will facilitate children's growth and development with activities that clarify, stimulate, and verify ideas and skills. Teachers will watch and listen to the children, provide resources, participate when appropriate, and validate their efforts and progress. The experiences allow children to contemplate, discover, and solve problems in an inviting environment. Professionals support possibilities for children with open-ended questions to expand their play, reinforce their language, and help them see relationships among

FIGURE 6–2   School Requirements

> **Some Schools Require Teachers to List the Title and Purpose of an Activity**
>
> Title: *Wet Sand and Dry Sand*
> Purpose: *Children will experience the difference in sand wet with water and sand that is dry.*
>
> **Some Schools Require Teachers to List the Title, Goals, and Materials**
>
> Title: *Wet Sand and Dry Sand*
> Goals: *To offer children opportunities to feel wet and dry sand.*
>   *To help children identify that wet sand is heavier.*
> Materials: *Sensory table with divider separating the wet and dry sand, sand shovels, measuring cups. Additional water as needed to keep wet sand damp.*
>   *Paper towels to wipe hands.*

people, objects, and ideas. For example, Teacher Marquez responds to five-year-old Jasmine, who pushes forward her potted, wilted plant: "What do you think the plant needs, Jasmine?" Later in the day he asks, knowing that she already watered the plant, "Jasmine, how is your plant doing now?"

It is essential therefore that activities identify goals to allow children to shape their own experiences. The process for designing the curriculum in general and activities specifically begins with a framework that is based on knowledge about child development combined with the respect for the uniqueness of the individual children enrolled in the program (Burts & Buchanan, 1998, p. 129). A **goal** is a general statement that defines an aim. Generally, the statement of purpose has an outcome in mind that specifies what you are trying to achieve (Ornstein & Hunkins, 1998, p. 272). Goals are written in sentences or phrases or can be stated with a single word. It is also acceptable to write goal statements that begin with the word *to* (infinitive verb), indicating that there is an expectation (Ornstein & Hunkins, 1998, p. 273). Objectives differ from goals because objectives must clearly identify an end product or the intended skill or behavior outcome (Arends, 1991, p. 39). Behavioral objectives require that the student's behavior, situation, and performance criteria are stated. A behavioral objective, as defined by behavioral theorists, would be stated in this way: the child, given a variety of ten pictures, will be able to identify four of the five

flowers correctly in twenty-nine percent of the opportunities (Arends, 1991, p. 45). Others argue that objectives can be written more generally and that an objective might specify that a child will understand and appreciate the diversity of the flowers presented in pictures (Arends, 1991, p. 46).

Activities designed around specific behavioral objectives require identification of the expected behavior change that will result from the planned experience. For example, a statement that the child will be able to point to the blue block is a behavioral objective. The observable behavior following the learning experience indicates that the objective has been met. It would also be necessary to indicate the conditions under which the child is expected to achieve the objective. An elaboration on the example given above might specify: The child will be able to point to the blue block after participating in the activity over a period of two weeks. A great deal of controversy remains regarding the use of objectives because they predetermine the child's actions, place unrealistic performance standards on the children, and cause teachers to design curricula with specific achievement outcomes. It is recommended that teachers of young children identify the goals for planned activities unless careful evaluation of the children's behaviors is required, utilizing accurate evaluation measures. For example, requirements for specific objectives may be specified for a child with disabilities in an individual educational plan.

Children are entitled to approach each activity in their own way.

Children will enjoy the freedom to wonder and explore when teachers avoid predetermining the specific use of materials. Goals for activities should define what the teacher will offer without indication of a measurable outcome. A predetermined measurable outcome will detract from the way children engage in the experience. Children are entitled to approach each activity in their own way. This requires that teachers allow children enough latitude to bring their own understanding and reality to the experience. We can't really know the interest level of young children when we begin to plan the activity. Stating in advance the behavioral objective will control the experiences with unrealistic and fixed outlooks about what the children should do, how they should think, and what they should feel. The teacher's responsibility is to provide the appropriate opportunities, materials, and guidance. We can anticipate and encourage children to engage in activities in their unique ways by allowing choices, by reinforcing the divergent use of materials, and by supporting the emergence of their actions.

Important Elements of an Activity

Now that you are well aware that there is no one correct strategy for planning and managing activities, consider what you need to shape an activity for young children in your group. What do you need to prepare? What do you need to have available? Exploring questions such as these will help you to begin to formulate the parts, or **elements**, of meaningful activities for young children.

When you plan an activity by considering the important aspects that shape each activity, you will confirm whether or not you are meeting your curricular guidelines. In addition, you will know if there is a balance of appropriate experiences needed to stimulate optimal learning.

What else would be helpful to know as you plan an activity about wet sand? Does the school have an organizing theme? Will the activity be offered in a specific Interest Center? Will you list the activity within a content area?

Managing curriculum effectively involves an investment of time in planning. Planning requires that a proposed activity be thoroughly examined. The outcome of the planning steps should be written documentation. Written documentation of an activity may minimally define the purpose of the experience or list numerous defining elements.

It is natural to resist changes. Not all teachers, especially experienced teachers, welcome the prospect of revising their entire curriculum. "We always do our lesson plans a certain way." "Filling out a long form for each activity seems time consuming." "Why should we spend so much time writing out all that information, I know what I need to do!" "This looks like a lot of work, is it worth it?" These remarks are typical comments from teachers, especially experienced ones. They enthusiastically welcome new ideas but clearly have limited time to spend revising their curriculum.

Efficient organization of curriculum plans actually creates additional time for busy Early Childhood teachers. Teachers interact with the children, with other staff members, with parents, and with volunteers. Each adult in the program requires a different degree of supervision and guidance. A teacher may spend five to ten minutes explaining how to set up and to facilitate an activity. Think about how many activities need to be arranged and how many times that same activity is reviewed with different staff members, volunteers, and parents. If the teacher documents the activity in writing, he or she provides the rationale thoroughly at one time. With an appropriately completed written form available, one that details the basic information, the teacher has more time to personally suggest helpful hints to the other adults.

Understanding the Elements

Consider many aspects of an activity when you initially plan an activity. You may or may not need to list all of the elements on an activity form. Curriculum elements refer to the parts of an activity, such as a title, a goal, and materials. Comprehensive curriculum designs detail elements and definitions to guide teachers in building appropriate and relevant activities for young children. The sixteen elements listed in Figure 6–3 create a starting point for teachers looking for strategies to plan and manage their curriculum.

How you use these elements in planning depends on your program and the need for written documentation. Once you understand the various elements needed for planning an activity, you should document the specified information in writing. You may find that listing the activity title and the materials is adequate to satisfy your program guidelines. Regardless of the goals or size of your school, you will learn to appreciate the value of building a framework for each activity. Identification of the elements will help validate purposeful teacher preparation. Most Early Childhood teachers spend time preparing for the children. The

FIGURE 6–3   Elements of an Activity

Activity Title	Name of the activity that describes the experience.
Activity Goal	A statement that describes the purpose of an activity. The goal relates what the teachers would like the children to experience.
Curriculum Area	A subject or content area; a discipline or area of study. Includes art, health–safety–nutrition, literacy, mathematics, science, physical movement, and social studies.
Developmental Focus	Indicates the primary focus of an activity to be within a developmental domain such as physical, affective and aesthetic, or cognitive and language.
Location/Interest Center	Recommends location for listed activity. Includes circle, outside, inside, art, dramatic play area.
Participants	Recommends the number of child participants for that listed activity.
Time	Estimated length of time that may be needed for the activity.
Age Range	Age range of children (3–4 years, 4–5 years) to help identify suitable experiences.
Materials	Suggested materials and supplies for the listed activity.
Preparation/Set Up	Preparation of materials needed and suggested steps for facilitating listed activity.
Teaching Strategies	Recommended actions for teacher who is guiding the activity. This may suggest sequence to follow in guiding a child's participation.
Possible Outcomes	Description of the behavior that a child may be expected to achieve after participating in the specific activity. May include concepts, skills, and vocabulary. **Concepts**—Single idea written clearly and simply for a child's understanding. **Skills**—Developing abilities related to a developmental focus area. **Vocabulary**—Words related to the activity to be used appropriately in conversation with the children participating in the activity.
Date:	Notation of the date when the Activity Guide was completed.

Source: Arce-Brooks Consultants (1997) Curriculum Manager.

majority of these remarkable teachers are not compensated for their time preparing curriculum activities. Advocacy is needed to speed the acceptance of compensation for curriculum preparation.

Listing details about activities is one way to invite positive parent involvement. Most parents are interested in the way that a school contributes to the growth and development of their children. A parent who becomes familiar with the concepts, the vocabulary, the songs, and the Interest Centers introduced to the children will be more apt to participate.

The first step in shaping an activity is to identify an *activity title*. The **title** also describes the experience that you are planning. A fitting title can be as creative as the activity or may just state what the experience will offer. The title of the experience detailed in Curriculum Activity Guide 3, Body Tracing, defines the activity. An activity title for another

experience, Valentine Friends, anticipated the outcome of the activity. This title does not specify what will happen as precisely but nevertheless is an effective and suitable title.

The **activity goal** is a statement that describes the purpose of the experience. The goal relates to what you will offer for children to experience. Goal statements usually begin with the word *to*. A typical goal statement that allows the children to direct their own behavior for the activity about wet sand might be "to experience touching and talking about the difference between wet sand and dry sand." The goal for an activity entitled Hole Punching might be "to have the opportunity to safely use a hole puncher." The goal for the activity entitled Valentine Friends could be "to become aware of the association of Valentine's Day and friendship."

The identification of the *theme,* although not listed as an element, may be important if your school uses the Thematic Approach to planning and organizing the curriculum. Specify project topic on an activity form if you use the Project Approach. An activity may relate to more than one theme; in many cases, an activity relates to all the themes. An activity that invites children to scoop out seeds from a pumpkin relates specifically to a Harvest theme. The activity Valentine Friends could relate to a theme about friendship or the February holiday. An activity entitled Hole Punching would fit with almost any theme because the experience supports small movement skills.

Listing of a *curriculum area* indicates that the activity focuses on a content category. Does the activity offer a specific experience in areas such as Mathematics, Art, or Movement? The curriculum areas listed should match the curriculum areas your school has identified for curricular guidelines, the mission statement, or in the school brochure. The curriculum areas commonly include Art, Literacy, Mathematics, Music, Physical Movement, Science, and Social Studies. Look back at the section on curriculum areas in Chapter 5 (see Figure 5–9). Which curriculum areas did you select? Which terminology best describes what you want for children in your center?

The Developmental Focus describes how an activity benefits children within a developmental area. The Developmental Focus lists three areas: physical, affective and aesthetic, and cognitive and language. Your school may identify alternative labels such as social-emotional, literacy, and motor development. Think about how the activity that you are planning to offer facilitates experiences within one of the Developmental Focus areas. Will the children have opportunities to develop large motor skills? If so, the activity's Developmental Focus area is physical. Many of the activities that you are planning may relate to more than one Developmental Focus areas. A mural-painting activity, using large house-painting brushes, could be offered to engage children in a social interaction. Therefore, the Developmental Focus of that mural painting activity might be listed as affective and aesthetic. This activity also offers large motor skill chances for young children, and therefore you may decide to offer this activity as a physical Developmental Focus. You either decide or consult with other teachers, especially if you are team teaching, how to focus the experience and how the experience satisfies the identified need of an individual child or group of children.

It is helpful to know in advance the location in which the activity will be presented. Listing of the **Location/Interest Center** permits teachers to determine if all areas of the classroom, inside and outside, are utilized effectively. The identification of the Location/Interest Center on a written form will help the teaching staff guide involvement of volunteers and parents as well. Programs that design their curriculum around Interest Centers will find that the Interest Center Guide (see Figure 5–21) in Chapter 5 is helpful. The activity planned in each activity area can be communicated verbally to the staff, volunteers, and parents. The Interest Center Guide acts as a visual backup to reinforce verbal explanations.

The **participants** element recommends the number of child participants for an activity. The number of children suggested provides guidance for the setup of activities and for maintaining appropriate supervision.

Time is the part of the activity guide that shows the length of time for the proposed experience. Identification of this element is applicable and realistic for managing a schedule while maintaining flexibility. The intent of the time marker is to allow appropriate participation, cleanup, and transition of the child or small group of children who join in the activity (see Curriculum Activity Guide 21 CAG).

Age range refers to the chronological ages of the children for whom you are planning activities. Remember that children, even though they are the same age, will have different needs and interests. Chronological age provides a general idea about the broad range of behaviors and skills that may occur during a particular age. You will plan some activities that are suitable for children of many ages, knowing that young children engage in guided experiences with their unique abilities. Suggested age range categories for Early Childhood include eighteen months to three years old; three-year-olds; three- and four-year-olds; four-year-olds; four- and five-year-olds; six-, seven-, and eight-year-olds; and OK for all ages. The identification of age range will also depend on the organization of the program and grouping of the children. Activities with the most flexibility welcome children with different interests and skills.

Another element in the planning process for activities is the definition of **materials.** Listing the materials for an activity can determine the success of that experience and the effectiveness of curriculum plans. Knowing in advance what suggested materials and supplies will be required helps the director and teacher to manage and prepare needed items.

The activity entitled Hole Punch will need the following materials: three to four hole punchers, three to four bowls, and small pieces of construction paper. When teachers plan curricula in advance and know which materials are required, it leads to successful curricular management and to successful experiences for the children.

Preparation/set up defines the suggested sequence of procedures or steps the teacher or assistant will follow to prepare the activity for participation by a child or children. The preparation/set up alerts staff regarding the preparation time needed to arrange the experience.

Teaching strategies recommend the actions to be taken for the teacher who is guiding the children in the activity. Teaching strategies describe the suggested teaching methods and procedures in facilitating the children's participation in the activity. This element is particularly important for teachers in preparation, volunteers, and parents participating in the school. The step-by-step procedures provide a flexible guide for inviting children to participate, engaging their involvement and supporting their self-initiated learning. Strategies for interaction and guidance could include: sit with children; listen to questions; pose and answer questions; engage in interactive questioning; encourage; support children's interaction; facilitate discussion; introduce new equipment; invite new children to join; offer to write down name and/or comments; and place materials

so they are readily available for children (Curriculum Activity Guides 25 and 26).

Possible outcomes describes the concepts, skills, and vocabulary that the activity will introduce or reinforce during the activity. **Concepts** are general ideas related to an activity. Because concepts are abstract ideas about objects or events, teachers need to present information for children to actively participate. This means that teachers need to consider what information is important about the activity and clarify that information in simple, concrete terms. Identifying concepts helps children to place objects into groups or classes. For example, the word *family* is used to define a group that includes separate, individual members (father, mother, grandma, grandpa, sister, brother, aunt, uncle, and cousins). The word *color* describes a group of objects that includes different shades of color such as red, blue, and green. You will help expand the children's discovery and learning by providing additional words for similar persons or objects, for example: "A car is also called an automobile and a truck is similar to a car." "Transportation gets us from one place to another." "An airplane is one form of transportation."

Concept development is more than just naming an object because an idea provides extra information and clarification. Children acquire abilities to think about objects belonging to classes or categories (Vance, 1973, p. 58), for example "my

This teaching strategy involves sitting with the children and answering questions.

bedroom is part of my home." Children also learn to generalize, for example, "Kittens and puppies are pets." In addition, children will develop skills in discriminating: "Calves are usually farm animals, not house pets." Lastly, relationships will become apparent among concepts, for example, the "keys unlock the wheel toy shed" (Figure 6–4).

Concepts must be introduced with concrete, hands-on examples. All children, as much as they are able, need to smell, see, touch, and handle an object to begin to grasp its abstract idea. Concept identification will assist you in helping children to see the many dimensions of one object. Expanding their awareness of the relationships among ideas

and objects will also increase their critical thinking and communication skills. For example, understandable concepts for young children about cats call upon the senses: a cat is furry; a cat purrs; a cat can be a family pet; and a cat has whiskers.

Skills are developing abilities in body movement, thinking and speech, or in social and emotional behavior. For example, an activity inviting children to participate in Pouncing Like a Cat offers chances to develop physical skills, Meowing Like a Cat offers opportunity to develop ability in language, and Imitating the Purring allows expression of feelings. There are consistent chances for skill enhancement within each Developmental Focus area. The value of an activity for young children may be identified by the skill that could develop as an outcome of participating in a particular activity. A list of skills categorized by Developmental Focus area will be useful as you initially write skills for activities (Figure 6–5). Review the Curriculum Activity Guides to add to your list about possible skill outcomes in each of the developmental areas.

Vocabulary identifies words related to an activity and to be used appropriately in coversation with the children participating in the activity.

DOCUMENTING ACTIVITIES WITH FORMS

Documentation of your curriculum plans, as you learned in Chapter 5, helps you to outline a balanced presentation of activities. Written plans will verify which children need more experiences and

FIGURE 6–4   Concept Statements

Categorizing or Classifying:

My bedroom is part of my home.
Forks and spoons are utensils for eating.

Discriminating:

Kittens and puppies are pets.
A potato is a vegetable, not a fruit.
The oven timer rings differently than the telephone.

Relationships among Concepts:

Keys unlock the wheel toy shed.
When I blow through a straw I can make bubbles in the water.
Paste makes some items stick to paper.
The magnifying glass makes objects look bigger.

FIGURE 6–5   Skills Categorized by Developmental Focus Area

Physical	Affective and Aesthetic	Cognitive and Language
Sensory discrimination	Decision making	Classifying
Eye/hand coordination	Cooperation	Comparing
Following directions	Self-expression	Discriminating
Fine motor control	Creative expression	Observing change
Sensory awareness	Independence	Exploring
Visual tracking	Understanding	Seriation
Coordination	Social play	Concept awareness
Nutritional awareness	Nurturing	Sequencing
Balance	Interaction	Expanding
Strength	Role-playing	Listening
Left/right movement	Making choices	Experimenting
Body awareness	Initiating	Print recognition

opportunities in certain Developmental Focus areas. Documentation of both prepared and spontaneous activities helps teachers to account for meaningful and flexible experiences. Written documentation of activities will help you to prepare more efficiently and increase your time with the children, their parents, and volunteers.

Written Curriculum Guides

Written forms for activities will be useful to both the teaching staff and to volunteers because they can inform the teachers and other adults supervising the children about the planned experience. A "visual" of a plan is like a map; it tells us and others where we might be going. The design arranges ideas and intentions, informing us if there is continuity and balance (Ornstein & Hunkins, 1998, p. 238). Basic information detailing the activity is practical and applicable when the emphasis is on flexibility. There are may ways to refer to a written description, including activity form, activity sheet, activity record, and activity guide. For the balance of this text an activity documented in print will be referred to as a Curriculum Activity Guide.

The practical value of a printed Curriculum Activity Guide is further extended when the form can be reused. An activity form with descriptive elements helps teachers manage their curriculum and alerts them to the important learning ideas that they can offer to the children during the experience. Curriculum Activity Guides that are reusable reduce the time-consuming task of writing and rewriting plans. An inclusive form, including all sixteen elements of an activity, is just one design for documenting an activity in writing. The activities displayed throughout the chapters use the form shown in Figure 6–6. A full-size, reproducible version of this form can be found in Appendix B.

Reusing and Displaying Curriculum Activity Guides

You will begin to appreciate the time you have spent on documentation when you begin to reuse the Curriculum Activity Guides. The initial investment for building a library of Activity Guides will involve concentrated time. However, when you adapt an activity idea to an individual child or the changing needs of your group of children, the major task of conceptualizing the activity will be

FIGURE 6–6   Curriculum Activity Guide

Title:		
Goal:		
Curriculum area:	**Developmental Focus:**	**Location/Interest Center:**
Participants:	**Time:**	**Age range:**
Materials:		
Preparation/setup:		
Teaching strategies:		
Possible outcomes:		
Concepts:		
Skills:		
Vocabulary:		

FIGURE 6–7   Curriculum Board

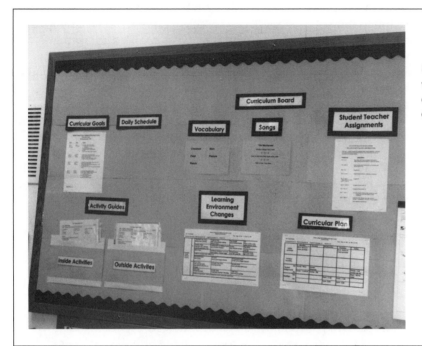

Use a bulletin board to present a visual of the curriculum plan and details of recommended experiences.

complete, and you will find that you are working much more efficiently.

Curriculum Activity Guides prepared on an eight and one-half by eleven sheet of paper or cardstock can be filed in a three-ring binder. Another documenting method that is popular among Early Childhood teachers is to document the information on index cards. Index cards can be laminated and filed in a box by curriculum area, developmental area, theme, or project. Index cards, especially those that are laminated, allow fewer chances to modify the experience. However, the index cards are easy to handle and can be readily available to staff members and volunteers for reference during the related activity.

If you have access to a word processor, type and file a template so you can reuse the format to type in activities. Store your activities in your computer document files, identified in a way that matches your curriculum organization.

Besides filing the written descriptions of activities and making them available for reference during the experiences, you may display Curriculum Activity Guides on a bulletin board to present a visual of the curriculum plan and details of recommended experiences. A large visual will allow teachers, parents, and volunteers to picture your map of intended experiences for the week (Figure 6–7).

IS THE ACTIVITY SUITABLE?

Knowing the children's capabilities directs the staff to arrange play experiences to support the children's acquisition of skills. The teacher should be supportive and have realistic expectations that anticipate the child's development through time. In this way, teachers can provide for the continuity and sequence of learning so "vitally needed" for children (Bloom, 1981, p. 109). But how will you know when an activity is suitable for a child?

As you learn to follow the development of a child over time, you will naturally begin to offer activities to meet the developing needs of the children. The more confident you become in your ability to apply child development knowledge and assessment findings, the easier it will be to arrange activities to match the child's progress. Catherine Landreth tells us, "What a young learner wants to do is what he feels ready and eager to master and what is just a little different from what he can do already" (1972, p. 33). Your task as a teacher is to plan activities to help the children understand their capabilities and be ready. You will give the curriculum credibility as you consider the sequence of activities (Landreth, 1972, p. 35). As you observe the children you will recognize their new behaviors, skills, and interests. You will recognize that the child is ready for a new experience. Reasonable expectations for young children guide you to plan some activities in sequence because the foundation for new learning is grounded on old learning (Essa & Rogers, 1992, p. 7). You will help children understand by presenting simple concepts first, then by moving toward more complex levels of understanding and skills (Gestwicki, 1999, p. 255).

Clustering Activities

When you think of a cluster you probably envision a group of people or objects that are related in some way. You may find this concept useful in organizing your curriculum. Consider **clustering** activities as a method to pattern suitable activities. Clustering implies that activities are related through time but not necessarily in a rigid order. You may find it useful to introduce an idea or concept and then return to it at a later time. Clustering activities supports grouping experiences to match the children's needs while maintaining a child-centered and process-oriented curriculum. Several Interest Centers may explore the same concept on a given day or week. Clustering encourages rotation and reinforcement of experiences within the different developmental areas. Integrated curriculum is supported by clustering activities with flexibility, learning, and skill development offered within the different Interest Centers and curriculum areas. Clustering allows you to implement experiences

sequentially with appropriate expectations for progression. Children benefit from repeated exposure to a skill or a concept. However, even after a skill is learned, children need chances to reinforce that skill or concept.

Some activities naturally flow from one another. In Chapter 5 there was discussion about trips to the neighborhood. It was stated that children need exposure to basic ideas about the post office before the visit, which demonstrates how patterning activities is more beneficial. Had the children toured the post office before preparatory activities such as reading stories and an initial visit to mail a letter, the tour of the facility might not have been as beneficial.

Clustering suitable activities will call on teachers to sequence some activities. The process of sequencing implies that skills and ideas progress from concrete, simple tasks to more abstract and complex activities. Think about offering fingerpainting with primary colors on day one and two. On days three and four, provide materials for mixing food color and water for children to experience discovering secondary colors. On the fifth day you might introduce experiences with felt figures of primary and secondary colors, along with modeling dough in primary colors. You would have clustered activities incorporating important aspects (Figure 6–8). These aspects remind us to incorporate the child's past experiences and her developmental level, to begin with concrete experiences, and to progress from simple to complex.

Clustering activities encourage arrangement of activities for children to experience new skills in different ways.

FIGURE 6–8 Considerations for Clustering Activities

Child's past experiences
Child's developmental level
Beginning with concrete activities
Progressing from simple to complex

Clustering activities encourages arrangement of activities for children to experience a new idea or skill in several different ways. Simply repeating the same activity over and over does not necessarily clarify learning, nor does it guarantee that a skill will be attained. Children will be more likely to remember and use an idea if they have been exposed to it in a variety of ways.

Three-year-old David's ability to distinguish the differences among textures of objects increases after experiencing several hands-on activities featuring rough and smooth materials. After many pleasurable but separate experiences with rough materials and smooth materials, David's understanding will be enhanced with activities combining both types of materials. The activities relate over time without necessarily requiring more complexity. In addition, the more senses that are called into action, the more David will become involved, retain ideas, and acquire skills (Figure 6–9).

Clustering activities also allows you to pattern experiences to progress from the simple to the more complex. Joe, age four years and three months, is observed recognizing all three of the primary colors: red, yellow, and blue. The next day, he is observed at the Outdoor Discovery Center mixing drops of primary colors into containers of water. His continued interest suggests to you that additional experiences related to color mixing may be warranted. Sec-

ondary colors are introduced during Grouptime using a flannel board and colored felt. Modeling dough made of secondary colors is added to the art shelf the next day. Joe pulls the purple modeling dough from the container, telling Angela, "I need the roller for my blue modeling dough." Additional activities to further reinforce the concept of the color purple could benefit Joe and Angela, who are acquiring an understanding of secondary colors. When they attend to the felt colors, use the primary-colored modeling dough, mix tempera paints, or listen to the book *Little Blue and Little Yellow* (Lionni, 1994), they progressively acquire concepts that reinforce the ideas experienced during the introductory fingerpainting activity.

Modifying Activities

A curriculum is successful when it is reviewed regularly. Ideally, informal reviews should occur each day. The staff needs to determine what worked, what did not work, and what needs to be changed. Informal daily reviews improve the quality of interactions between the teachers and children.

How many children participated in the Dramatic Play area since new props were added? Formal and informal observation will give direction for the modification of the curriculum. For example, during staff discussion it was noted that only two children during that day used the suitcases placed in the Dramatic Play area. Further staff collaboration leads to plans to introduce the suitcases during the next grouptime to create interest in the props. Continuing observation may determine that those props are not needed at this time. Evaluation determines what equipment should be rearranged, what materials should be added or removed, and whether the experiences offered are meeting children's needs.

More formal evaluation may involve video recording of activities. Teachers who listen and observe the children's responses will gain insight into their level of understanding. Check the children's involvement and progress to determine whether to repeat certain activities or add new ones. Written reviews on the back of Curriculum Activity Guides provide critical insight for planning and actual modification of the experience. Did children respond to the teacher strategies, and were possible outcomes noted?

Listen to children and watch them participate. Review their participation, recognize their interest, and note their readiness. Modify curriculum plans to more effectively present activities that are suitable for the children enrolled in your program.

FIGURE 6–9 Clustering Activities

Concept: Rough	**Concept: Smooth**
Activities:	**Activities:**
Touching sandpaper	Enjoying fingerpainting
Sorting dry dog food	Washing river rocks
Stacking tree bark	Testing hand lotions

Combining Concepts: Rough and Smooth

Activities: Fingerpaint corrugated paper
Wash sea shells and rocks
Rub ice cubes on sidewalk

It is important for teachers to listen to children and watch them participate.

SETTING UP ACTIVITIES

What Is Needed?

The *curriculum plan* outlines the essentials. This is a guide that allows you to access or plan activities that help you to accomplish the curricular guidelines set for the week, weeks, or month. The plan establishes a guide for the specific activities and alerts the director about the materials and supplies needed. The use of facilities and scheduling extra staff and volunteers are also noted.

Second, the Curriculum Activity Guides provide specific listings of the materials, locations, and staff members needed to implement the experience. Third, staff meetings allow teachers to review the plans and guides in order to ensure that modifications are made as needed. The plan and guides together create a map guiding your direction. Lastly, you will set up suitable activities when preparation time is supported by the program (Figure 6–10).

Adapting the Plan to the Day and Moment

Since the curriculum plan serves as a map, you make the decision whether you need to change your direction. The curriculum plan provides credibility and order and helps you to facilitate the program goals. However, you are a teacher and therefore respond to children because you listen,

FIGURE 6–10   Essentials for Setting Up an Activity

Curriculum plan
Activity guides
Staff collaboration
Preparation time

observe, and understand what you know to be appropriate for their growth and development.

Although we desire to facilitate an accountable program, we also need to ready ourselves to adapt the plan and activities to the moment and day and then document the change. Children's needs change, staff members' needs change, and circumstances in families and communities change. Adapting plans will not compromise the integrity of your teaching, but rather will place you among other remarkable Early Childhood teachers who suitably support children's growth and development in all developmental domains.

LABELING AND STORING CURRICULUM MATERIALS

Busy teachers need efficient methods to implement their plans. Teachers require sufficient and accessible storage for the curriculum supplies, materials, and equipment.

Efficient storage also positively affects the children because it models organizational skills (Greenman, 1988, p. 126). Labeling specific materials and supplies encourages children to return items to designated places. "Classrooms that are cluttered with material, walls completely covered with display, and overflowing storage bins contribute to chaos making it difficult for children to select activities" (Dodge, Jablon, & Bickart, 1994, p. 95).

If you are trying to maximize your storage, you will want to carefully select your materials initially. Roger Neugebauer, publisher of the *Child Care Information Exchange,* recommends to teachers who are considering the purchase of equipment that they question whether vendors are capable of providing support and if the product can be tried out before purchase (1998, p. 67).

In a quality child-care and education setting, the environment is scaled to and accessible for the children. However, your environment "must have some inaccessible storage areas like closets and high book shelves for securely stowing supplies, nap mats and folding cots, teachers' belongings, medical kits, and cleaning supplies" (Caples, 1996, p. 16). Storage will help you organize similar materials together. The location of materials, whether the storage is fixed or movable, creates a pattern of movement. Question whether the supplies are truly accessible and that they do not disrupt other children who are engaged in an activity (Loughlin & Suina, 1982, p. 154). Some storage is fixed and some is movable; for example, a hinged cabinet unit on wheel casters stores woodworking equipment well, safely locks, and wheels out into the Interest Area as needed. Whether the storage is for multiple or specialized items, creating efficient storage requires that it is aesthetically pleasing, creative, and in close proximity to the area in which items are needed (Greenman, 1988, p. 126). Effective storage will improve the management of curriculum ideas.

REVIEW

Planned activities will evolve from the children's questions and from more formal assessment methods that identify relevant topics. Activities are experiences that actively engage children. The sixteen elements of an activity will help you document meaningful experiences, helping you to prepare and increase your time with the children.

A Curriculum Activity Guide is a printed form with descriptive elements designed to help you manage the curriculum efficiently. The initial investment for building a library of Curriculum Activity Guides involves concentrated time. However, when you adapt an activity idea to an individual child or the changing needs of your group of children, the major task of conceptualizing the activity will be complete.

Clustering, or sequencing suitable activities, reinforces individualized curricula and allows rotation and reinforcement of activities. It also supports integrated curricula with flexibility in creating experiences for learning and skill development.

A curriculum is successful when teachers review it regularly. Assessment determines whether equipment should be rearranged, what materials should be added or removed, and whether the experiences offered are meeting children's needs. Curriculum Plans and Activity Guides establish a guide for the setup of activities. Staff collaboration and preparation time will help adapt the plans and activities to the moment and day.

KEY TERMS

activity	materials
activity goal	participants
age range	possible outcomes
clustering	preparation/setup
concepts	skills
Curriculum Activity	teaching strategies
Guide	title
elements	vocabulary
Location/Interest Center	

RESPOND

1. Write activity titles and goals for the following two activities:

   A. Activity Description: Washing tricycles in the outside area with sponges, soap, and water.

      Title: _____

      Goal: _____

   B. Activity Description: Matching shapes found in the outdoor environment with photographs.

      Title: _____

      Goal: _____

2. Copy the Activity Guide on page 237. Complete the form designing a Science activity for preschool children. The children have shown need for more large movement activities.

3. Identify three activities that will introduce the concepts of hard and soft. Refer to the section in this chapter titled "Clustering Activities."
4. Collect and review two activity forms from directors or teachers. Write a one-paragraph response analyzing the portions or the form that you could use and explain why.

REFERENCES

Arends, R. I. (1991). *Learning to teach* (2nd ed.). New York: McGraw Hill.

Barnhart, C. L., & Barnhart, R. K. (Eds.). (1990). *The World Book Dictionary.* Chicago: World Book.

Bloom, B. S. (1981). *All our children learning: Primer for parents, teachers, and other educators.* New York: McGraw-Hill.

Bruner, J. S. (1960). *The process of education.* New York: Vintage.

Burts, D. C., & Buchanan, T. K. (1998). Preparing teachers in developmentally appropriate ways to teach in developmentally appropriate classrooms. In C. Seefeldt & A. Galper (Eds.). *Continuing issues in early childhood education* (2nd ed.). Upper Saddle River, NJ: Merrill.

Caples, S. E. (1996). Some guidelines for preschool design. *Young Children, 51*(4), 14–21.

Dodge, D. T., Jablon, J. R., & Bickart, T. S. (1994). *Constructing curriculum for the primary grades.* Washington, DC: Teaching Strategies.

Essa, E. L., & Rogers, P. R. (1992). *An early childhood curriculum: From developmental model to application.* Albany, NY: Delmar.

Gestwicki, C. (1999). *Developmentally appropriate practice: Curriculum and development in early education* (2nd ed.). Albany, New York: Delmar.

Greenman, J. (1988). *Caring spaces, learning places: Children's environments that work.* Redman, WA: Exchange Press.

Landreth, C. (1972). *Preschool learning and teaching.* New York: Harper & Row.

Lionni, L. (1994). *Little Blue and Little Yellow.* New York: Mulberry.

Loughlin, C. E., & Suina, J. H. (1982). *The learning environment: An instructional strategy.* New York: Teachers College Press.

Neugebauer, R. (1998, March/April). Guide to early childhood curriculum products. *Child Care Information Exchange, 126,* 67–71.

Ornstein, A. C., & Hunkins, F. P. (1998). *Curriculum: Foundations, principles, and issues* (3rd ed.). Needham Heights, MA: Allyn & Bacon.

Vance, B. (1973). *Teaching the prekindergarten child: Instructional design and curriculum.* Monterey, CA: Brooks/Cole Publishing Company.

CHAPTER 7

Physical Development:
Health, Safety, and Nutrition;
Movement; and Music
and Rhythm Activities

Curriculum Profile

Koula hops through the door and hands Teacher Sal a picture. She says, "This is me when I was a baby. I was learning to walk."

Koula unzips her jacket, hangs it on her cubby space hook, and then places her snack box on the counter. Koula looks around the room, slides to the circular art table. There are aprons on each chair. She pulls the apron over her head. Koula sits down at the table, cuts with the scissors, squeezes the glue bottle, and places fabric and buttons on her paper. Koula writes her name after asking the student teacher for help. Before the hour is over Koula has moved from the manipulative table, where she fitted puzzle pieces and stacked shapes, to the sensory table, where she sifted sand and poured water. Koula returned to the art area to mold modeling dough. She pinched and pounded the dough. As the sun warmed the outdoor classroom, the sliding doors were opened, signaling to Koula that she could play indoors and outdoors. She walked outside, climbed the slide steps, slid down the slide several times, and then ran toward the wagon. She pulled the empty wagon around the path once before inviting Jane for a ride. She pushed the wagon before skipping to the outside Listening Center where she turned the knobs to adjust the sound. Koula washed her hands after toileting, then joined the cooking experience group, where she mixed, stirred, and cut. The small Grouptime invited Koula to move her fingers and hands rhythmically to action songs. The Grouptime discussion included a large flannel board story about crossing streets safely.

Chapter Outline

Physical Development
   Large Movement: Possible Outcomes and Activities
   Small Movement: Possible Outcomes and Activities

Connecting Curriculum for Physical Development
   Integrating Activities
   Teaching Strategies

Physical Development with Health, Safety, and Nutrition
   Healthy Habits for Young Children
   Safety for Young Children
   Nutritional Awareness and Cooking for Young Children

Physical Development with Movement
   Movement and Perceptual Motor Development for Young Children: Possible Outcomes and Activities

Physical Development with Music and Rhythm Activities
   Music and Rhythm for Young Children: Possible Outcomes and Activities

Study Guide

As you study the sections in this chapter, you should be able to:

- Understand the large and small physical development movements.
- Learn how to integrate activities to facilitate movement experiences for young children.

- Consider ways to contribute to the children's understanding of health, nutrition, and safety.
- Know about relevant safety topics.
- Become familiar with skills related to nutrition and cooking.
- Recognize movement categories and motor skills.
- Identify concepts and topics related to music and rhythm.

PHYSICAL DEVELOPMENT

Development occurs when the brain and body mature, initiating changes in abilities and behaviors. Physical development of children refers to their basic physiological changes and motor skills. Children acquire skills sequentially, yet the acquisition of skills and changes in the body are unique for each child. Individuality in skill acquisition results from a person's heredity and environment. Children will acquire skills to balance a three-wheel toy before a two-wheel toy. They will dump a bucket of sand before pouring the contents of the bucket into another container. As children acquire basic motor skills during the early childhood years, they gain more control and confidence to try new tasks. Activities help children develop their capabilities.

The Curriculum Profile at the beginning of this chapter demonstrated numerous ways in which Koula moved as she participated in different experiences. A variety of experiences help children develop physically. Active involvement is beneficial because it provides children with chances to increase important behaviors and to develop physical skills (Figure 7–1).

Large Movement: Possible Outcomes and Activities

Two-year-olds, three-year-olds, and four-year-olds generally are in motion. That is what makes young children so observable. They are developing rapidly

FIGURE 7–1   Children Develop Skills and Behaviors through Physical Development Experiences

agility	fitness
balance	flexibility
cooperation	involvement
confidence	motivation
creativity	participation
endurance	relaxation
expression	strength

during the preschool years and exhibiting ranges of physical abilities and capabilities.

Motion requires muscular activity. When the large body muscles are in motion, it is called **large movement,** which is also referred to as gross motor skills and gross motor development. Children use large movements for walking, running, climbing, pedaling, and throwing. They are developing their dexterity, and skills in general body movements by participating during active experiences. As coordination, balance, and control mature, children's participation in large movement activities increase. Appropriate environments for young children need indoor and outdoor climbing structures, large blocks, carpentry materials, swings, wheel toys, and space to move, run, and dance.

Skills: Possible Outcomes

Children acquire specific motor skills by engaging in physical movement. Motion permits them to feel their bodies, move, and begin to understand their bodies' capabilities and changes. A variety of large movement activities helps children to develop self-confidence and is necessary for healthy physical development. Large movement experiences give children opportunities to release large muscle energy, relieve stress and tension, achieve relaxation, and develop large motor skills (Figure 7–2).

Large Movement Activities

Teachers who plan specific large movement activities in the outdoor environment expand on routine experiences with wheel toys and climbing structures. An obstacle course challenges large muscles while requiring a child to problem solve. A bean-bag toss obligates a child to stretch, throw, and toss (Curriculum Activity Guides 27 and 28 📖). Teachers

Large movement experiences contribute to children's physical development.

who schedule large movement activities indoors modify the experience to the space available. Each child will benefit from a program with opportunities to meet their individualized needs and capabilities. Adaptations to the environment, with specific consideration for the kind of impairment, will allow greater participation of children with disabilities. For example, children in wheelchairs who are unable to build blocks on the floor may be able to use a rectangular board with casters, allowing them to lie on their stomachs on top of the scooter boards and propel themselves with their hands or elbows and use blocks or manipulative toys (Spodek & Saracho, 1994, p. 221)

Large movement experiences will contribute to 3the children's physical development with or without specific equipment. Lifting and placing unit blocks, running, waving long streamers with outreached arms, running with the wind to music, and scooting on boards are all large motor activities.

Small Movement: Possible Outcomes and Activities

A baby's first grasping motions trigger the beginning of natural exploratory behaviors. Curiosity continues to drive infants, toddlers, and preschoolers to investigate every item in their surroundings. Children use their small muscles in their arms, hands, fingers, and faces to interact and to respond. Motor behavior involving the small muscles is called **small movement,** or fine motor development.

Skills: Possible Outcomes

Many chances exist throughout the daily program to facilitate small movement development. Children

FIGURE 7–2   Children Develop Skills and Behaviors Through Large Movement Experiences

crawling	pulling	galloping
walking	throwing	skipping
jumping	kicking	tossing
hopping	hanging	wiggling
running	sliding	climbing
carrying	balancing	swinging
pushing	lifting	rolling
pedaling	stretching	leaping
swaying	catching	bouncing

engage their small muscles when they manipulate puzzles, interlocking pieces, unit blocks, and art materials. Self-help skills expand when children use their growing small motor skills to zip zippers, to button shirts, and to brush their hair and teeth.

You will be able to utilize the natural opportunities in both the indoor and outdoor environments to encourage the children's participation in small movement experiences. Placing props, such as toy people and animals, in the sand area extends children's opportunities for exploration and creative play. There are opportunities for creative interactions at the manipulative table equipped with magnifying tools. This Discovery Center invites children to examine bugs, leaves, and dirt. Small motor activities tend to establish relaxing, slower-paced options for children, especially in the outdoor classroom, where large movement activities tend to dominate. Inviting children to pour, dig, place, hold, stack, reach, and assemble helps them develop their small muscles and improves their small movement skills (Figure 7–3).

Staff recognizes that there are wide variations of fine motor skills among preschool children. Equipment modifications designed for children with disabilities allow them to participate and maximize their potential for developing small motor abilities. Adaptations to the activities, individualized for the child with special needs, benefits children. The teacher's adaptations in the presentation of activities will be valuable to children with disabilities by ensuring that a child can see your face and gestures if he is hearing impaired; using physical prompts until the verbal prompts can be followed for the visually impaired child; assigning another child to be a caller for a motor impaired child; and giving directions slowly and one-at-a-time for a learning-delayed child (Cook, Tessier, & Klein, 1996, p. 303).

Small movement activities such as keyboarding influence development.

Small Movement Activities

Small movement activities influence other areas of development. As children develop physically, they become more aware of their own body movements and the consequences of their body motions. Letting go at the top of a slide helps them to acquire concepts of movement and speed. Turning the water faucet many ways before the water flows allows them to practice a skill. Pressing the computer mouse causes a particular function to activate on the computer screen. Placing puzzle shapes into the correct spaces requires them to make judgments before fitting the pieces. Plan activities to build on the skills that children are naturally developing in the environment throughout the day: letting go, turning a faucet, pressing a button, and placing a puzzle. Eyedroppers and Soap Suction and Tweezers and Ice Cube Trays are two activities that will develop small motor development and increase attention span and concentration (Curriculum Activity Guides 29 and 30 [CAG]).

CONNECTING CURRICULUM FOR PHYSICAL DEVELOPMENT

Physical development experiences must be incorporated within the curriculum through activities that fit the child's natural need for large movement. Physical development activities support the

FIGURE 7–3 Children Develop Skills and Behaviors Through Small Movement Experiences

holding	plucking	squeezing
fitting	zipping	pinching
placing	painting	keyboarding
clapping	washing	tracing
coloring	smiling	steering
pouring	chewing	writing
cutting	shaking	typing
buttoning	steering	whistling

children's physiological needs for activity, sensory stimulation, fresh air, rest, and nourishment (Bredekamp & Copple, 1997, p. 17)

Integrating Activities

Movement skills are recognized as fundamental factors for a child's physical growth. Some programs organize the activities by Developmental Focus area. Others organize activities by curriculum area or theme. Programs meet the children's needs in many ways with a variety of planning approaches. Your decision to integrate curriculum planning will place you among a growing number of Early Childhood professionals who strive toward an emergent and integrated curriculum (Chapter 5, "Establishing and Recording a Curriculum Plan and Schedule"). As you continue to observe and listen to the children, you will find that there are meaningful activities to connect Developmental Focus areas, curriculum areas, and a theme (Figure 7–4).

Springtime brings awareness of growing and planting. During a story time, Jodie leans toward Teacher Tomas and whispers, "My papa has a big garden." During the weekly staff meeting Teacher Tomas shares Jodie's comment about her papa's garden. A student teacher comments that she has also heard several children in the sand area referring to plants and seeds during the week. The staff organizes experiences for children translating their interests into large movement activities. Skills develop when children rake, dig, and hoe a garden. Awareness of the health benefits of preparing food

from the garden is a bonus with a gardening theme. Appreciation of plants—water, dirt, sunshine—directs children's attention toward the curriculum area of Science.

Teachers who manage activities thematically may find that there are certain themes that facilitate physical development activities. The theme Sports for Everyone, for example, will expose children to and incorporate events held as part of the Special Olympics sponsored by many communities for children with disabilities. The number of sports introduced should depend on the children's developmental level and interest. A theme such as Exercising complements experiences that introduce children to occupations related to physical fitness (Figure 7–5).

Teaching Strategies

Children's continuous movements create a natural setting to facilitate their physical development. Your role as a teacher is to ensure safety in a motivating environment. The children will need sufficient time for active participation to refine and expand their physical abilities. A general understanding of the sequence of physical skills and appreciation of each child's unique timetable keeps the experiences flexible and appropriate for the group of participants.

Movement contributes to growth in all areas of development. The guidelines for physical education, from preschool through high school, were established in 1990 by the National Association for Sport and Physical Education. Reference to regular physical participation for a healthy lifestyle is highlighted. Teachers are warned to avoid many of the traditional games in which children are singled out, eliminated with no chance to re-enter the activity, and required to perform predetermined moves. Teachers are encouraged to promote positive attitudes to guide discovery and exploration

FIGURE 7–4   Activities Integrate Developmental Focus Area, Curriculum Areas, and Theme

Developmental Focus Area	Physical
Curriculum Areas	*Health, Safety, Nutrition* Activity: Cooking fresh carrots
	Movement Activity: Preparing outdoor garden area
	Science Activity: Planting and observing plants grow
Theme	Gardening

FIGURE 7–5   Themes Facilitating Physical Development

Large Movement	**Small Movement**
Sports for Everyone	Carpentry
Exercising	Tools and Small Machines
Hiking	Stitching and Sewing
All About Me: My Body	My Senses: Touch
Summer Safety	Plants

and to de-emphasize competition (Pica, 2000, pp. 295–303).

Teachers who gently guide and model skills create an atmosphere for child-centered movement play. Helping children feel competent about themselves during early childhood has lifetime value. Beneficial lifetime experiences include active participation and appreciation of walking, climbing, gardening, and sports. The positive effects are immediately apparent in elementary school for the children who have acquired the fundamental motor skills, such as balancing, throwing, and skipping. Verbal reinforcement helps children feel successful. Activities that are slightly ahead of the children's developmental reach bring new ideas and challenges as they practice and gain movement skills (Bredekamp & Copple, 1997, p. 19).

PHYSICAL DEVELOPMENT WITH HEALTH, SAFETY, AND NUTRITION

Healthy Habits for Young Children

Planning specific activities related to the curriculum area of **Health, Safety,** and **Nutrition** facilitates young children's potential for physical well-being and fitness. Children benefit from programs that offer activities introducing concepts to encourage healthy and safe practices. Familiarity with good health, safety, and nutrition practices establishes healthy habits for the entire life span. Appropriate and meaningful experiences help children to understand more about themselves and their relationships with others. Begin by securing safe environments and by modeling healthy practices. Keep accident prevention as a high priority. You will need to give careful attention to accident control, knowing that accidents are the leading cause of death during preschool years. By modeling healthy and safe behaviors, teachers offer beneficial practices that children and parents can use outside the program.

Each child needs to learn about and appreciate his own body functions and needs. This awareness will contribute to a sense of self and to good mental health. Lee learns that his mouth is dry and that his body needs water. He learns that he is sweating and may need to move to a shady spot in the sand area. He learns that washing his hands before eating a snack helps to prevent illness. He is rewarded with the teacher's recognizing smile when he waits patiently at the drinking fountain for his turn.

Health: Possible Outcomes

Children benefit from routine schedules that contribute to healthful habits. Washing hands before mealtimes and cooking experiences provides positive outcomes. Some teachers schedule health-related routines with direct guidance and beneficial results. Children learn that brushing their teeth and resting their bodies are important ways to sustain their health. Early learning experiences should be planned to encourage possible outcomes, including introduction to concepts related to healthful habits (Figure 7–6).

You will contribute to the children's understanding about health by using appropriate vocabulary related to the activities. The vocabulary list that is identified for each planned experience lists recommended words that may be used by the teacher or other adult participating with the children in the experience. Vocabulary is one of the elements of the Curriculum Activity Guide

FIGURE 7–6   Possible Outcomes: Concepts Related to Healthful Habits

Activity Title	Concept
Charting Growth	Babies are little. Baby photographs of the children in your program demonstrate growth.
Illness Control	Washing hands is a healthy habit. Using nose tissues may help to prevent illness. Washing tables keeps them clean. Resting gives me energy.
Regular Checkups	A visit to the doctor is for a checkup. Regular checkups contribute to wellness.

Children benefit from healthy habits.

FIGURE 7–8   Healthy Habit Topics for Young Children

Charting Growth	Measuring, weighing, and charting growth Displaying baby and toddler photographs
Illness Control	Washing hands Identifying and discussing allergies Using tissues Washing tables Scrubbing tricycles, equipment, materials Resting Going to the doctor
Regular Checkups	Medical—visitor or trip Dental—visitor or trip

(Figure 7–7). The vocabulary can be printed in parent newsletters and displayed on bulletin boards as a way to expand awareness and reinforcement outcomes of activities.

Healthy Habit Topics and Activities for Young Children

The topics for healthy habits and the activities will be determined by the children's responses to the initial activities that you schedule. Events and occurrences in the children's lives will influence the direction of the curriculum plan. Begin with topics most familiar to the children, such as washing hands and using tissues to wipe noses (Figure 7–8). A child's absence from school, caused by a long-term illness, may stimulate an activity, a theme that involves **integrating activities,** or a project related

FIGURE 7–7   Possible Outcomes: Vocabulary Related to Healthful Habits

Activity Title	Good Posture and Position	
Vocabulary	posture	stretch
	straight	body functions
	align	body needs: food, water
	spine	fatigue
	exercise	rest
	elimination	

to health. A pet's illness could also generate interest in a topic related to healthy habits that questions whether pets get colds and the flu like children. An activity about height will help children become more aware of their own bodies (Curriculum Activity Guide 31 [CAG]) and an experience learning about exercise and heart beats supports movement and health curriculum areas (Curriculum Activity Guide 32 [CAG]).

Safety for Young Children

A safe environment, designed for young children, establishes a sound foundation for safety awareness. For example, positioning paper towels near the sink and within reach of the children eliminates some of the dripping water that makes floors slippery and unsafe. The setting and schedule should be arranged for prevention of accidents. You will be able to effectively model safe practices within environments that focus on the developmental needs of the children enrolled in your center.

Safety: Possible Outcomes

The Safety activities that you plan will be influenced by your curricular guidelines and the curriculum approach adapted by your school. The planned and spontaneous experiences will integrate experiences across the curriculum.

Safety topics that are suitable for young learners should be reviewed by the teaching staff. Some topics may also require input from families with the intent of keeping the activities relevant to the children's world. Expectations for possible outcomes suggest inclusion of simple concepts related to the topics. Once considered, concepts can be documented on the Curriculum Activity Guides for reference during the specific activities (Figure 7–9).

The vocabulary related to Safety activities assists teachers and adults guiding the experiences for the children to expand learning opportunities. Watching and listening to the children will give teachers insight about the children's use of language and provide ideas about ways to encourage their vocabulary in relation to specific activities (Figure 7–10).

Safety: Topics and Activities for Young Children

The program guidelines, curriculum plan, children's needs, and local community emphasis affect the selection of the topics for activities related to safety. Safety education topics can be divided into several categories. Program guidelines and regional emphasis affect the selection of Safety topics (Figure 7–11).

Preplanning activities will help you to manage a curriculum to include Safety and will increase your time. Teachers who listen to children's conversations and elicit parental input find that activities are more emergent. The curriculum plan should allow flexibility to incorporate activities that respond to the current needs of the group. Examples

FIGURE 7–10 Possible Outcomes: Vocabulary Related to Safety

Observed Behavior	Wide-eyed Hyung rushes into the center and says, "The car door closed on my hand."
Title	Clap and Close
Goal	To practice clapping and relate to a way to increase safe practices while loading into a car.
Vocabulary	clap car door loud wait sound safe close

FIGURE 7–11 Safety Topics for Young Children

Environmental	indoor outdoor
Ecological	pollution
Emergencies	first aid 911 calls
Fire	exit plans fire fighters prevention
Food	containers/labels discoloring
Lost/Found	locate appropriate adult hug a tree OK to talk to police officer
Neighborhood	neighborhood watch play area
Pedestrian	walking paths (ramps, light) right of way parking lot safety
Poison	plants cleaning products unmarked containers
Transportation	seat belts signs bike helmets
Weather	appropriate clothing weather reports, warnings shelter

FIGURE 7–9 Possible Outcomes: Concepts Related to Safety

Activity Titles	Concepts
Floor Safety	Floors can be slippery. Water on the floors makes them slippery.
Locking Gates	The gate is locked to keep me inside and safe. Keys unlock certain gates.
Emergency Help	911 number is used when no one can help. Looking for an adult first is important.
Fire Engine Siren	The fire engine siren sounds loudly because it is rushing to help. Cars stop when the siren is sounding.

Nutritional Awareness—children enjoy preparing and eating food.

of two teacher-directed experiences include Dial 911 (Curriculum Activity Guide 33 ⟨CAG⟩) and Medicine is Not Candy (Curriculum Activity Guide 34 ⟨CAG⟩). Once introduced by the teachers in a Grouptime, the materials may be provided in an Interest Center to allow children to initiate their own participation and choice of experiences.

Safety procedures help to manage Interest Centers and activities. Specifying the number of children to participate in an activity is one way that the environment signals safety. The sign secured to the loft shows that three friends can be in the loft at one time. The laminated chart also pictures one child climbing on the ladder. **Cooking** experiences incorporate safety messages with specific procedures that list hand washing, number of participants, and caution with electrical appliances and cooking utensils. A picture hangs on the cage showing the safe way to feed and hold the guinea pig. Reinforcement for Safety throughout the schedule is beneficial.

Nutritional Awareness and Cooking for Young Children

"It is a watermelon inside," Catherine excitedly shouts when the large, green, round watermelon was cut in half by the teacher. Four other children gathered around the table, waiting for a small wedge to be placed in their Styrofoam bowls. The children washed their hands before joining the snack table activity. Catherine indicated that she

has eaten watermelon before and that the black seeds were hard to pick out. This was the first time she observed a whole watermelon cut into pieces. Participation in meal preparation helps children to expand their knowledge about food: where it grows, what it does for their bodies, and ways to prepare healthful foods.

Nutrition education outlines activities that help children enjoy food preparation and mealtime. Children learn to appreciate different foods and identify cultures with favorite foods. Experiences emphasizing Nutrition education encourage children to try new foods and to listen to their bodies telling them when they have had enough to eat. Nutrition education extends to parents, first by involving them in planning initial goals. When parents volunteer at your center during cooking activities they provide the needed extra staff and, more importantly, share foods familiar to their families and cultures.

Nutrition and Cooking: Possible Outcomes

As children learn about food, a familiar topic, they participate in emergent learning. Nutrition education broadens mealtime and Cooking activities to help children understand statements such as, "Eat your food, it is good for you." Nutrition education encourages pleasurable mealtimes with conversation and adults modeling appropriate table behaviors. Early care and education professionals must also maintain a method to carefully monitor children's food allergies, keeping all personnel informed. This awareness should extend to include the children's Cooking experiences that are provided during open activity time, when children are encouraged to participate in activities that they choose.

Food preparation designed for young children offers pleasures to all of the senses. Children can squeeze floured dough, taste the fresh pineapple, watch the pudding thicken, smell the strawberries boil, and crunch the coconut texture in the banana bread. Cooking experiences offer the optimum way to introduce new foods and new preparations of familiar foods. Children's appetites and preferences change. They may say they do not like a food because they have never tried it, but the same food prepared differently may be more appealing. If available regionally, artichokes are more fun to eat after snipping off the thorny tips with the help of a watchful teacher and gloves for protection.

Food preparation activities integrate curriculum areas while meeting children's developmental needs. Children develop small motor skills when they use cooking utensils. They follow directions when they read the picture recipes. Mathematical awareness is enhanced when children measure, count, and monitor time during Cooking experiences. Food preparation activities also require safe and sanitary conditions that add benefits related to Health and Safety (Figure 7–12).

Nutrition Topics and Cooking Activities for Young Children

Full participation ensures that the experience offers hands-on opportunities. Teacher preparation establishes procedures that facilitate positive outcomes. Children will enjoy preparing foods, whether the experience relates to a curriculum theme, emerges from their interests and needs, or is part of an Interest Center. Preparation initially

FIGURE 7–12   Possible Outcomes: Skills Related to Nutrition and Cooking

Skills	Nutrition and Cooking Activities
baking	scones
comparing	Italian gnocchi, latkes, and American dumplings
counting	number of cherry tomatoes for an individual salad
cooperating	at Cooking Center with other children
cutting	soft strawberries and hard apples
harvesting	fresh squash from school garden
mixing	tofu burgers
observing	flour mixing with the egg and milk
following	recipe directions
shelling	fresh, whole peanuts
squeezing	grapefruit and oranges for juice
spreading	cream cheese on bagels
stirring	fresh peaches and shaved ice for peach freezes

should include basic foods that will encourage children to appreciate and enjoy nutrition. The activities you plan and add for the moment and the day will enhance children's knowledge about food sources and nutrition. There are many different topics related to Nutrition education and Cooking that can be developed into meaningful activities. Experiences that fit within many curriculum areas help facilitate skills within developmental areas and can be organized around a theme or project (Figure 7–13).

Preparing a nutritious snack using Individual Snack (Curriculum Activity Guide 35 [CAG]) and Food Collage (Curriculum Activity Guide 36 [CAG]) offers children activities within the curriculum area of Health, Safety, and Nutrition.

FIGURE 7–13   Nutrition Education and Cooking Activity Topics for Young Children

Nutrition Education	Cooking Activities
observing others eat	growing fruits and vegetables
eating and enjoying meals	planning meals and menus
exploring origins of food	presenting appealing food
appreciating cultural preferences	recognizing food allergies
experiencing healthy foods	selecting appropriate ingredients
becoming an aware consumer	balancing food selections
storing food safely	placing leftover pancakes in bags

PHYSICAL DEVELOPMENT WITH MOVEMENT

Children keep their bodies in motion and, as they do, begin to understand who they are in relationship to their surroundings. Movement directs children's interactions and thinking behaviors. The basic fundamental movements that develop first, such as throwing, stacking, running, and squeezing, establish a base for the more complex movements. Children's motor patterns develop progressively, beginning with simple movements and advancing to more complex behaviors that combine basic motions to achieve a purpose. In the Curriculum Profile at the beginning of this chapter, Koula achieved many movements through experience, such as climbing, sitting, balancing, and pushing, before combining these basic movements in moving down the slide.

Planning appropriate movement activities requires that you consider experiences to include all children. When children are asked to move from one area to another, additional space is needed to allow the preschooler in a wheelchair to participate. A ringing bell signals to a visually impaired child the direction in which he needs to move (Curriculum Activity Guides 37 and 38 [CAG]).

Movement and Perceptual Motor Development for Young Children: Possible Outcomes and Activities

The common denominator in each age group is movement (Cherry, 1971, p. 6). When a child moves her body to change her place or position she completes a movement. Societal concerns for physical fitness validate your planning **movement and perceptual motor development** activities on a daily basis. Teachers need to encourage confidence and competence of children, rather than to structure their participation in games.

A child changes his place of location and body position in distinctive ways. Austin moves to another place by walking. He stretches his legs while remaining in the same position. He lifts a heavy block from the grass. Austin completed movements as he walked, stretched, and lifted. These motion behaviors categorize into three types of basic movement: **locomotor,** nonlocomotor, and **manipulative** (Pica, 2000, p. 92; Flinchum, 1975, p. 54) (Figure 7–14). Plan experiences for children to move from one place to another (walk, roll, jump forward, backward, sideways); move body parts while staying in the same place (twist, toss bean

FIGURE 7–14   Basic Movement Categories

Locomotor	Body moves to another place.
Nonlocomotor	Body moves while remaining in the same place.
Manipulative	Hands and feet move to operate and control objects.

bags, bat a plastic ball hanging from a string); place; and use their hands and feet to touch and control different objects (place pegs in specific holes).

A child acts and interacts throughout the day with his or her senses. What the child senses—sees, hears, touches, tastes, smells—depends on previous experiences, current needs, and cognitive awareness. Three-year-old Rita approaches a popcorn-stringing activity differently than four-year-old Joseph. Joseph approaches the table with confidence, having experienced popcorn stringing on numerous occasions during his two-year enrollment. Rita's perception of this activity is different because she is newly enrolled and does not have the prior experience with this activity.

Perceptual abilities determine how well children discriminate with their eyes and hands. The experiences during early childhood are most important because children develop their capabilities to sense, judge, apply, and coordinate incoming sensorial messages. Planned experiences give children advantages for discriminating size, shape, distance, and depth. Appropriate activities help children integrate the stimuli so they can make adjustments to their movements in response to their surroundings (Flinchum, 1975, p. 62). As children engage in movement, they improve their abilities to judge the signals and to anticipate the needed movement.

Experiences such as jumping over a tire and maneuvering a tricycle on a path will contribute to the children's awareness of the space around them and how they fit into it (spatial awareness). Throwing a balloon up into the air gives information about the quality of force. Touching hidden objects gives information about shape, texture, and structure. Selecting specific sizes of beads for stringing develops eye–hand coordination. A wide range of perceptual experiences contributes to the attainment of purposeful movement as a child acts and reacts to achieve a relatedness with her surroundings (Gerhardt, 1973, p. 26).

Movement: Possible Outcomes

Support for creative and self-directed movement allows children to express their feelings and enjoy locomotor, nonlocomotor, and manipulative motion. Guidelines are also important because they give inexperienced children a starting point, offer comfort, and build confidence (Cherry, 1971, p. 6). A curriculum plan should include activities to balance fast–slow and loud–quiet experiences to support movement and perceptual motor skills (Figures 7–15 and 7–16).

Movement Topics and Activities for Young Children

Body movement is essential to a person's ability to handle everyday activity; it stimulates thinking, yet the goal of movement development is competence rather than participation in structured games. Movement activities will contribute to basic movement skills by offering fundamental patterns naturally throughout the day. Diverse experiences motivate young children when they are challenged with opportunities to discover because these activities minimize frustration and de-emphasize competition, helping children to enjoy movement and gain basic movement skills (Gerhardt, 1973, p. 3).

Watch children moving under, over, and around. As they do, they begin to sense feelings about space. For example, Austin is in the box. He feels the box is around him. Koula jumps into the box with him. They get out of the box, then move behind the box and begin to become aware of location. They can adjust their bodies to assume a different shape when they crawl through a tunnel. Finally, Koula rolls the ball a short distance to Austin.

FIGURE 7–15   Possible Outcomes: Perceptual Motor Skills

Skill	Developing Perceptual Awareness
Choosing	Choosing pieces for an art wood sculpture.
Matching	Matching sizes, shapes.
Moving	Moving in response to judged distance on an obstacle course.
Stacking	Stacking blocks by shape and size.
Touching	Touching and describing objects with touch.
Turning	Turning pages while listening to a story.

You will continue to support the children's spontaneous motions with appropriate planned activities. The children's movements will provide you with additional clues about their interests and needs and will help you to balance locomotor, nonlocomotor, and manipulative movement experiences (Pica, 2000, pp. 93–98) (Curriculum Activity Guide 39).

When children use more than one of their senses during a movement, they have an opportunity to advance their perceptual skills. Name of the Animal is a teacher-directed activity that invites one child at a time to reach into a bucket of Styrofoam to locate a plastic animal. Each child

FIGURE 7–16   Possible Outcomes: Movement Skills

Movement Category	Movement Skills
Locomotor (Large motor)	crawling walking running jumping rolling climbing hopping leaping galloping sliding skipping
Nonlocomotor (Large and small motor)	stretching bending clicking with fingers sitting shaking swaying falling pointing pulling pushing swinging turning twisting
Manipulative (Small motor)	lifting pushing pulling throwing kicking catching ball rolling bouncing

FIGURE 7–17   Discovering Spatial Awareness with Movement

Balance	Balancing small box on head.
Time	Sprinkling the water hose quickly over the flowers.
Direction	Hopping over the tires.
Size	Tiptoeing tiny steps.
Shape	Wiggling like a worm.
Distance	Rolling the ball one foot.
Area	Sitting inside a box.
Volume	Filling the wagon with blocks.

listens to the sound the hidden animal makes and then names the animal. Once the child names the animal he or she pulls the plastic animal out of the bucket and visually examines the model. This game requires coordination of three senses, giving clues through touch, sound, and sight. There are many ways to facilitate children's discovery of spatial awareness by arranging movement opportunities (Gerhardt, 1973, pp. 136–137) (Figure 7–17).

Children also develop concepts about space, direction, and size as they move, gaining the confidence to continue exploring movement when the equipment is safe and varied. Staff support spontaneous motions, complemented with ap-

Riding a tricycle contributes to this child's awareness of the space around him.

propriate planned activities, by carefully assessing children's interests and needs. Careful observation results in activities that are meaningful to the children enrolled and offer a balance of locomotor, nonlocomotor, and manipulative movements.

PHYSICAL DEVELOPMENT WITH MUSIC AND RHYTHM ACTIVITIES

Music is the common thread that links different languages, cultures, and ages. Programs traditionally and consistently include **music and rhythm skills** for young children because young learners generally respond to melodies, instruments, songs, fingerplays, and rhythmic motion.

Music and Rhythm for Young Children: Possible Outcomes and Activities

You will enjoy music and rhythm by creating an environment that allows children to explore, to express, and to create. Music, singing, and fingerplays signal transitions and help children to settle-down and to relax. Musical and rhythmic experiences established to meet developmental needs help children enjoy musical and rhythmic experiences throughout the day (Figure 7–18). Playing soothing music when welcoming parents and children at their early morning arrival helps to begin the day with a relaxing climate. Display photographs of pianos when piano recordings play and pictures of mariachi bands when playing Latin ballads.

Children naturally express rhythmic sounds and patterns, especially when the staff secures an environment that welcomes and encourages music. Music and rhythmic activities accommodate curricular planning approaches. Teachers who plan programs with activities within curriculum areas will discover that numerous resources provide songs that develop children's music awareness and appreciation related to specific curriculum areas. For example, an Art activity set up for children to paint a mural together while listening to the music of the *Grand Canyon Suite* (Groff) favors creative expression. Children who participate in a fingerplay, Five Little Apples, experience mathematical skills in counting and sequencing. A story with actions, Going on a Picnic, engages children's listening and rhyming interests within the

FIGURE 7–18   Music and Rhythm Experiences Meet Developmental Needs and Goals

Developmental Focus	Goals
Affective and Aesthetic	To experience dancing near a partner
	To participate in a group activity
	To express feelings through body movements
Cognitive and Language	To have an opportunity to change sounds into action
	To experience new movements
Physical	To become aware of control of body
	To appreciate feeling of body in space

curriculum area of Communication and Literacy. Invite children to add movements to the songs and fingerplays (Figure 7–19a and Figure 7–19b).

Music and Rhythm: Possible Outcomes

The benefits of music and rhythm contribute to a recognized tradition in early care and learning programs. "Music not only provides pleasure and comfort; it also helps improve a child's ability to concentrate and discriminate" (Croft, 1990, p. 68).

FIGURE 7–19a   Going On a Picnic

Tune: *She'll Be Comin' Round the Mountain*

We'll be going on a picnic, that's today, yeah, yeah.

We'll be going on a picnic, that's today, yeah, yeah.

We'll be going on a picnic, we'll be going on a picnic, we'll be going on a picnic, that's today.

We'll be taking six big lunches when we go, yum, yum.

We'll be taking six big lunches when we go, yum, yum.

We'll be taking six big lunches, we'll be taking six big lunches, we'll be taking six big lunches when we go.

We'll be eating all our lunches way out there, chomp, chomp.

We'll be eating all our lunches way out there, chomp, chomp.

We'll be eating all our lunches, we'll be eating all our lunches, we'll be eating all our lunches way out there.

Teachers listen and watch children to assess their reactions and needs. Some children need time to observe the activities before joining the group. Activities can contribute to the development of skills such as concentrating, discriminating, exploring, and listening (Figure 7–20). Appropriate teacher guidance respects the observers and welcomes them when they are ready. Younger preschoolers will move their hands and fingers while quietly watching the teacher and listening to the words of songs. Days and weeks may pass before children coordinate hand movements. Teachers extend participation of all the children by providing appropriate props to the music and rhythm experiences. Teachers create a welcome atmosphere by projecting positive attitudes toward singing and creative movement. Teachers model, suggest, and describe movements that respond to the

FIGURE 7–19b   Four Juicy Apples

Tune: *Five Little Speckled Frogs*

Four juicy apples hanging on a tree
Four juicy apples smiling at me
I shook that tree as hard as I could
Down came one apple. Mum, was it good.

Three juicy apples hanging on a tree.
Three juicy apples smiling at me.
I shook that tree as hard as I could,
Down came one apple. Mum, was it good.

Two juicy apples hanging on a tree.
Two juicy apples smiling at me.
I shook that tree as hard as I could,
Down came one apple. Mum, was it good.

One juicy apple hanging on a tree.
One juicy apple smiling at me.
I shook that tree as hard as I could,
Down came no apples just for me.

FIGURE 7–20   Possible Outcomes: Music and Rhythm Skills

Concentrating	on number of drum beats the words of the song
Creating	a new fingerplay to a familiar chant words to a familiar tune
Discriminating	sounds from tambourine and cymbals high-pitched tones and low-pitched tones
Exploring	fast and slow movements musical instruments
Expressing	feelings in rhythmic movements mood changes
Listening	words and timing in a responsive song to pitch and tone of songs
Relaxing	to flute music to tunes and melodies sung in different languages
Respecting	songs and dances from many cultures creative musical expression
Rhyming	stories and fingerplays with action

children's developmental levels. Describing and suggesting a movement (hop like a popping corn kernel or jump quickly) are more successful strategies for encouraging children's participation than modeling alone (Andress, 1991). An activity such as Dancing with Scarves supports children's creative expressive as well (Curriculum Activity Guides 40 and 41 [CAG]).

Interest in movement will also be supported with the arrangement of an Interest Center giving children changes to develop their movement skills (Interest Center Guide 1).

Music and Rhythm Topics and Activities for Young Children

Music and rhythm activities provide chances for children to appreciate the music that families enjoy. As young learners enjoy children's songs and rhythmic movements from other cultures, they acquire knowledge about the world outside their immediate community. The pleasurable use of basic instruments, such as drums, gives hands-on experience with music. Comments about the historical and cultural origin of drums give an added benefit to music exploration. While exploring topics related to the wider world of music, the primary focus must remain on the significance of the experiences to the participating children's interests (Figure 7–21).

Instruments add to children's knowledge. They learn that a triangle makes one sound that lasts for a long time. A tambourine makes two sounds because it is a little drum with jingles on the

FIGURE 7–21   Music and Rhythm Activity Topics

Fingerplays	Simple hand, finger, and arm movements. Gestures dramatize words to music and songs such as *Open, Shut Them.*
Instruments	Instruments such as drums, bells, rhythm sticks, cymbals, tambourines, and triangles may be purchased. Staff and volunteers can make clappers, drums, and shakers. Teachers use autoharp or guitar to accompany children's songs. Guests invited to introduce instruments such as harp, piano, guitar, flute, and saxophone.
Records, Tapes, CDs	Recorded music (record albums, tapes, and CDs) played for a specific musical experience, as a child-directed individual activity, or for background music. Selection variety should range from international folk songs to classical and instrumental.
Rhythmic Activities	Beats in patterns provide rhythmic experiences. Rhythmic patterns found throughout indoor and outdoor classrooms: rainwater dripping down pipes and bubbling aquarium. Child can clap hands and stomp feet to copy rhythmic pattern.
Songs	Simple, repetitive words using familiar words and objects. Spontaneous singing, initiated by children and teachers, of traditional and creative songs planned for Grouptime, transition, and special activities.

Interest Center Guide 1

Interest Center   *Outside Large Motor*   **Theme**   *Unselected*

Art	Cooking	Literacy	Quiet Reading	Outside Art	Outside Large Motor
Block	Computer	Manipulatives	Science	Outside Circle	Outside and/Water
Circle	Dramatic Play	Music/Rhythm	Sensorial	Outside Garden	Trike Path

Interest Center Guidelines   **Approximate Age Range**   *3–5*

To become aware of the concepts of in and out using various body movements.

Developmental Focus | Physical | **Affective**   **Cognitive**

Curriculum Area   *Movement*

Interest Center Materials

   Constant   *Obstacle course*

                                Grassy area

   Featured   *Cardboard boxes (different sizes and large enough for children to climb*
                                  in and out)
                                  Tires
                                  Tunnel
                                  Hoops

   Preparation/Set Up   *Place cardboard boxes, tires, tunnels, and hoops to grassy area. Place two*
                                  signs, "In" and "Out"

Teaching Strategies

Introduce boxes, tunnel, and hoops during Grouptime with focus on the concepts of in and out.

Teacher presence and supervision guides children's in and out movements through tunnels, boxes,

and hoops during participation in obstacle course.

Possible Outcomes for the Child or Children

   Concepts   *I can climb in and out; I can move into and out of a tunnel; I can jump*
                                  into and out of a hoop.

   Skills   *spatial awareness, large motor development, movement exploration*

   Vocabulary   *in, out, through, tunnel, inside, outside*

Child Participation   **Date**

side. Drums produce many sounds, quiet when the fingers tap and louder if hit with a stick. Instruments integrate well with creative movement activities to extend children's awareness of their body rhythms. Curriculum integration occurs as themes and curriculum areas blend with the provisions for activities that meet the developmental needs of children (Curriculum Activity Guides 42 and 43 [CAG]).

REVIEW

A variety of active experiences help children to develop physically. Large and small movement activities facilitate outcomes in skill development. Integrating activities across the curriculum areas and Developmental Focus areas further supports physical development. Teachers are encouraged to promote attitudes to guide discovery and exploration and to de-emphasize competition.

Physical development is facilitated with activities in the curriculum area of Health, Safety, and Nutrition. Appropriate and meaningful experiences help the children to understand more about themselves and their relationships with others. Safety topics range from environmental to emergencies; while Nutrition includes knowledge about healthful eating and cooking experiences.

Basic movement categories include locomotor, nonlocomotor, and manipulative. Knowing the way children act and interact through the day signals additional ways to contribute movement and perceptual motor activities.

Because music is a common thread that links different languages, cultures, and ages, it is suitable for young children. Music and rhythm help children to relax, express themselves, and feel pleasure. Fingerplays, instruments, records, tapes, rhythmic activities, and songs contribute to the list of appropriate activities for physical development.

KEY TERMS

Cooking
Health
integrating activities
large movement
locomotor
manipulative
movement and
   perceptual motor
   development

movement skills
music and rhythm
   skills
Nutrition
Safety
small movement

RESPOND

1. Consider suitable activities for children, ages three to five, specially designed to support their physical development. Prepare a list to include three activity topics for small movement and three for large movement.
2. Make three copies of the Curriculum Activity Guide (page 237). Complete the forms with the theme of Fitness as a guide. One form is for a Health activity, the second for a Nutrition activity, and the last for a Safety activity.
3. Review Figure 7–17 "Discovering Spatial Awareness with Movement." Prepare an activity, completing a Curriculum Activity Guide, using an activity idea from the list.
4. Call up one of the following Web sites on the Internet. Describe in a paragraph the available resources to enhance a curriculum facilitating physical development and the related curriculum areas:

Center for Disease Control and Prevention
http://www.cdc.gov/

KidsHealth. Org
http://www.kidshealth.org/

PE Central
http://pe.central.vt.edu/

PE Central is designed for elementary school–age children. Survey the ideas provided and modify three of the activity ideas to suit preschool–age children. Modify one of the selected activities to accommodate children with limited visual ability.

REFERENCES

Andress, B. (1991). From research to practice: Preschool children and their movement responses to music. *Young Children, 47*(1), 22–27.

Bredekamp, S., & Copple, C. (Eds.). (1997). *Developmentally appropriate practice in early childhood programs* (Rev. ed.). Washington, DC: National Association for the Education of Young Children.

Cherry, C. (1971). *Creative movement for the developing child: A nursery school handbook for non-musicians* (Rev. ed.). Belmont, CA: Fearon.

Cook, R. E., Tessier, A., & Klein, M. D. (1996). *Adapting early childhood curricula for children in inclusive settings* (4th ed.). Englewood Cliffs, NJ: Merrill.

Croft, D. J. (1990). *An activities handbook for teachers of young children* (5th ed.). Boston: Houghton Mifflin.

Flinchum, B. M. (1975). *Motor development in early childhood: A guide for movement education with ages 2 to 6.* St. Louis, MO: Mosby.

Gerhardt, L. A. (1973). *Moving and knowing: The young child orients himself in space.* Englewood Cliffs, NJ: Prentice Hall.

Pica, R. (2000). *Experiences in movement: With music, activities and theory* (2nd ed.). Albany, New York: Delmar.

Spodek, B., & Saracho, O. N. (1994). *Dealing with individual differences in the early childhood classroom.* White Plains, NY: Longman.

CHAPTER 8

Affective and Aesthetic Development: *Art, Creative Dramatics, and Social Understanding Activities*

Curriculum Profile

Julie, a second-semester student teacher, arrived at the practicum seminar without her expected bright smile. She remained quiet during the opening discussion. Hearing the predictable question, "Did you experience a situation that made you uncomfortable at the training center?" Julie shifted her position, leaned forward, and said, "Yes, now I understand that poem you read in class about the little boy."

Julie's field assignment takes her into the community twice a week. At the site this morning a craft experience was arranged by a substitute teacher. Julie related the following incident:

"The children joined in at the craft table, where they shaped and twisted crepe paper. The staff directed the children, before they left the art table, to glue the flowers on a stick and push the stick into the glob of modeling dough they placed inside a small flowerpot."

Julie sighed and continued, "It is not that the activity itself was so off . . . it is what happened at the end of the day. I was assigned to help the children retrieve their 'art' just before their parents arrived. When I handed Ryan his flowerpot he immediately shook his head saying, 'That's not mine, that's not mine.' I showed him that his name was written on the bottom of the pot. Ryan stood very still, shaking his head, and repeating, 'That's not the one I did.' His eyes watered when he saw his dad walk through the door. Not knowing what to do, I handed the pot to Ryan's father. Ryan walked away, ignoring the flowerpot. When I went to the workroom, I realized why Ryan was so upset. The substitute teacher was there continuing to reshape and to rearrange the children's paper flower creations. So, the flowerpot I tried to hand to Ryan was not his . . . it was an adult's finished product. Ryan didn't recognize the flowerpot because it was different from the one that he created."

Chapter Outline

Study Guide

As you study the sections in this chapter, you should be able to:

- Examine the definition of affective and aesthetic development.
- Analyze the possible outcomes for emotional and social growth.
- Understand the skills children develop while enjoying art activities.
- Review Creative Dramatics to understand the benefits of dramatic play, guided drama, puppetry, and sociodramatics.
- Recognize Social Understanding as a valuable curriculum area in Early Childhood.

AFFECTIVE AND AESTHETIC DEVELOPMENT

In the Curriculum Profile, Ryan rejected the flowerpot because it was not the one that he created. The influences affecting his behavior started early as he interacted with his family. He started preschool with abilities that allowed him to adjust to new people and to express his feelings. Ryan's affective development is healthy for a four-year-old preschooler. Early Childhood teachers respond to the changing emotional, social, and aesthetic needs of children by planning appropriate experiences that encourage their development.

Most activities planned in the curriculum areas have potential for promoting emotional and social development. The affective and aesthetic focus in this chapter is on three relevant subjects, the curricular areas that particularly encourage the development of children affectively and aesthetically: **Art, Creative Dramatics,** and **Social Understanding.**

Centering on affective and aesthetic development calls for you to look at the changes in children's psychological, social, emotional, and creative behaviors. The intended outcomes of sensitively planned experiences contribute to the ability of the children to achieve healthy personalities, positive relationships, and creative outlooks.

Play and creative expression offer the best ways to encourage children's achievement of affective and aesthetic goals. During play episodes, children learn about the opinions and feelings of others. Interaction allows children to express their own feelings. Materials that call on the senses offer chances for the overwhelmed behaviors of children to relax. Children need abundant support and understanding to ensure that their unique identities emerge.

Emotional Development: Possible Outcomes and Activities

Some children run into the center with excitement. Other children cry when their parents depart. Children let family members and teachers know how they feel when they cry, suck their thumb, smile, frown, and laugh. Children react to anger, fear, surprise, and pleasure, to name just a few emotions. Adults gain insight into children's emotions as the children respond to people, events, and the environment. Emotionally healthy children will learn early to express themselves with the guidance of adults, who model acceptable ways. As a result, comments such as, "I am sad that I can't take the fish home" and "I want to use the hammer and I don't want to wait" can be heard throughout the day.

The foundation for healthy emotional behavior and personality begins in infancy with the development of a sense of trust. The stages of **social development** and **emotional development** delineate tasks and achievements specific to each stage of development (Erickson, 1996, p. 6). Parents hold dreams that their children will experience life's positives, such as inner confidence, sense of purpose and involvement, meaningful, constructive relationships with others, successful school and work experiences, and "most of all—happiness." Evidence is available to validate a formula for happiness that is more likely for children who have high self-esteem. (Briggs, 1970, p. 2). Self-esteem is an attitude that equates to a sense of self-respect and a feeling of self-worth. Children's judgment of themselves, how they feel, and their emotional reactions and expressions influence the kinds of friends they will choose and how they get along with others and direct the productivity of their lives. Children's feelings of self-worth form the core of their personalities and determine what they make of their aptitudes and abilities (Briggs, 1970, p. 3). They have a growing need for independence that is moderated by the adults in their environment and their own temperament. During the early childhood years, children learn to handle a broad range of feelings, including happiness, sadness, anger, distress, and joy, within the cultural context of their family and community. Children learn to express their feelings with distinct differences about likes and dislikes, again influenced by the culture, the region, and the era. In today's society children express fear about abduction or killer robots (Craig, 1996, p. 299).

Skills: Possible Outcomes

Early childhood is a critical time for children to achieve a growing sense of self and an appreciation for others in their surroundings. Affective and aesthetic experiences help children to adjust to separation from home, gain self-confidence, and achieve competence. Teachers respect and value children; in turn they feel proud of themselves: "Ron, thanks for scrubbing the snack table, it looks really great, doesn't it." Children begin to appreciate different religions and cultures: "Jana, we are so glad you brought your grandfather's hat from Bolivia." Staff support opportunities for children to make choices and to resolve conflicts by setting limits and accepting feelings: "I can see, Beverly, that it makes you unhappy to have to wait. But, there is only room for four friends in this block area."

Teachers encourage emotional development with nurturing and sensitive behaviors and experiences. When you respond to the children as individuals, as members of families, and as a group interacting within your Early Childhood setting, the **possible outcomes** will lead to children acquiring emotional development **skills** (Figure 8–1).

Emotional Development Activities

Children who feel valued and capable begin to develop significant concepts of themselves. Opportunities in school settings further enhance positive self-concepts within the environments that encourage children to explore and communicate. When children know what to expect they respond more effectively both to routine and to changes. Specific activities, such as water play and fingerpainting, tend to relieve tension and build skills that help children to handle new situations.

A variety of activities allow children to select experiences when they are ready. For example, stretching exercises not only contribute to the development of self-esteem but also offer an alternative for children who feel anxious about "messy activities." You will enhance children's self-esteem by modeling behaviors to encourage empathy and problem-solving skills. Experiences that emerge from the children's interests and needs integrate learning (Curriculum Activity Guides 44 and 45 [CAG]).

FIGURE 8–1 Possible Outcomes: Emotional Development Skills

> Accepting limits
> Appreciating pleasurable experiences
> Establishing self-regulating behaviors
> Expanding or achieving a sense of trust
> Expressing and clarifying feelings positively
> Recognizing personal abilities

Social Development: Possible Outcomes and Activities

Early care and education programs traditionally initiate children's first group situation with individuals outside the family and home. These provide daily opportunities for children to learn to cooperate and to function as members of the group. They become aware of one another's thinking and different perspectives about the same topic and share their own thinking with the adults and other children in small group. The size of a small group varies, depending on the age of the children and the type of activity. Smaller groups of one to four for three-year-olds and five to eight children for four-year-olds will allow children to have a greater opportunity to interact with each other in a positive social gathering. Early Childhood settings provide smaller versions of society, which allows children to gain social competence among their peers.

Experiences planned for social development enable children to react and interact in social situations. They need to listen, consider, and make decisions. Developing a sense of community, particularly a positive community, may help shield children from the societal changes that are negatively affecting the social health of children and families. Children need adult supervision and cooperative activities (Garbarino, 1998, p. 9). Teachers will help reduce the vulnerability to the negatives in the social environment with school settings that support interaction and recognition of the children's caring behaviors. For example, Tre directs Tasha to take one of his biscuits from the basket he is holding. Later in the morning, Tasha runs over to help Tre when he falls off a tricycle. The teacher's approving smile and availability encourages Tasha and Tre to continue their nurturing gestures toward each other.

Skills: Possible Outcomes

Children acquire social skills as they mature and become less centered on their own needs and thoughts. Growth contributes to their developing capabilities to understand the point of view of others. Interaction with other children, in an environment that is suitably organized and supervised, further motivates them to cooperate and communicate using acceptable behaviors. Prosocial skills equip children with behaviors needed for responsible group participation while they are in school and throughout their lives.

Teachers who reinforce desirable behaviors find that young children capably demonstrate em-

pathy, sensitivity, and negotiating skills. For example, Enry handed Pat her large house-painting brush when his brush fell on the ground. She commented, "You can use mine and I'll get another from Teacher Jane." Enry showed concern and empathy for Pat's needs. Watching cooperating behaviors, participating in family-style meals, and receiving guidance to control natural impulses lead to the acquisition of desirable social skills (Figure 8–2).

Social Development Activities

Benjamin, Christian, and John rapidly move large flannel shapes of furniture on a chart of a house that is secured to the outside of the wheel-toy shed. The boys laugh, talk, and cooperate as they fill the delineated spaces with the flannel furniture. This activity meets several social development goals. The boys acquire decision-making skills as they determine who selects and who places the furniture shapes on the chart. The experience allows them to cooperate and communicate because there is ample space for them to move freely without bumping into each other. This activity provides appropriate supervision from adults who are supporting the small group interaction. Another experience, When I Was a Baby, increases children's awareness of themselves and their own growth, which contributes to the children's self-concept (Curriculum Activity Guide 46 [CAG]). This experience, like any of the other teacher-guided experiences, may be converted to a child-initiated experience and placed in an Interest Center. An expansion on When I Was a Baby can initiate a project in the Dramatic Play area with special baby props and mini-albums of the children when they were babies (Interest Center Guide 2). The activity Litter Patrol creates an opportunity for children to interact in a group while developing a sense of pride and responsibility for their community (Curriculum Activity Guide 47 [CAG]).

FIGURE 8–2 Possible Outcomes: Social Development Skills

Using empathetic words and gestures
Cooperating
Learning about their community
Making appropriate choices
Participating with others and in a small group
Respecting differences

Interest Center Guide 2

Interest Center   *Domestic Scene - Baby Nurturing*   **Theme**   *I'm Me, Special*

Art	Cooking	Literacy	Quiet Reading	Outside Art	Outside Large Motor
Block	Computer	Manipulatives	Science	Outside Circle	Outside and/Water
Circle	Dramatic Play	Music/Rhythm	Sensorial	Outside Garden	Trike Path

Interest Center Guidelines   **Approximate Age Range**   *3–5*

Baby props to be introduced at Grouptime, then added to Dramatic Play Interest Center area.

Developmental Focus   **Physical**   Affective and Aesthetic   **Cognitive and Language**

Curriculum Area   *Social Understanding*

Interest Center Materials

   Constant   *Play food and dishes*
              Adult dress-up clothing

   Featured   *Baby props, dolls*
              Nonbias photos of families nurturing babies
              Baby bed, rocker, books

Preparation/Set Up

1. *Locate and laminate pictures/photos*
2. *Locate baby props; prepare labels for shelves*
3. *Add baby props to Dramatic Play Interest Center*

Teaching Strategies

1. *Introduce baby props during grouptime.*
2. *Teacher helps children set up props in area.*
3. *Teacher facilitates children's understanding of baby nurturing with appreciation of diverse ways to hold and carry babies.*

Possible Outcomes for the Child or Children

   Concepts   *All babies need special care.*
              Mothers, fathers, and relatives care for babies.

   Skills   *Social understanding and caring*
              Social interaction

   Vocabulary *mother, father, baby, care, relatives, hold, soothe*

Child Participation   **Date**

Aesthetic Development: Possible Outcomes and Activities

Aesthetic expression is natural and spontaneous for some children. Children can create sounds, move their fingers through the sand, and draw on frosty windows. A setting needs to nurture children's natural drive to imagine, create, and express. Teachers who enrich the environment give children choices of materials that are pleasing to all the senses. There will be a positive impact on the development of the creative processes of children when they use materials, interact with people, and react to events (Rogers, 1961, p. 350).

Aesthetics is an essential part of the curriculum. An Early Childhood program caters to aesthetics with consideration for the ways that children experience the world with their senses. Surround children with many opportunities to appreciate and to explore the favorable aspects of their world: the sights and sounds with physical contact. Enjoy, with the children, a spider web, the design of a poster, a cloud formation, the feel of a seashell, and the sounds of a violin.

Skills: Possible Outcomes

Appreciation of nature and beauty is one of the beneficial outcomes of experiences designed to invite the participation of children. Additional values and possible outcomes include the enhancement of favorable emotional behaviors, enjoyment, observational skills, and originality (Figure 8–3).

Aesthetic Development Activities

The potential for children to develop aesthetic awareness increases when teachers help children explore and respond to the beauty in nature and art. Child-initiated and teacher-guided types of activities foster a sense of both wonder and enjoyment (Curriculum Activity Guides 48 and 49 ⌨).

FIGURE 8–3   Possible Outcomes: Aesthetic Development Skills

Appreciating nature and beauty
Enjoying sounds, music, and rhythm
Expressing originality
Observing color, shape, and form
Releasing and expressing feelings
Recognizing musical variations
Responding to other's feelings and behaviors

CONNECTING CURRICULUM FOR AFFECTIVE AND AESTHETIC DEVELOPMENT

The goals for affective and aesthetic development require staff members to concentrate on the process of activities rather than on the product. Benjamin, Christian, and John enjoyed placing the flannel figures on the chart. In doing so, they gained skills in cooperation. The experience also contributes to their acquisition of prosocial skills. Experiences that remain open-ended allow children to enjoy opportunities to make choices. Teachers who demonstrate supportive behaviors toward affective and aesthetic development redirect behavior, provide props and equipment to enhance play opportunities, and model language and communication. Preschoolers gain prosocial behaviors in settings where adults offer explanation and reason. Children will begin to establish a sense of wonder about nature and beauty within a nurturing and sensitive environment.

Integrating Activities

Observations of the children will indicate the direction of the activities for affective and aesthetic development. Comprehensive curriculum planning suggests that you balance among the curriculum areas as you meet the developmental needs. The integration of relevant experiences pattern the goals of the program and observed behaviors. For example, a teacher observation of Lew revealed that he returned to the flannel furniture activity three times to watch Benjamin, Christian, and John. Lew remained on the tricycle, paused on the trike path to watch the boys. An additional activity might emerge from the observation of Lew and still integrate with the theme, curriculum areas, and Developmental Focus areas that you have scheduled to guide the curriculum plan. An activity such as Designing a Trike Path Detour invites the participation of Lew, who is on a trike, and welcomes the trio leaving the flannel furniture activity. This activity could be one of many identified with a Developmental Focus area, work well with activities in other curriculum areas, and tie in with a theme like Transportation (Figure 8–4). Lew's participation may remain minimal, but this activity allows him to directly experience group interaction. The other three boys model social skills such as problem solving, negotiating, and cooperation.

FIGURE 8–4   Activities Integrate Developmental Focus Area, Curriculum Areas, and Theme

Developmental Focus Area	Affective and Aesthetic
Curriculum Areas	*Health, Safety, and Nutrition* Activity: Safety on the path *Social Understanding* Activity: Sharing rides with friends *Mathematics* Activity: Counting passengers in vehicles
Theme	Transportation

Themes relating to children's emotional needs, such as Rain, Wind, and Thunder, create opportunities for you to support affective and aesthetic development with subjects such as family, celebrations, emotions, and character-building (Figure 8–5).

Teaching Strategies

Teachers and care providers are second only to parents and other primary caregivers in the amount of direct influence they have on the children's identity and the development of their social behaviors. The attitudes and values of the staff affect the tone and rhythm of a center. Teachers who enjoy and understand the curiosity and activity level of children respond by creating supportive, safe environments that encourage exploration. When children feel secure, they gain the confidence to explore. Teachers who address the goals of affective and aesthetic development will anticipate the needs of children and then respond with relevant experiences. Children who know what to expect adjust more readily to the rules needed for participation and interaction in a group setting. Flexible teachers respond to the changing needs of children and the program by maintaining a consistent yet relaxed atmosphere.

AFFECTIVE AND AESTHETIC DEVELOPMENT WITH ART

Art for Young Children

Appropriate Art activities encourage relaxation, exploration, and pleasure. Children benefit from Art experiences when activities are soothing and developmentally focused. Children who engage in Art experiences develop concepts in other curriculum areas. Mural painting involves measurement tasks, such as securing a long piece of butcher paper to fit across a fence, that give children exposure to beginning mathematical concepts. Children who paint murals become aware of Science-related ideas as they observe the changes in colors as they mix tempera paint into the paint extender. Children who are allowed to be expressive through Art are more likely to attain positive feelings about themselves and others as they together brush paint on the same stretch of paper.

Bulletin boards and home refrigerators are testament to the priority that parents give to art work. Teachers for young children favoring best practices encourage appreciation for the process rather than the end product of the artwork. The process embraces the way that children express themselves, explore the paste, and move the paintbrush across the mural paper. Squeezing, pulling, patting,

FIGURE 8–5   Themes Encouraging Affective and Aesthetic Development

Social	Emotional	Aesthetic
Helping My Community	Rain, Wind, Thunder	Colors Everywhere
Friends	Family Traditions	Art in Our Museum
Celebrations	Feelings	Music We Like
We Are Alike and Different	Family Members	Sculptures in Our Park

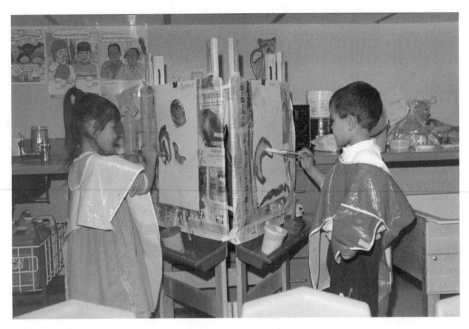

Art activities encourage relaxation, exploration, and pleasure.

pounding, and rolling clay or hanging, collecting, and painting are more important to the children's development than the final product. Programs that value the artistic processes limit materials that require children to copy adult models. As a teacher of young children, you need to place emphasis on manipulation, exploration, and expression.

Art: Possible Outcomes

Physically, Art promotes fine-motor coordination and sensorial discovery. The cold earth clay smells different and feels good to children who squeeze, pinch, and pull the damp ball of clay. Art activities encourage the development of affective and aesthetic skills (Figure 8–6).

FIGURE 8–6   Possible Outcomes: Skills Related to Art

Activity Title	Skills
Taking Photographs of Flowers	Appreciating nature
Mixing Modeling Dough	Coordinating small movements
Painting with Foaming Soap	Expressing feelings
Seashell Collage	Making choices

Younger preschoolers approach new activities tentatively, at first experimenting by touching, dipping, and spreading the paste. Skills continue to develop when children experience the same materials repeatedly, preferably with creative variations. Painting a mural encourages group interaction with two or more children involved in a large area for drawing, painting, and collaging. You need to vary painting activities by providing different surfaces for the paint, chalk, and felt-tip pens. When burlap is substituted for paper, children enjoy watching the paint absorb and adhere differently to the burlap than it does to paper.

The strength of your indoor and outdoor environments will influence how smoothly the Art activities unfold. The Art Interest Center should have low tables, easels, sinks with running water, and open-organized shelves that are stocked with basic art materials. The open shelves allow children to select and use the materials during time planned for activity centers. Smocks and aprons protect children as they enjoy Art activities that tend to be messy. Water buckets and sponges, placed near the Art activities, encourage independence and responsibility. Paintbrushes with shorter handles reduce spills and facilitate small movement coordination. Your preparation needs to include activity plans that list materials and procedures needed for each activity.

Children's reactions to Art materials depend on their previous experiences with paper, pencils, glue, and paint. In a suitably arranged and supervised setting, children discover many ways to use the materials. Creating collages with paste is different than creating with glue. When your attitude allows space and time to explore, children begin to master Art materials (Figure 8–7).

Art Topics and Activities for Young Children

Your selection of activities that allow children to make choices contributes to their sense of responsibility, confidence, and creativity. Proud feelings show when Damian glues the plastic shapes. Teachers encourage children so that they find their own creative inner self. Children feel encouraged to explore when adults supportively guide the children who ask for help with suggestions such as, "What do you think will happen when you try that," or "Try wiping the brush on the side of the container if you want less paint." Remain sensitive also to the cultural needs of the children and families by cautious consideration when using food material for Art activities. The culture, traditions, and religions of many families could prompt them to find this wasteful and contrary to their respect for food.

Art, as a curriculum area, should not be limited to the use of Art materials. Children will

FIGURE 8–7 Basic Art Materials

Material	Activity Use
Clay	Manipulating and molding
Collage	Miscellaneous items such as buttons, golf tees, magazine pictures
Crayons	Drawing and rubbing
Chalk	Drawing Dip in starch and draw
Pencils/Markers	Drawing Tracing Writing
Glue	Constructing
Paint	Fingerpainting Roller painting Sponge painting String painting Cotton swab painting
Paper	Collage Cut Paste Paint
Prints	Shaped sponges Wood blocks Rubber stamps Objects
Modeling Dough	Mold prepared modeling dough Make modeling dough
Scissors	Cutting

Children benefit from working with all types of Art materials.

benefit from exposure to various art forms. An early introduction establishes a good foundation for an appreciation of art. Appreciation of art helps children to use their senses by reacting to what they see, hear, and feel in their surroundings. Aesthetic awareness becomes a critical component of art appreciation. You can contribute to the children's abilities to see beauty in nature, in their communities, and within their cultures. You can find art in the design of buildings, automobiles, and clothing. Children also learn to appreciate each other's artwork. Display the work of noted artists and designers famous for different forms of creativity as well as the work of children.

Art defines cultures and lifestyles and has a place in the curriculum that seeks to meet the needs of all children. Drawings of animals and children found on ancient pottery offer interesting visual experiences for young children, even though the time concept is beyond their perceptions. Remember to list and watch for hints from the children. This will continue to give you direction as your curriculum plan unfolds with a balance of stimulating and suitable Art activity topics (Figure 8–8).

In settings where staff members respect the children's work and their reactions to the art that surrounds them, enthusiasm to explore continues. The experiences may relate to a theme gen-

FIGURE 8–8 Art Experiences for Young Children

Big picture reproductions of noted artists
Children's art display
Collage
Cutting and tearing
Drawing—chalk, crayons, felt pens, pencils
Gluing and pasting
Mobiles—chain, nature
Molding—clay, modeling dough
Painting—fingerpainting, object, roller, sand, soap, tempera
Printmaking—stamps, rollers, objects
Sculptures—object, clay, modeling dough, paper, Styrofoam, wood
Taking photographs—instant or disposable cameras

erated from direct observation of the enrolled children or offered within an established interest center. The Art Interest Center would accommodate the activities Tissue Paper and Starch Art, Tire Track Art, and Nature Collage (Curriculum Activity Guides 50, 51, and 52). You will encourage art expression when you are familiar with the children and plan meaningful activities to integrate the curriculum. The Nature Collage is one example of integrating the curriculum because materials are offered that will give children the opportunity to creativity express themselves while exploring items from nature.

AFFECTIVE AND AESTHETIC DEVELOPMENT WITH CREATIVE DRAMATICS

Creative Dramatics for Young Children

The term Creative Dramatics has different meanings to programs and schools. The definitions and guidelines are determined by program expectations and the age of the children. However, you will find that the words *pretend, imagine,* and *play* appear frequently in the description of Creative Dramatics. Creative Dramatics is adapted in this textbook as a general term to organize four categorizes of activities that significantly contribute to affective and aesthetic development of young children. The four organizing categorizes within Creative Dramatics are Dramatic Play, Guided Drama, Puppetry, and Sociodramatics.

The terminology, as with so many other Early Childhood program descriptions, varies from one professional to another and from one program to another. The content of the four Creative Dramatics categories remains essentially stable with the focus on pretending, playing, creating, and imagining. This is especially true when the expectations for developmentally appropriate curriculum construct the foundation for experiences related to Creative Dramatics. You will find that the categories overlap in content and purpose; therefore you can locate ideas for Creative Dramatics activities indexed under the subjects of movement, literature, social studies, and play.

Creative Dramatics: Possible Outcomes

Creative Dramatics allows a child to playfully pretend to be someone or something else. Children are able to act out and pretend to be like people they know or have encountered. Children also can imagine being an animal or an object while gaining valuable skills, and in this way, Creative Dramatics is a "powerful learning tool" (Johnson, 1998, p. 2; Smilansky, 1968, p. 14). (Figure 8–9).

FIGURE 8–9   Possible Outcomes: Skills Related to Creative Dramatics

Collaboration
Cooperation
Combine ideas
Concentration
Creativity
Flexibility
Imagination
Interpersonal relations
Language and vocabulary
Pretending
Problem solving
Satisfaction

Creative Dramatics Topics and Activities for Young Children

Dramatic Play, Guided Drama, Puppetry, and Sociodramatics are organized activities that prepare children for the challenges of real life. The experiences contribute to their development with opportunities to develop skills in collaborating and cooperating with other children. Dramatic Play, Guided Drama, Puppetry, and Sociodramatics activities can be flexible, stimulating the imagination while encouraging language and vocabulary skills. The children can practice problem solving, especially when they engage in Guided Drama and Sociodramatics while gaining satisfaction from group interaction.

Dramatic Play

Children can find satisfaction through **Dramatic Play** as they demonstrate their creativity and sociability. Children imagine as they replicate roles of their parents and teachers and friends. They satisfy their own wishes as they pretend, allowing them to participate, observe, and perform (Smilansky, 1968, p. 6). Children learn about concepts, discover how objects function, and model and practice roles. You will find children pretending and imagining primarily in the Interest Center delegated for Dramatic Play. Children will imitate voices and gestures and dress up in the clothing and use the props that you provide. However, we are cautioned to avoid overwhelming children with too many props that might distract and confuse them (Croft, 1990, p. 110). Instead, it is recommended that staff introduce the simple props first, then add new props to keep the play interesting (Schickedanz, 1999, p. 4) or reflect a current theme.

During Dramatic Play, children replicate roles of their parents, teachers, and friends.

Guided Drama

Guided Drama is the pantomiming and acting out of a poem, short story, or rhyme. This active experience encourages children to dramatically and creatively act with guidance from the teacher or another adult. The children's ages clearly determine the guiding procedures. You might begin with the younger preschoolers by suggesting that they show you "How does a worm wiggle?" As children become more comfortable, you might ask the group to act out a few pages of a favorite story.

For older preschoolers and school-age children a set of guiding components are recommended for implementing Creative Dramatics. These include providing a degree of structure to guide the children. This may include modeling or demonstrating actions and sounds. Second, the curriculum should remain open-ended to encourage exploration and alternative variations. A safe environment is suggested and with time set aside for feedback from the children (Johnson, 1998, p. 4).

Linda Carol Edward's description of guided fantasies indicates that the creative dramatic experience is planned and usually centered on one idea or topic. The experience gives the children chances to experiment and originate images by pretending. Experiences for younger children need to be simple and familiar. Walks, trips, and visitors stimulate guided fantasy activities. Staff should maintain open participation so that no child is mandated to participate and allow a reflection time to bring children back to the "here and now" (Edwards, 1990, p. 15). A trip to the local bakery might stimulate a guided fantasy experience, for example, "pretend you are a muffin in the oven and you are baking." "Pretend you are the cats in the story, show me how they curled up to sleep after enjoying their milk."

Puppetry

Puppetry, which has a long history as a method of entertainment for adults in many cultures, continues to excite children's imagination and creativity. There are many types of puppets, some you will purchase, many you will design, and some you will spontaneously create to expand an idea. Introducing puppets in three stages is suggested: model use of puppets, create and use puppets together; and allow children to make and interact with puppets (Jackman, 1997, p. 110).

Puppets can help children develop skills in the Developmental Focus areas (Figure 8–10).

Sociodramatics

Children pretend to be moms, dads, sisters, bakers, teachers, and cats during **Sociodramatics.** They participate voluntarily in a social play activity by taking on a role and by pretending with the props and imaginary objects (Smilansky, 1968, p. 7). Social play related to specific roles is also influenced by the community and regional locations. Playing forest ranger is relevant to some children, while becoming a beach lifeguard is more specific to others and weather reporter may be more meaningful yet. Sociodramatics (Figure 8–11) helps to clarify concepts and contributes to the children's understanding of their community: Where does Bobby's mother work? Elaine's father takes a bus to work to manufacture jackets. The newspaper editor came to school to take our pictures. Teachers could invite the lead firefighter, whose name is Sharon. Curriculum plans should indicate how to highlight the work of the new family, who moves as the agricultural picking seasons dictate. Children will learn that work and jobs require specific training, not specific genders. In Sociodramatics children acquire negotiating skills when they interact. The children's play during Sociodramatics helps them to acquire concepts about the many roles and occupations available to them in their communities and outside their immediate area.

FIGURE 8–10   Puppets: Enhancing All Developmental Focus Areas

Puppets hold a unique fascination for young children, a fact that insightful teachers will use to good advantage. Puppets provide a nonthreatening avenue for children to consider ideas, express creativity, explore emotions, and participate in problem solving.

Teachers routinely use puppets to focus Grouptimes, introduce concepts, and facilitate transitions, and may have specific puppets designated for these purposes. Initially, it is helpful to identify a Grouptime puppet, complete with a name and personality (don't forget it, as the children won't!). Examples of how a Grouptime puppet can facilitate and enhance Developmental Focus areas are:

Affective:	A "shy" puppet learns the names of all the children and leads a name song.
Cognitive:	A puppet encourages communication and enhances language acquisition by engaging children in conversation.
Physical:	A puppet can be used to lead children in large motor exercises. In addition, fine motor development is increased by the child's own manipulation of a hand or finger puppet.

Teachers are sometimes self-conscious about using puppets and altering their voices. Remember that young children provide a very forgiving audience. For those who remain apprehensive, try a "shy" puppet who only whispers in the teacher's ear. You'll gain the children's rapt attention as you build your own confidence.

Kathy Barry, MA—Shasta College

FIGURE 8–11   Sociodramatic Role-Play Prop Boxes

Social Roles	Role-Play Props
Auto service/mechanic	Tools, mechanic skate, credit cards, hoses, pumps, tires, patches, empty oil cans, work clothes, rags, window cleaner, buckets, signs, hats, money, cash registers, charge cards.
Baker	Toastmaster (without electrical cords), baking pans, utensils, muffin tins, cash register, bags, display case, aprons, signs.
Forest ranger	Shovels, flashlights, hats, maps, badges, boots, tents, signs, jacket, brochures, photographs.
Gardener	Wheelbarrow, buckets, gloves, blunt clippers, branches, flowers, potting soil, rake, hoe, watering cans, seed packets, hoses, hats, tools, nozzles, sunscreen, planters.
Grocer	Signs, folding shelves, empty food and can samples, bags, cash registers, grocery cart, play money, markers, signs, stickers for pricing, plastic produce and food.
Librarian	Books, shelves, tables, rug, counter, posters, stamps, paper, library cards, rolling cart.
Veterinarian	Stuffed toy animals, linen, bandages, pet food samples, posters, cages, flashlights, medical jacket, collars, leash, appointment book, telephone, index cards for records.

AFFECTIVE AND AESTHETIC DEVELOPMENT WITH SOCIAL UNDERSTANDING

Social Understanding for Young Children

The curriculum area of Social Understanding ideally supports affective and aesthetic development. Social Understanding helps the children understand themselves, their families, and their community. Early childhood is the appropriate time for children to begin to acquire prosocial skills. Acquisition of prosocial skills is the link to becoming good citizens who are capable of predicting and reacting appropriately in social situations.

Families, communities, and the larger society establish social practices. Early Childhood curriculum that promotes healthy socialization features goals to recognize the importance of families, communities, and cultures. This thoughtful balance helps children achieve patterns of behaviors within our pluralistic society. Because children's primary experiences are in their homes, they bring the perspectives of their families to the preschool and child care centers. The children must adjust to new people, routines, and food. We can facilitate the transition by bringing more of the children's home values and practices into the school setting. The Montessori Method arranges practical life exercises for children. These tasks help teach the children about themselves, grooming, dressing, shining shoes, and care of their indoor and outdoor environments. This is accomplished by fostering an environment in which children can practice washing, sweeping, table setting, and weeding and raking (Orem, 1974, p. 68).

The conventional reference to this curriculum area, Social Understanding, is Social Studies. Lessons about people in society can be arranged into subcategories such as society and communities, geography, history, political science, economy, and languages. Preschool children have limited comprehension of historical events and distant places, but helping them put the initial building blocks in place through activities to help them understand themselves, their families, and the people in close community proximity will be the foundation for future learning. Helping children to understand themselves and others facilitates their affective and aesthetic development. Children demonstrate emotional behaviors early, yet the part of the brain that controls emotions continues to develop during most of the adolescent period. Worthwhile experiences, planned for your group's interests, benefit the children's emerging identities. Children need frequent opportunities that stimulate emotional development because early emotional status is critical as it predicts achievement in school, work, and relationships throughout life (Pool, 1997, p. 74).

Social Understanding: Possible Outcomes

Consider the curriculum area of Social Understanding and the way it can be applied appropriately for young children. Children need to become more aware of themselves, their families, and their communities. You can facilitate this awareness by broadening the traditional social studies unit with subcategories. You can plan activities to benefit children as they learn to accept new routines (self-understanding). For example, at home Marty can sit wherever she wants. At school she will learn to accept the chair that is empty and available. Marty is the youngest child in her family. Her older siblings respond to her desires without her verbal requests. At the center, Marty needs to verbally express her wishes to inform either the teachers or other children (Social Understanding). Guidance from the teachers positively promotes Marty's personal awareness and interpersonal skills. Relevancy increases when you respond to children positively in an environment in which choices are the preference when possible. Marty chooses to sit in the group-time where a guest, a police officer, is talking about uniforms (Community Understanding). (Figure 8–12).

Communication and literacy skills will also improve as you add meaningful vocabulary to the Social Understanding–related activities (Figure 8–13).

Social Understanding Topics and Activities for Young Children

Although the study of people in society covers a broad array of topics, you will maintain an emergent curriculum by keeping focused on meaningful activities that integrate different curriculum

FIGURE 8–12   Possible Outcomes: Skills Related to Social Understanding

Self-Understanding	Social Understanding	Community Understanding
Accepting	Appreciating differences	Accepting others
Comforting	Collaborating	Cooperating in community
Expressing	Distinguishing right/wrong	Developing responsibility
Initiating	Empathizing	Expanding viewpoint
Making choices	Interacting with others	Helping
Motivating	Predicting consequences	Locating community places
Nurturing	Problem solving	Participating
Separating	Respecting differences	Visiting

FIGURE 8–13   Possible Outcomes: Vocabulary Related to a Social Understanding Activity

Activity title	When I Am Afraid	
Vocabulary	feelings	scared
	afraid	reaction
	alarmed	response
	fearful	solution
	frightened	well-being

areas yet focus on the children enrolled in your program, their families, and their communities.

Topics to enhance Social Understanding, are often sensitive issues that may require you to establish some guidelines. Pets die. Family members become ill. Children experience trauma and violence. Thoughtful consideration also must be given to developmental, cultural, and religious concerns. During early childhood, children begin to clarify gender roles as they relate to their families values and societal standards. We need to provide experiences that are nonstereotypic and bias-free. Encourage positive self-esteem while respecting the children's home practices, and encourage community awareness and responsibility (Figure 8–14).

Social Understanding topics and activities will allow collaborative efforts to grow because children will begin to respect others with your guidance. Some schools disallow war toys altogether and give children alternative adventure material. The ultimate goal is to help them develop sensitivity and empathy while learning to understand consequences (Wichert, 1989, pp. 36, 43). Ask children for their ideas to encourage a democratic vote. Bobby came up with several ideas, but agreed with Elaine's idea to move the cage under the shady tree.

Children are affected by the violence in society. The primary response of teachers must be to provide safe and secure environments in school programs. Children need emotional stability in set-tings where they are unhurried and benefit from sufficient number of staff who attend to the needs of individual children, and in long-term relationships with the staff (Jackson, 1997, p. 69). In a perfect society, we want peaceful and nurturing models for our children. We want television to be void of violence and with programming that represents all children and people with respect. While we advocate nonviolence in the lives of children, it is suggested that we promote children's "values and critical thinking by extending their interests," even if some of these interests include Power Rangers. Reinforce the children's positive comments by reflecting on their open communication; show that you are pleased that they shared their thoughts. Respond enthusiastically about any of the comments that may be nonviolent (Greenberg, 1995, p. 61). Give children substitute words for "language filled with violent allusions . . . such as 'break a leg' or 'I'm gonna knock 'em dead . . . moving [them] away from our violent idioms,'" recommends Wilma Gold, who chairs the NonViolence in the Lives of Children Project for the California Association for the Education of Young Children (1999, p. 4–5).

Continue to formulate new ways to promote cooperation. Themes, topics, and activities specifically planned will help to open children's views and expand their prosocial abilities. The theme *Learning About My Friends* introduces children to beginning concepts that identify both similarities and differences: "Once we were all babies; we have different hair; Lettie sees with glasses; Bobby has one brother like me." Some themes and topics emerge from observation of the children, while other relevant topics remain stable in programs for young children (Figure 8–15).

Activities to Strengthen Connections

Social Understanding, lastly, although not to infer that it is less important, is a sound curriculum area in which to recognize multicultural values. This

FIGURE 8–14   Activities Promote Community Responsibility Meeting Developmental Needs

Developmental Focus	Activity Title	Activity Description
Physical	Helping Families	Place collected food in bags for families after a disaster (fire, flood, twister, or earthquake).
Affective and Aesthetic	Snack with Friends	Visit senior citizens for snack time meal together.
Cognitive and Language	Helping Too!	Visit toddler area to put away sand toys and rake the sand.

FIGURE 8–15   Social Understanding Topics for Young Children

Topic	Conventional Reference
When I Was a Baby	History
Plans for Tomorrow	History
Finding Home and School	Geography
Responsible to My Community	Civics/citizenship
Friend Photo Match	Civics/citizenship
Workers at My School	Social Studies
Jobs in My Community	Social Studies
Visitors Share Their Work	Social Studies
Together We Decide	Political Science
Family Celebrations	Anthropology
Where Do Babies Sleep	Multicultural
Families Have Favorite Foods	Multicultural
Family Day Visit	Anthropology
Earning and Spending Money	Economics
We Are in the News	Journalism
Only Special TV Programs	Journalism

may be a good time for you to reread the section titled Strengthening Connections: Harmony, Equity, Respect, in Chapter 1. It is the family influences that directly influence the way that the child views the world. School is the place where you learn to appreciate the differences and similarities.

Design curriculum to respond to the great diversity of homes and communities with authentic inclusion. Authentic inclusion recognizes children and families with positive regard for identity, language, and values. Nonbiased, nonstereotyping activities will call on you to research new resources (Figure 8–16) to achieve harmony, equity and respect.

As you discover the resources, adapt the suggestions to fit your local community. While we can respect and appreciate our differences, it is also valuable for us to emphasize our similarities as humans. We are more alike than we are different. Essentially, there is great variation among people of the same racial, cultural, or ethnic group. You will benefit from learning about families, cultures, languages, and religions, but avoid holding a fixed description of any child. There are many factors that influenced who you are and with which culture you identify. These include, but are not limited to, your education and the availability of education to your parents, social economic status, regional location, and generational changes (Garcia, 1994, p. 55). Everyone has a culture with meaningful and rich customs for all to appreciate (Figure 8–17).

Nadia Saderman Hall presents creative activity ideas that will encourage recognition of simi-

FIGURE 8–16   Resources for Authentic Inclusion

Anti-Bias Curriculum: Tools for Empowering Young Children, Creative Resources for the Anti-Bias Classroom by Louise Derman-Sparks and the ABC Task Force (1989).

Looking in, Looking Out: Redefining Child Care and Early Education in a Diverse Society by Hedy Nai-Lin Chang, Amy Muckelroy, Dora Pulido-Tobiassen (1996), A California Tomorrow Publication.

Creative Resources for the Anti-Bias Classroom by Nadia Saderman Hall (1999).

Teaching and Learning in a Diverse World: Multicultural Education for Young Children by Patricia G. Ramsey (1987).

Roots & Wings: Affirming Culture in Early Childhood Programs by Stacey York (1991).

larities: matching pictures of traditional holiday dress; hair beading on wigs representing diverse backgrounds; and books in braille (Hall, 1999, pp. 120, 156, 173). Plan activities to promote community awareness and responsibility (Curriculum Activity Guide 53 CAG). Design experiences to encourage cooperative behaviors and a positive sense of self (Curriculum Activity Guide 54 CAG). Arrange opportunities for children to resolve conflict in communicative ways (Curriculum Activity Guide 55 CAG).

FIGURE 8–17   Celebrating Children and Families: Curriculum Topics to Recognize Similarities

We Are All People	What We All Need	What We All Can Do
Skin Colors	Food and Water	Communicate
Hair	Homes	Celebrate
Thumb Prints	Families	Work
Names	Love	Worship

REVIEW

Affective and aesthetic development focus on the changes in children's psychological, social, emotional, and creative behaviors. Early Childhood programs are well positioned to offer nurturing and sensitive activities to support positive affective and aesthetic skills.

Art, as a curriculum area, has long been recognized as beneficial for young children. Appropriate materials and activities encourage relaxation and exploration. Because art defines cultures and lifestyles, art experiences can extend beyond the creative manipulation of materials to art appreciation.

The curriculum area of Creative Dramatics playfully invites children to experience Dramatic Play, Guided Drama episodes, Puppetry, and Sociodramatics. Sociodramatics integrates activities with emphasis on learning about social roles.

Activities within the curriculum area of Social Understanding ideally support affective and aesthetic development with recognition of the self, the family, and the community. Experiences extend beyond the traditional social studies units. Social Understanding supports activities that relate to acceptance, appreciation of differences, and community participation.

KEY TERMS

Art	Puppetry
Creative Dramatics	skills
Dramatic Play	social development
emotional development	Social Understanding
Guided Drama	Sociodramatics
possible outcomes	

RESPOND

1. Visit an art museum either in person or through the Internet. Visit a school library if these resources are not available in your community. Inquire about the programs available for young children. Specifically ask questions about art appreciation, inquiring about the availability of prints of famous artwork from around the world. If the museum does not have a lending program for the prints, check with the educational outreach department in an elementary school district.

2. Research the topic of Puppetry. Prepare a two-page report that can be used as part of an in-service training for teachers at your school. Create two puppets for a Grouptime demonstration during an in-service session.

3. Connect with as many of the Web sites listed below that are currently active as possible. Gather appropriate activity ideas and resources to integrate authentic and sensitive curriculum activities. Multicultural resources need to represent families and their celebrations without bias and stereotypes.

Multicultural Awareness Activities

http://curry.edschool.Virginia.EDU/ gomulticultural/activityarch.html

Multicultural Calendar

http://www.kidlink.org/KIDPROJ/MCC/

New Zealand Perspective to Early Childhood Education Curriculum

http://members.xoom.com/koaroha/index.htm

REFERENCES

Briggs, D. C. (1970). *Your child's self-esteem.* New York: Dolphin.

Chang, H. N. L., Muckelroy, A., & Pulido-Tobiassen, D. (1996). *Looking in, looking out.* San Francisco: California Tomorrow.

Craig, G. J. (1996). *Human development* (8th ed.). Upper Saddle River, NJ: Prentice Hall.

Croft, D. (1990). *An activities handbook for teachers of young children* (5th ed.). Boston: Houghton Mifflin.

Derman-Sparks, L., & The ABC Task Force. (1989). *Anti-bias curriculum: Tools for empowering young children.* Washington, DC: National Association for the Education of Young Children.

Edwards, L. C. (1990). *Affective development and the creative arts.* Columbus, OH: Merrill.

Erickson, E. H. (1996). A healthy personality for every child. *In sources: Notable selections in early childhood education.* Guilford, CN: Dushkin Publishing Group.

Garcia, E. (1994). *Understanding and meeting the challenge of student cultural diversity.* Boston: Houghton Mifflin.

Garbarino, J. (1998). Raising children in a socially toxic environment. *Child care Information Exchange, 122,* 8–12.

Gold, W. (1999, Fall). Nonviolence in the lives of children. *Connections, 28*(2), 4–5.

Greenberg, J. (1995). Making friends with the power rangers. *Young Children, 50*(5), 60–61.

Hall, N. S. (1999). *Creative resources for the anti-bias classroom.* Albany, NY: Delmar.

Jackson, B. R. (1997). Creating a climate for healing in a violent society. *Young Children, 52*(7), 68–70.

Johnson, A. P. (1998). How to use creative dramatics in the classroom. *Childhood Education, 75*(1), 2–6.

Jackman, H. L. (1997). *Early childhood curriculum: A child's connection to the world.* Albany, NY: Delmar.

Orem, R. C. (1974). *Montessori: Her method and the movement.* New York: Capricorn.

Pool, C. R. (1997). A safe and caring place. *Educational Leadership, 55*(4), 43–77.

Ramsey, P. G. (1987). *Teaching and learning in a diverse world: Multicultural education for young children.* New York: Teachers College Press.

Rogers, C. R. (1961). *On becoming a person: A therapist's view of psychotherapy.* Cambridge, MA: Houghton Mifflin.

Schickedanz, J. A. (1999). *Much more than the abc's: The early stages of reading and writing.* Washington, DC: National Association for the Education of Young Children.

Smilansky, S. (1968). *The effects of sociodramatic play on disadvantaged preschool children.* New York: John Wiley & Sons.

Wichert, S. (1989). *Keeping the peace: Practicing cooperation and conflict resolution with preschoolers.* Santa Cruz, CA: New Society Publishers.

York, S. (1991). *Roots & wings: Affirming culture in early childhood programs.* St. Paul, MN: Redleaf Press.

Cognitive and Language Development: *Literacy, Mathematics, and Science Activities*

Curriculum Profile

"How will I know she is learning?" "What should I do to make sure that he will talk?" "When should I start her reading?" "When, how, what, and where should I be *teaching* so that my child will learn?" These questions have not varied significantly over time. Parents want the best for their children. They want them to do well in school and succeed in life. Early Childhood educators support parents by helping them to appreciate and hold reasonable expectations for the development of their own children. When parents begin to see the connections among the planned curriculum and learning, the entire program benefits.

Parents become supportive of reading, communicating, questioning, and discovering. They begin to use letters and numbers as they fit into the daily lives of their children.

Parents need reassurance that the early years are the learning years. Early Childhood professionals can reassure parents by pointing out how children acquire basic ideas on which other knowledge will be built. The eighteen-month-old's pleasure in placing a wet washcloth on the chair shows her natural motivation to accomplish a task. She is so careful as she places the washcloth, after opening the folds, on the top part of the wooden chair. She watches the washcloth slip down, smiles, and picks it up again and begins to drape it on the chair another time. Over and over, over and over, Brooke seemingly enjoys the task with her whole body, taking pleasure in the repetition, not yet knowing or caring that she is learning. As she begins to demand that her parents, "read it again" it will not be an attempt to stay awake longer. Her interest in books will contribute to her understanding of herself, her family, her pets, and her surroundings even before she joins an early education program. Brooke will begin to show preferences for certain books. Will she like *Are You My Mother, Goodnight Moon,* or *Little Blue and Little Yellow?* It will not matter to Brooke that listening to her parents and teachers read to her will positively affect all aspects of her development. Encouraged to explore and experience, Brooke will remain curious and happy—that is what learning is about.

Chapter Outline

Cognitive and Language Development
  Cognitive Development: Possible Outcomes and Activities
  Language Development: Possible Outcomes and Activities
Connecting Curriculum for Cognitive and Language Development
  Integrating Activities
  Teaching Strategies
  Technology
Cognitive and Language Development with Communication and Literacy
  Communication for Young Children: Possible Outcomes and Activities
  Literacy for Young Children: Possible Outcomes and Activities
Cognitive and Language Development with Mathematics
  Mathematics for Young Children: Possible Outcomes and Activities
Cognitive and Language Development with Science
  Science for Young Children: Possible Outcomes and Activities

Study Guide

As you study the sections in this chapter, you should be able to:

- Recognize the value of cognitive and language experiences during Early Childhood.
- Learn to write possible skills and concepts for cognitive and language development activities.
- Evaluate the inclusion of technology as an additional learning tool in Early Childhood settings.
- Identify experiences that will support communication and literacy.
- Understand the activities that will promote mathematical skill development for young children.
- Consider ways to maintain curiosity about Science.

COGNITIVE AND LANGUAGE DEVELOPMENT

The noise level and busy behavior of children demonstrate in an environment planned to meet their needs that they are motivated to learn. Abilities to communicate and to reason expand rapidly during the early childhood years as children play individually and in small groups. **Cognitive** development is about knowing and thinking. It relates to knowledge and how that knowledge is acquired. As you begin to plan for children in this Developmental Focus area, consider children's development of mental abilities, **language,** memory, conceptualizing, creativity, **Communication,** and **Literacy.** The setting that enhances cognitive development is one that provides engaging and relevant opportunities for children to develop their thinking and communication abilities.

As you prepare your facility for children, do so by creating an environment with varied experiences. Some activities are specific to a curriculum area, for example, matching toy horses with numbers offers a **Mathematics** experience for older preschoolers. Other activities will integrate curriculum areas, for example, planting and charting the growth of carrot seeds. These are the types of experiences that expose children to concepts related to Mathematics and **Science.**

Teachers should encourage children to reason and to communicate throughout the day with exploratory and manipulative materials. Cognitive growth progresses as children acquire skills in critical thinking and language. You will support children in their **cognitive development** and **language development** by helping them to recognize new ideas and by reinforcing their original and creative ideas.

Cognitive Development: Possible Outcomes and Activities

Play allows the child to think critically—to see, to explore, and to reason. The natural curiosity of children directs their interest in solving a problem: matching and sorting gardening tools, investigating bird nests, and stacking the blocks so they do not tip over. The manipulating and exploring of real objects encourages children to discover, to inquire, to remember, to classify, to label, to compare, and to see cause and effect. These are critical thinking skills that emerge when children are allowed to experiment and make meaningful choices.

For example, Emma's discovery of ice in the water table outside begins a conversation: "Who put the ice outside?" Discussion about temperature and water leads Teacher Millie to suggest to Emma that she take some of the ice inside the classroom. The ice is placed on sturdy paper plates and taken inside. Although other children excitedly make predictions, Teacher Millie encourages Emma to watch her ice. Ice cubes taken from the kitchen freezer are placed on another paper plate.

Skills: Possible Outcomes

The teacher is ready to facilitate, to expand, and to enrich every opportunity for learning. Designing activities that facilitate, expand and enrich increases the likelihood that a child will acquire critical thinking skills in a nurturing environment.

Consider the way children demonstrate their emerging capacities for cognition. Are they curious about new people and materials? How do they explore and experiment? Do their attention spans allow them to stay with a particular activity and concentrate on it? What do they remember? (Cohen & Stern, 1983, p. 124).

Appropriate curriculum for young children supports cognitive development by providing concrete child-initiated and child-directed experiences

FIGURE 9–1 Possible Outcomes: Cognitive Development Skills

seeing	labeling
hearing	observing
touching	organizing
tasting	problem-solving
smelling	remembering
classifying	reasoning
comparing	seeing cause and effect
discovering	exploring
exploring	inquiring

that are relevant. There is great probability that children will begin to understand number concepts, spatial awareness, and ideas about time when activities are appropriately planned with individually appropriate and age-appropriate activities. We help children understand these concepts with our language. "The trike is next to the path" (spatial concept); "We need one chair for each friend" (number concept); and "Your dad will pick you up after snack" (temporal concept) (Figure 9–1).

Cognitive Development Activities

Children will let us know that they are challenged by certain activities because they will enjoy repeating the tasks over and over. Organize encounters with objects in the setting that allow them to discover similarities and differences, to see cause and effect, and to gain a sense of space, sequence, and time. Feature many chances for them to see colors, shapes, sizes, and patterns, and encourage them to use symbols to represent their emerging ideas (Cohen & Stern, 1983, pp. 125–134). An activity such as Fix-It Shop introduces concepts about repair and tools (Curriculum Activity Guide 56 [CAG]). Participation by children may stimulate the need to create a project about repair (Interest Center Guide 3). The activity Growth Sequence acquaints the children with sequence and ordering (Curriculum Activity Guide 57 [CAG]).

Language Development: Possible Outcomes and Activities

Babies begin the process of language development by communicating with their cries. The language or languages a child acquires are the first and most apparent outcome that indicates cognition is developing. The capability to think about ideas and then to communicate those ideas in words is a significant

A baby's cries begin the process of language development.

cognitive achievement. Language is the foundation to a child's interaction with family and peers. Language affects emotional behaviors as well.

During play episodes, children reveal their wishes, their feelings, and their understanding and desire to understand their world. Language is so tied with how we think and who we are that it compels careful attention from you as the Early Childhood teacher. The acquisition of language has lasting influences that are apparent in regional accents and the usage of words that are learned from parents, siblings, and the extended family and community (Weiner & Elkind, 1972, p. 92). As children learn their primary language, they acquire a set of beliefs, expectations, and practices from their family. They bring the values and experiences of the home to the school, where teachers respectively bind the diverse ways and languages (Fillmore, 1993, p. 12).

Skills: Possible Outcomes

The child needs to be immersed in a language-rich environment to stimulate the formation of vital communication skills. The adult models language and accepts the child's language by creating ongoing and informal opportunities to enhance a child's language abilities—both spoken and symbolic representation. Symbolic representation is called the printed word. There are numerous ways that teachers facilitate the development of a child's language skills. We answer requests and questions. We invite discussions and conversations. We express our ideas and words and accept the child's expressions. We listen and we encourage each child to listen. We provide names for objects, peo-

ple, and events. We observe and provide opportunities for children to observe. We question to stimulate thinking and language. We help the child recall and remember what he said or saw. We enrich the day with rhyming words. We speak to other children, to staff, and to parents.

The entire environment becomes an Interest Center for language with printed labels and signs with words placed within the children's view to encourage Literacy development. Teacher-guided memory games enhance the critical thinking skills of children. Interactive charts allow children to see big print, finish sentences, create endings, and place pictures with words into the story. Laminating and binding materials allows routine "publishing" of children's illustrations and stories. These child-initiated and teacher-guided games enrich the environment and support important cognitive development skills (Figure 9–2).

Language Development Activities

Appropriately planned activities encourage a child's verbal fluency, which is his ability to speak. When a teacher writes down what the child says about an activity or experience, it is called dictation. Dictation, included with an Art experience such as fingerpainting, records what the child says about that particular activity. The teacher asks the child about her work and whether she wants her

FIGURE 9–2   Possible Outcomes: Teacher's Comments Facilitate Language Development Skills

Answering	"Yes, Sally Jo, hang your jacket in this cubby hole."
Expressing	"I see you have a cap. Is it new?"
Listening	"You can hear the hummingbird's wings."
Naming	"That is a marigold. This flower is called a poppy."
Observing	"You are riding the tricycle smoothly."
Questioning	"Do you prefer the orange juice or the cranberry juice?"
Recalling	"Yesterday, the bus driver enjoyed eating a snack with us."
Rhyming	"Yes, the cat sat on the mat."
Speaking	"It will be clean-up time in five minutes."

Interest Center Guide 3

Interest Center *Construction/Fix-It* **Theme** *Community Workers*

Art	Cooking	Literacy	Quiet Reading	Outside Art	Outside Large Motor
Block	Computer	Manipulatives	Science	Outside Circle	Outside and/Water
Circle	Dramatic Play	Music/Rhythm	Sensorial	Outside Garden	Trike Path

Interest Center Guidelines **Approximate Age Range** *3–5*

Set up special Interest Center for construction in outside large motor area to give children opportunities to repair.

Developmental Focus **Physical** **Affective and Aesthetic** **Cognitive and Language**

Curriculum Area *Social Understanding and Movement*

Interest Center Materials

Constant *Obstacle course, table, chairs, grassy area*

Featured *Prepare and place Fix-It Shop sign on rearranged obstacle course ladders to replicate a shop. Add tools, broken (but safe) small appliances, short pieces of wood, wire, glue.*

Preparation/Setup

1. *Prepare Fix-It Shop sign.*
2. *Prepare appliances—remove cords, loosen screws.*
3. *Outline tools on trays.*
4. *Arrange shop.*

Teaching Strategies

1. *Introduce safe use of tools in Interest Center as children select to participate.*
2. *Supervise, interactive questioning as children take apart and "repair" appliances. (How would you tighten that screw?)*

Possible Outcomes for the Child or Children

Concepts *Tools can take apart appliances*
Construction workers and repair persons use tools.

Skills *Fine motor development, social understanding, role playing, problem solving, confidence.*

Vocabulary *tools, repair, construction, fix-it*

Child Participation **Date**

description written down. An experience such as the activity Telephone Partners invites children to chose to use the telephones with the teacher adding interactive questions: "What do you think the person will say when they answer the phone?" "Was there a busy signal?" "Tell me how that sounded?" (Curriculum Activity Guide 58 [CAG]).

CONNECTING CURRICULUM FOR COGNITIVE AND LANGUAGE DEVELOPMENT

The "Guidelines for Decisions about Developmentally Appropriate Practice," in the revised edition of *Developmentally Appropriate Practice in Early Childhood Programs,* provide direction for appropriate experiences to enhance cognitive development. Curriculum will meet the children's needs when teachers respect the intelligence of the enrolled children and build on what they already know. The activities should be based on the children's interests and respect their familial and linguistic diversity. Teachers will more likely achieve developmentally appropriate practice when they offer young children choices and time to explore relevant and purposeful activities. Experiences will further cognitive development for young children when new concepts support enjoyment of learning and allow the children to be involved in the planning and review of their work (Bredekamp & Copple, 1997, pp. 15, 18, 126–127).

Integrating Activities

The guidelines presented in the previous section emphasize curriculum planning implemented with considerable attention to the children's home experiences with their families and communities. Activities planned with cognitive and language development in mind will easily integrate across the curriculum. An activity about the post office provides the children with opportunities that may develop their skills in critical thinking and language. They will also gain information about social roles and therefore experience activities within the curriculum area of Social Understanding. Activities about the post office will cross over to Mathematics (counting letters) and Art (appreciating design of postage stamps). Play experiences related to the post office facilitate children's abilities in Communication and Literacy. You can plan activities related to the function of a post office or the role of a postal clerk when the theme of post office is selected by the teaching staff. Or you can plan an activity because a child has shown an interest in letter writing and delivery. The post office activity or theme offers children benefits in language development. A specific activity (letter writing) features Literacy readiness. Activities can focus on a Developmental Focus area and curriculum areas and connect with a theme (Figure 9–3).

Projects, themes, and Interest Centers support the development of cognition and language in different ways. A theme that features a specific curriculum area, such as Day and Night, may be more relevant to the development of critical thinking (cognition). Another theme, Celebrations, favors experiences related to language development. Most themes will provide an integrated curriculum plan with beneficial activities related to many curriculum areas and themes (Figure 9–4).

Teaching Strategies

Parents ask what they can do to ensure that their children will do well in school. This inquiry is often about intellectual functioning because society

FIGURE 9–3   Activities Integrate Developmental Focus Area, Curriculum Areas, and Theme

Developmental Focus Area	Cognition and Language
Curriculum Areas	*Communication and Literacy* Activity: Writing Letters
	Movement Activity: Walking to the Post Office
	Social Understanding Activity: Sociodramatic Play—Mail Carrier
Theme	Community Helpers— Mail Carrier

FIGURE 9–4   Themes Enhancing Cognitive and Language

Cognitive	**Language**
Water Safety	Celebrations
We Are Alike/Different	Adventures—Outdoors
Make Believe	Drama/Fine Arts
Day and Night	Family Gathering

places great emphasis on academic achievement. To enhance cognitive development you will need to first know each child's needs and encourage each child's curiosity and confidence. Validate the process of acquiring a skill, rather than expecting a finished product from an activity. Look at inventive ways to enhance the children's critical thinking, Communication, and Literacy. Design activities to encourage children to observe, listen, speak, and write. Avoid structuring unrelated experiences that push children to acquire meaningless facts, such as memorizing isolated facts, letters, and numbers. Practices that ignore exploration put the children's motivation at risk. The developmentally appropriate practice guidelines describe giving children choices, providing activities that cover concepts based on prior knowledge, problem-solving, and plans for children to review and work as the suitable way to enhance cognitive activities.

Technology

Joey brings his envelope to the student teacher and asks for help with the computer label printed with his name. As they walk back, Joey says, "This is for my grandpa, he's in the hospital and needs it right now, so I don't want the label, I want to fax it, OK?" The student teacher leads Joey to the fax machine, where he watches her input the numbers and listens to the static sounds during connection. When the machine beeps, Joey knows that a printout will be his record that he sent a message to his grandpa. Later, during activity time, Joey and Gail are busy printing out a page from a teacher-selected Web site on the Internet and notice that they have run out of paper. Once again, Student Teacher Shelly is there to offer to assist Joey with the technological equipment.

Technology is about machines, tools, products, and devices that assist children and their families in daily life activities. Technology is constantly changing and continually affects children in homes, schools, and communities. In just one day a child may observe his teacher scan his drawing into the computer, send an e-mail, see the grocery clerk electronically debit items, and watch the numbers on the digital gas station pump that also prints a receipt. Technology enables children with disabilities to access and participate in the community and school programs. Assistive technology improves the operation of wheelchairs, hearing aids, and on-screen keyboards specially designed for individuals who cannot use hands and fingers.

Technology integrates into every aspect of the Early Childhood curriculum and needs to be viewed as a tool to enhance skills. Technology, particularly the microcomputer, helps us to access information. Today, most children have significant and direct experiences with technology on a daily basis. Most were born in hospitals with sophisticated medical technology. Technological inventions extend our abilities to see (batteries and lights); to hear (telephone and stereo speakers); to remember (camera and camcorders); to medically heal (lasers); to cook (microwaves); and to travel (airplanes).

Technology includes and expands Mathematics and Science awareness. Children develop a technological attitude by planning, predicting, and participating in activities. A walk to the library begins with a planning session with discussion about the number of books, the return walk, and a stop at the cafeteria to pick up a snack. Predicting that the books and snack may be heavy, children suggest bringing the wagon to carry the books and snack. Children are introduced to two concepts about technology: a wagon is a tool to help us carry heavy items, and a wagon has wheels that allow the wagon to move when we walk. Planning for a subsequent walk leads the children to "discover" and "invent" another device to keep the books from sliding around in the wagon. Two plastic tubs from the water play area are dried and placed into the wagon. Photographs of the wagon with the two tubs are placed in the discovery center and labeled with a sign prepared and printed by the computer—"Invention." Children continually gain awareness of technological concepts as they interact in an enriched environment (Figure 9–5).

FIGURE 9–5 Technology Enhances Cognitive and Language Development

Skill	Teaching Activity
Planning	Walks to the fire department; auto repair shop
Predicting	Which wheel turns faster
Participating	Lifting objects with a pulley
Creating	Pictures of the pets with computer graphics
Comparing	Whipping cream with hand and electric beaters
Exploring	Tools that drive nails into wood
Inquiring	About water available in homes
Investigating	Adding machines and calculators
Observing	Products of telecommunications

COGNITIVE AND LANGUAGE DEVELOPMENT WITH COMMUNICATION AND LITERACY

Communication and Literacy combine as a curriculum area to help organize plans for facilitating children's cognitive and language development. You may have been introduced to Literacy as a series of subjects in grade school (spelling, reading, and writing) unless you were in a whole language school where emphasis was on "writing across the curriculum." Because we integrate the curriculum areas, Early Childhood is indeed whole language. Add to this feature the advantages of emergent curriculum and acceptance of multi-linguistic abilities and we have an edge on reaching appropriate goals. You will hear many teachers refer to this category as language arts, with traditional promotion of speaking, listening, writing, and reading.

Communication for Young Children: Possible Outcomes and Activities

Children begin to communicate first with their family members. The way children communicate sounds and words with particular tempos and pitches is a result of their interactions during those critical first two years. Innate temperament also influences the outcome of Communication, with the home language exerting tremendous influence. Teachers who support and respect linguistic diversity ensure optimal learning opportunities in Communication for the children enrolled in their programs. Diversity of language may bring the entire group of children into learning new languages and other forms of Communication. This validates respect and preservation of the children's home languages. Languages are tied to our personal identities, which can be shared. When languages are shared children learn that there are many forms of expression and gain beneficial experiences as members of an inclusive community (Seefeldt & Galper, 1998, p. 254).

Communication: Possible Outcomes

Communication skills include more than just speaking. In addition, they develop skills to answer, discuss, express, listen, name, observe, question, recall, and rhyme. Teachers planning activities that offer varied linguistic experiences allow communicative interaction that is meaningful for the children in the program, for their parents, and the staff. Conversations that foster interactions call on teachers to use simple sentences and to speak slowly and clearly,

varying their tone of voice and the words that they use. It is also important to pause between sentences and to use concrete vocabulary by avoiding using the word *that* to describe objects that have a name or label. Children's communications skills will be facilitated when teachers accept and build on the children's phrases; follow their topic of interest, and "comment more than question" (Kratcoski & Katz, 1998, p. 31). Interactive questioning encourages teachers to pose comments that challenge the children to think about, wonder, and discover: "Imagine what it might look like if ten butterflies landed on the plant," "Think about the way we should walk into the library," "What might happen if we didn't mix the liquid into the bowl?"

Children become aware of other people speaking different languages, that some communicate with their hands, and that our words can be recorded by writing them down, recording them into a machine, or clicking buttons on a computer. Communication also involves listening and observing. Young children develop the capability to store and remember ideas and images. This is called recall. You will enrich the communication skills of young children with a wide variety of linguistic experiences as you interact and converse with them throughout their preschool years (Figure 9–6).

Communication Topics and Activities for Young Children

Observe and listen to the children to identify behavior that will direct the development of appropriate activities. You can meet the needs of children by planning activities from a Thematic Approach, from a Developmental Focus area approach, or within Interest Centers. As you already know, validate children's emerging capacities with assessments of their behaviors and interactions. Nathan cuts a piece of paper in half. He walks to Shelby, hands her the paper, and says, "This is your ticket to the fair, we gonna go to the fair." The teacher is provided with a clue to Nathan's interest and can foster communication skills within a theme or interest center (Figures 9–7 and 9–8) (Curriculum Activity Guides 59 and 60 [CAG]).

Literacy for Young Children: Possible Outcomes and Activities

"That's my letter." "Write my name." "That says stop." Children have formed varying awarenesses of the printed word. We live in a literate society with expectations for reading and writing performance. As an Early Childhood educator, you are

FIGURE 9–6   Experiences Support Communication

Creative Dramatics	Role playing—acting like a cat, moving like the wind.
Interactive software	Computer software invites child's verbal response.
Dictating stories	Adult records in writing child's words and stories.
Discriminating	Perceiving and responding to different sounds and letters.
Discussing	Teacher-guided during mealtime and Grouptime.
Feeling box	Feeling and describing objects concealed in a special box.
Large movement	Walk up and down; crawl in and out; hop front and back.
Memory games	Show three items. Hide in basket. Can you remember?
Puppets	Speak, listen, and tell a story, poem, or teach a song.
Sequence stories	Tell part of familiar story. Child continues or completes.
Telephones	Connected to another phone in indoor area; dramatic prop.
Tape recorders	Records a child's messages; available for interactive stories.

FIGURE 9–7   Activities Contribute to Communication Skills

Observed Behavior: Nathan cuts a piece of paper in half. He walks to Shelby, hands the paper to her, and says, "This is your ticket to the fair, we gonna go to the fair."

Theme or Interest Center: County Fair

Activity	**Skills**
1. Ticket booth large box for ticket booth; rubber stamp; fair brochures; play money; music; money and ticket collection box; maps; employee hats.	Asking for ticket Discussing maps Listening to ticket requests
2. Amusement Games Bean bags and cardboard target; ping pong balls and metal bucket; hidden treasure; pictures of prizes; tickets; ticket box; large boxes and tables.	Observing target Recalling hidden items Listening-balls in bucket

FIGURE 9–8   Experiences Expand Multilingual Communication

My Name in Many Colors	Prepare name tags with the children's names written (manuscript or DeNealian) in several different languages. Color code each language in a specific color or colors. Introduce name tags during a Grouptime. Demonstrate the teacher's name tag first then the children's in multiple languages. Allow children choices to select name tags in language preference.
Same Tune, Different Words	Sing familiar songs in primary language spoken by the majority of children. Sing the same songs in another language helping children to recognize that the tunes are the same.
Signing the Song	Guide the children in learning to sign a familiar song in American Sign Language, Signing Essential English, or Signing Exact English.
What do you Call Your Grandmother?	Display pictures of grandmothers. During a grouptime present photos of grandmothers representing diversity. Provide the word for grandmother in many languages. Ask children what they call their grandmother. Follow-up activities may include grandfather, aunt, uncle, etc.

already sensitive to societal demands for reading and writing skills. You know the importance of discovery and readiness. The challenge is to help parents appreciate the way that you will guide the children's encounters to fit the way they learn best. Competence without pushing inappropriate school tasks is the rule if we want to increase the probability for children to succeed. Literacy can secure a strong educational base as long as best practices are maintained.

The International Reading Association (IRA) and the National Association for the Education of Young Children (NAEYC) adopted a joint position paper. This statement clearly indicates that reading aloud to children is the most important activity to support their understandings and skills. In addition, it was pointed out that it is during the preschool years that children benefit from exposure to print as long as the experiences are appropriate and positive and "challenging but achievable with sufficient adult support" (NAEYC, 1998, pp. 31, 33). The America Reads Challenge, sponsored by the United States Department of Education, asks all persons to identify what they can do—personally and professionally—to help create communities of strong readers. "As Early Childhood Specialists, you understand how important it is to provide children with solid language and listening skills as the means to future success in reading. Your expertise and close working relationship with families and caregivers provides you with opportunities to make a significant contribution toward preparing young children for reading readiness in their earliest education setting," stated Carol Hampton Rasco, Director of the America Reads Challenge (Rasco, 1997, p. 1) (Curriculum Activity Guide 61 [CAG]).

Literacy: Possible Outcomes

Focus on the rewards and pleasures of reading, writing, and labeling. Look at Literacy as another way to communicate feelings, needs, and plans. As you help children along the pathway to Literacy, accept their words and introduce them to new ideas and concepts. A concept is actually just an idea about an object, person, or event that the child encounters or experiences. Children explore their world with their senses, gaining distinct information about each item. Children learn to respond to common elements. As children begin to discriminate the features of objects they also make associations among objects. You can help the children to organize and to classify these generalizations and relationships. When children see how objects relate, ideas are formed and concepts learned.

As the children's teacher you will support concept learning with emphasis on verbal and written language. Begin by labeling objects in the environment: "This is a gate." "Gus is our guinea pig." "Our guest today is a Postal Clerk. Her name is Ella." Over time, as you provide descriptions of the objects and things such as, "The gate is metal," "The gate surrounds our play area," "The gate is gray," "The guinea pig is furry," "The guinea likes celery," the children will learn more ideas and begin to group these ideas. Children also need to understand how the objects work and what animals do. So, you continue to communicate ideas verbally and labeling in writing, "The guinea pig wiggles her nose. Stacy fed the guinea pig today." Then, you can identify similarities and differences of the idea or object (Read, 1976, p. 232). In this way you expand children's comprehension of concepts and you support Literacy (Figure 9–9).

FIGURE 9–9 Concept Learning Contributes to Literacy Readiness

Concept:	Fruit		
Label	**Description**	**Features**	**Similarities/differences**
Orange	Round	To eat	Round like an apple
	Smells	Squeeze for juice	Smells like a lemon
Concept:	Animal		
Label	**Description**	**Features**	**Similarities/differences**
Guinea pig	Furry	Squeals	Looks like a cat
	No ears	Wiggles nose	Is not a rabbit

FIGURE 9–10 Appropriate Vocabulary for An Activity

Activity Title	Cooking Pasta, Fideo, and Noodles	
Vocabulary	noodles	heat
	pasta	stir
	fideo (Spanish—a type	sieve
	of noodle)	drain
	boil	soft
	sautée	long

Art extends children's oral language and literacy because they can express their feelings and ideas to others while being creative.

You will also facilitate Literacy by adding lists of the appropriate vocabulary in the weekly and monthly parent newsletters and placing the lists on bulletin boards. This display and the Curriculum Activity Guides bring parental attention to the children's curriculum (Figure 9–10). Parents becoming aware of the vocabulary will be able to reinforce the use of words and labels and contribute Literacy development.

Literacy Topics and Activities for Young Children

Your Early Childhood setting features Literacy for young children because you provide realistic experiences for the age group. Build on the children's previous experiences related to their everyday lives. Literacy will develop in settings where children are given ongoing opportunities to use language throughout the day. Literacy experiences relate to the overall physical arrangement of the environment, to routines, and to materials and resources specifically planned by early care and education professionals (Schickedanz, 1999, pp. 136–137). Teachers who enjoy literature and read a variety of books will project a positive attitude about Literacy to the children and their parents. Children who are regularly exposed to books during the early childhood years will develop reading abilities earlier and more successfully for both pleasure and information (Lay-Dopyera & Dopyera, 1982, p. 339). Studies also indicate that many types of experiences give children a verbal advantage; therefore they are more ready to read. Other activities planned to support Literacy development need to be with concrete materials to enrich and enlarge their daily experiences. If they are unable to visit a zoo, books with many pictures of zoo animals will substitute (Coody, 1992, p. 91). The value of literature crosses over into many areas of the curriculum and is supported by the educational recommendations for Literacy across the curriculum. For example, Art activities extend children's oral language and Literacy because they can express their feelings and ideas to others while developing skills in creative expression. Cooking activities are versatile and cohesive with Literacy. Award-winning books for young children (Figure 9–11) will stimulate cooking

FIGURE 9–11 Young Children's Picture Books and Cooking Experiences

Blueberries for Sal by Robert McCloskey. (1948). New York: Viking.

Bread and Jam for Frances by Russell and Lillian Hoban. (1964). New York: Harper & Row.

Chicken Soup with Rice by Maurice Sendak. (1962). New York: Harper & Row.

Stone Soup by Marcia Brown. (1947). New York: Charles Scribner's Sons.

FIGURE 9–12   Experiences Support Literacy

Bulletin board	Children place photographs or drawings of their pets under the words dog and cat.
Dictation	Adult writes down child's words, story.
Dramatic play props	Food orders, catalog orders, debit and charge receipts.
Labels	Meaningful word labels throughout indoor and outdoor environment.
Literature	Child listens to stories and books read by adult (picture books or Big Picture Books). Asks questions before, review story after.
Matching games	Purchased or prepared games allow matching similar pictures.
Microcomputer	Software for child or small group.
Object hunt	Searching for identified and labeled items familiar to children.
Observing adults	Writing, pointing to words in Big Books during story; writing child's name on work; writing messages from left to right, top to bottom.
Puppets	Manufactured and created, used to tell story or have children use to relate a story to be dictated. Can introduce an idea or open a Grouptime.
Sign-in	Clipboard with children's names in large print for optional check off upon arrival and departure when parents sign in.
Storytelling	To small groups; may use flannel board or props; not essential. Children need to see and be able to listen to storyteller.
Backpack/briefcase	Writing materials, rubber stamps, rulers, books.
Visual charts	Charts for activities, such as cooking, that have pictures and words. Experience charts with children's descriptions of an experience.
Waiting lists	Waiting lists of children interested in participating in popular activities are maintained.
Writing center	Desk with variety of writing tools to include templates, magnetic letters, index boxes of each child's favorite letters or words.

experiences and contribute to Literacy development (Coody, 1992, pp. 115, 141, 148, 165).

Reading books, storytelling, and use of puppets and flannel boards, visual charts, and labeling support the development of Literacy skills. Ideas and words can be represented in books, charts, and labels (Curriculum Activity Guides 62, 63, 64 [CAG]) (Figure 9–12).

COGNITIVE AND LANGUAGE DEVELOPMENT WITH MATHEMATICS

Asking children to place one napkin by each chair helps them to understand one-on-one correspondence. Setting up an activity for children to walk up and down steps helps them become aware of their relationships to objects in a given space. Providing a modified measuring tape to determine length of legs gives the children chances to learn about their bodies and about measurement. What you plan and how you arrange the environment will establish important beginnings for children to construct mathematical awareness. These beginnings are needed for later, more formal mathematical operations. This curriculum area will be enjoyable to you and to the children because you and staff arrange for exploration and discovery. Encourage children to be inventive as they discover connections and spatial relationships. Mathematical experiences will enhance children's critical thinking, reasoning, and problem solving skills.

Mathematics for Young Children

Numbers are everywhere, and children are exposed early to ideas about numbers, size, and amounts. Numbers are on television sets, ovens, watches, price tags, money, and clocks. Numbers describe a child's age, older brother's size, how long it takes to get to school and the cost of a yogurt cone. Children learn early what *more* means and the significance of *big*. Discovering the relationships of objects in our environment and finding order are basic processes of Mathematics. Teachers who encourage curiosity will find that young children continue to look, to explore, and to discover experiences throughout the day.

The Mathematics program for children three to five years of age requires hands-on resources for children to explore informally, in planned experiences, and in Interest Centers. Children need to be able to use, store, distribute, and replace the manipulatives when they have finished using them (Charlesworth, 2000, p. 326). Selection of appropriate mathematical materials should include review of recommended criteria to ensure that the resources are sturdy and versatile, fit the program guidelines and children's developmental stages, and are safe, easily supervised, and bias-free (Charlesworth, 2000, p. 331).

Mathematics is easily integrated throughout the curriculum and the children's day. For example, Teacher Betsy comments, "I see four children in the block area"; "Check the sign and see if there is room for you"; "You can cut this apple in half so that there is one piece for you, Michael, and one for Megan." Activities in the Interest Centers encourage sensory experiences and create numerous chances for the children to measure rice, shift sand, and pour cups of cornmeal. Materials placed in a Mathematics Interest Center, or the Manipulative Center, need to be organized in containers and displayed on low, accessible shelving. Teachers should rotate the mathematical manipulatives periodically as the children's interests and development change or to relate the mathematical materials to a theme or project (Charlesworth, 2000, p. 329) (Interest Center Guide 4). Routine classroom experiences also promote awareness of Mathematics, "Chae, the goldfish needs just one ounce of food" (Figure 9–13).

Mathematics: Possible Outcomes

Children become aware of mathematical concepts and discover concepts by manipulating real materials in self-directed activities and teacher-guided activities. Experiences that develop mathematical awareness should be featured throughout the day. Interest Centers offer many experiences for interaction with mathematical concepts adding to mathematical skills, such as arranging buckets, ordering tricycles, and patterning or sequencing the drum beats (Figure 9–14).

Mathematical activities, even though you have an overall curriculum plan to guide the concepts and skills to be presented, should emerge from the children's interests and needs. Observe the behavior of the children. Listen to their language. Then, plan experiences that contribute to development of specific mathematical skills (Figure 9–15).

Interest Centers offer many experiences for interaction with mathematical concepts.

FIGURE 9–13   Interest Centers Offer Mathematical Experiences

Interest Center	Recommended Materials for Rotation
Manipulative	Pegboard, geoboard, nesting blocks, puzzles, cubes, rods, stringing beads, mazes, linking blocks, magnet shapes, sorting-grouping-matching games, clocks, scales, measuring tapes and cups, spoons, timers, play money, calculator, shapes, tiles
Unit block	Unit block and storage shelf in carpeted area, play people, block size vehicles, signs, tracks
Cooking	Cooking utensils to include bowls and pans in various sizes, measuring spoons, scale
Large motor outside	Obstacle course, rebounder (counting and sequencing jumps), stop watch, ladder and steps (going up and down)
Dramatic Play	Play money, calculators, receipts, checkbooks, maps, address books, compass, odometer, scale, stop watch, calculator, adding machine, credit cards, stamps
Sensorial area	Sand, water, textures, jars (to explore color, size, shape, size)

Interest Center Guide 4

Interest Center *Mathematics*   **Theme**   *I'm Growing*

Art	Cooking	Literacy	Quiet Reading	Outside Art	Outside Large Motor
Block	Computer	Manipulatives	Science	Outside Circle	Outside and/Water
Circle	Dramatic Play	Music/Rhythm	Sensorial	Outside Garden	Trike Path

Interest Center Guidelines   **Approximate Age Range** *4–5*

To provide experiences for children to measure and monitor their growth.

Developmental Focus   **Physical**   **Affective and Aesthetic**   Cognitive and Language

Curriculum Area Interest Center Materials

Constant   *Puzzles, cylinders, Legos, matching cards, unit rods, cubes, patterning and matching lottos.*

Featured   *Trays with mirrors, measuring tapes, cotton string, envelopes, scissors, index cards, felt pens, bath scale, pictures of hands, legs, heads.*

Preparation/Setup

1. Add materials to trays.

2. Set trays on shelves in manipulative or sensorial area.

Teaching Strategies

1. Introduce new materials during Grouptime. Show pictures, measuring tape. Measure finger with tape and string.

2. Provide guidance and assistance for children as they request when measuring and cutting string the size of their foot, leg, or fingers.

Possible Outcomes for the Child or Children

Concepts   *Fingers, legs, and arms are different sizes. A measuring tape tells the amount of inches or feet.*

Skills   *measuring, comparing*

Vocabulary *measure, length, inch*

Child Participation   **Date**

FIGURE 9–14 Possible Outcomes: Mathematical Skills

Arranging	Sand buckets from smallest to biggest
Ordering	Grouping, sorting, classifying objects that look alike; all tricycles to the wheel-toy garage.
Pairing	One space for each tricycle; one-to-one correspondence.
Patterning	Repeating sequence of drum beats.
Comparing	There are four flowers on that plant, two on this one.
Measuring	Amount of flour needed to make modeling dough.
Reversing	Following the path back to the preschool.
Analyzing	Whose plant is taller?
Graphing	Visually graphing children who drink juice or milk.

FIGURE 9–15 Possible Outcomes: Mathematical Concepts for an Activity

Observed Behavior:	Joey, using the telephone in the Dramatic Play area, says, "I'm going to visit my grandpa in the hospital." Gail asks, "What's a hospital?"
Activity Title	Walking to the Neighborhood Clinic
Mathematical Skills	**Mathematical Concepts**
Pairing	Everyone walks with one friend.
Seriating	First we pair into twos, then we walk to the clinic. Next we look at the items, then we walk back.
Classifying	There are four waiting chairs and two examining rooms.
Predicting	Will the bus have room to park?

Mathematics Topics and Activities for Young Children

Joey seems very excited that Teacher Naomi has planned to visit the neighborhood medical clinic. He is thinking and talking about his grandpa often and has told many children that he's going to visit his grandpa in the hospital. The planned activity, a neighborhood field trip, responds to Joey's and other children's needs to know more about medical facilities. In addition, there are opportunities to expand their mathematical awareness and specific mathematical skills. Introduction of mathematical concepts needs to be suitable for the children's developmental stages. Activities need to remain simple and concrete because many mathematical concepts require a level of abstract thinking that the preschool children may not possess (Ault, 1977, p. 51) (Figure 9–16).

The entire environment will become learning places for mathematical learning. You will be able to plan informal, unstructured, or teacher-guided Interest Centers for individual or small groups, the key aspect of which will be to establish mathematical activities as hand-on activities (Figure 9–17).

Manipulative Mathematics engages the children as they handle, store, distribute, and replace the material. Rosalind Charlesworth's book, *Experiences in Math for Young Children*, remains a solid resource for activity ideas for Mathematics (2000, p. 326) (Curriculum Activity Guide 65, 66, 67 [CAG]).

FIGURE 9–16 Introducing Mathematical Concepts—Activity Topics

classification. Grouping objects with similar characteristics and features. Putting child-size shoes into one category or box and adult size shoes into another category or box.

conservation. Understanding the amount does not change even though it may appear that way. Manipulating materials provides foundation for the skill to understanding that when five buckets are spread out across the sand box or next to each other, there are still only five buckets.

seriation. Ordering or sequencing objects or events. Each day when the child arrives she checks off her name when her parent signs-in, then puts away her jacket into their cubbyhole, then enters the indoor activity area.

concepts about time. Also called temporal concept. "When will my daddy pick me up?" "It is clean-up time in five minutes, the big hand will be on the 12."

concepts about numbers. Stand with one friend for the walk. There were four large beds.

concepts about space. The lab for nurses is next to Jan's mother's classroom. The stethoscope was around the teacher's neck. Each preschooler sat on top of the hospital bed.

FIGURE 9–17 Activities Contribute to Mathematical Awareness

Activity	Skills
Big, Small, Medium Envelopes	sorting arranging ordering
Organizing Mail for Delivery	analyzing comparing

COGNITIVE AND LANGUAGE DEVELOPMENT WITH SCIENCE

Children learn about science whenever they actively experience and enjoy the natural phenomena in their immediate surroundings. Hands-on activities favor children's way of learning in the Science curriculum. Science is happening all around the children. Support their natural curiosity, interest, and awe by taking pleasure in the way they see surroundings with fresh and observant wonder. There will be daily unexpected opportunities to answer the many "why's," to enjoy the new spring blossoms, to touch piled sand in the desert playground, to scoop the snow left on the climbing structure.

The study of science systematically organizes information about the world. Science is divided into two broad fields, biological science and physical science. The biological sciences include study about growing and living elements of the world.

Physical science includes study about the causes and effects of matter, energy, and space.

Science for Young Children

Experiences remain child-focused if they are simple and real. Listen to what children are really saying and asking. Remain well acquainted with the children's homes because their comments are based on their prior experiences, most of which have been primarily outside the school environment. As a teacher, your role is to guide discovery. Meaningful discovery is possible when relevant activities take children beyond simple observation. Introduce children to experiences that allow them to mix, pour, stir, float, dissolve, and monitor. Watch their reaction. Listen to their comments. Ask the children questions that allow them to "see" connections and consequences. For example, do you acknowledge the children's reactions to the experience? Do you reflect on their comments and behaviors? Comment on and help them think about the sand that feels and moves differently after the rain shower. Clarify misconceptions—"The sand does feel different, but no one was outside to pour water on the sand pile. What happened when we were indoors?" Alert children to be cautious in their exploration of Science materials, including animals that they do not know, plants that may not be all right to touch and eat, and smelling items in unknown containers. In this way you will integrate concepts of Health and Safety with Science to help children

FIGURE 9–18   Early Childhood Teacher's Roles for Science

Guide	Introduce
Watch	Listen
Ask	Clarify
Alert	Integrate

to become aware of hazards in their surroundings. For example, rapidly moving water is not safe. Food that is discolored is not healthy to eat (Figure 9–18).

Science: Possible Outcomes

Observing, classifying, quantifying, and communicating are skills that three-, four-, and five-year-olds will use as they participate in Science activities throughout their early childhood years. These are processes that help them to gather information, inquire, and investigate—find out what and how. Observation is the most basic element of this process. Children look, hear, smell, taste, and feel. They use their senses to observe. Then they can communicate about what they see and hear in their surroundings, sharing messages with descriptions using vocabulary and ideas. They begin to classify these concepts, finding similarities and differences. Classification helps children to make sense out of the objects that they do see and describe by organizing and sorting objects according to the observable characteristics. When children begin to quantify, they compare, count, and measure. How much space did we need for the butcher paper? Was it hotter yesterday than today? Quantifying relates to the children's skills at observing, classifying, and describing objects more precisely (Neuman, 1978, pp. 23–27). Inferring (thinking and talking about

what might happen) and applying information are more abstract tasks reserved for older preschoolers and primary children. Emphasis in Science is on emergent experiences, not isolated tasks and preconceived experiments.

Acceptable Science topics in Early Childhood Education need to be useful for the children; good, basic science; help to build useful skills; and allow children to discover (Neuman, 1978, p. 30) (Figure 9–19).

Relevant, well-planned Science activities contribute to the development of concepts and promote cognition. Conceptual awareness increases as children become increasingly more perceptive of their surroundings. Planned activities can introduce children to both the biological sciences, including plants and animals, and the physical sciences, including heat from the sun and falling objects (Figure 9–20).

Your positive attitude about Science will keep the children open to natural and physical phenomena. For example, five-year-old Ray brings a picture taken on a vacation to his uncle's ranch. He points to sheep in the picture that are corralled in a field. Ray is excited about the wire that created a temporary corral. Ray shouted loudly, "we can't go near because the wire will hit us." Children remain gathered around Ray to listen to his comments about the ranch, the sheep, and especially the hot wire. The afternoon Grouptime opened a chance to talk about the sheep and to clarify misconceptions about the hot wire corral. The teachers also agreed that a visit from a sheep rancher needed to be arranged (Figure 9–21).

Science Topics and Activities for Young Children

Children's natural curiosity initiates ideas for numerous Science activities. Your curriculum approach identifies strategies for presenting Science experiences to children. Plan activities with familiar and natural materials that give children

FIGURE 9–19   Possible Outcomes for Young Children: Science Skills

Exploring	sounds created by tapping on metal, plastic, wood.
Observing	the guinea pig eats lettuce.
Communicating	labeling, questioning, and talking about flowers in window box garden.
Organizing	rock collection.
Applying	experiences about healthy eating to classroom pets.
Relating	frozen bird bath to very cold weather/temperature.
Inferring	the wood block will sink and the feather will float.

FIGURE 9–20   Science Concepts within Major Science Fields

Biological Science	Physical Science
Our bodies grow	The sun heats up metal tricycles
Pets need food, water, care	Blowing on a pinwheel makes it move
Some plants can be eaten	Warmed juice dissolves gelatin
Trees provide shade	The moon looks different at night
Creek water comes from snow	A wood block falls faster than a feather

FIGURE 9–21   Activities Offer Science Concepts and Vocabulary

Activity Title	Visit From a Community Helper: Sheep Rancher Brings Lamb
Concepts	Sheep ranching is a job and business
	Lambs are baby sheep
	Mother sheep feed their babies
	Sheep and lambs are sometimes kept in a barn on the farm
	Sheep are sheared for their wool
	Sheep eat grass
	Sheep are moved to different places so the grass can grow again
	Wire and electricity can create a hot wire corral
	Hot wire means that the sheep will get a shock or jolt
	Children should not touch hot wires, electricity can shock

Vocabulary	rancher	corral	grazing
	sheep	hot wire	wool
	lamb	electricity	shear
	barn	section	weave
	livestock		

opportunities to see, to hear, to taste, to smell, and to touch. Exploration and discovery of concrete experiences validate that children actively build knowledge for themselves. Scientific inquiry is fun and exciting when children observe cause and effect as they directly experience natural events (cloud formation) and arrange materials in their environment (smelling different fruit). Children develop Science skills and begin developing positive attitudes in preschool because you help them to see natural phenomena. Interest Centers create places for Science with manipulative materials and overlap and integrate with other curriculum areas and Interest Centers (Figure 9–22). As children explore ideas (where does rain go), their critical thinking and language (timing and changes of stop lights) abilities develop. Teachers plan activities to enhance possibilities for cognitive development (Curriculum Activity Guides 68, 69, 70 [CAG]).

Science activities contribute to the development of concepts and promote cognition.

FIGURE 9–22   Interest Centers Support Science

Interest Center	Recommended Materials for Rotation
Manipulative	Color paddles, prisms, weights, scales, lenses, sundial, sponges, magnets, puzzles, microscope, flashlights, compass, magnifiers
Discovery/Sensory	Weights, collections (shells, rocks, soil, textures), microscope, water (coloring, sponges, eyedroppers, straws), objects (touching, seeing, tasting, smelling, hearing), ant colony, aquarium, ant and silkworm farms, terrarium (plant and worm)
Cooking	Cooking utensils and appliances
Pets	Staff preference and commitment to pet care and available space determines selection. May include guinea pigs, birds, and fish—indoors
Gardening	Indoor safe plants throughout center; herbs; outdoor garden area—shovels, trowels, rakes, watering cans, hose, signs, sun hats, soil, seedling containers, gloves
Dramatic Play	Clothing and props for Science-related occupations: gardener, horticulturist, botanist, meteorologist, geologist, astronomer, chemist, chef, veterinarian, engineer

REVIEW

There is strong evidence for cognitive and language development to remain strong components of the Early Childhood program. Cognitive development refers to knowing and thinking and ties closely with language acquisition. As children see, hear, touch, taste, and smell their world, they begin to acquire cognitive skills. They also listen, answer, name, observe, question, recall, and speak increasingly during early childhood, especially when there are supportive adults guiding language development.

An increasingly important factor in the access of information is technology. Technology integrates every aspect of the curriculum and serves as an important tool to enhance skills. There are three curriculum areas that particularly fit well within discussion of cognitive and language development: Communication and Literacy, Mathematics, and Science. All three curriculum areas facilitate critical thinking, concept formation, and communication.

The curriculum area of Communication and Literacy has focused attention with the position paper jointed prepared by the International Reading Association and the National Association for the Education of Young Children. The message delivered indicates that reading aloud to children is as important as early but appropriate exposure to print.

Mathematics experiences will allow children to discover connections, numbers, and spatial relationships. Teachers' responsibility for Science activities includes introducing children to concepts and watching and listening to them as they explore their surroundings.

KEY TERMS

cognitive
cognitive
  development
Communication
language

language
  development
Literacy
Mathematics
Science

RESPOND

1. Observe two preschool-age children. Prepare two activities for them to support their Literacy development. Specify the skills and concepts for each activity.
2. Design and document in writing a Mathematics activity that will help parents understand the value of hands-on, manipulative material for young children. Copy the Curriculum Activity Guide form for the written documentation. This prepared activity is to be presented during class.
3. Access one of the following Web sites. List three Science activities that could be suitably adapted to meet young children's needs. If these sites are not active, locate another Web site that lists Science or Mathematics activity ideas.

http://www.exploratorium.edu/science_explorer/

http://photo2.si.edu/dino/dino.htm

http://www.ciera.org/

REFERENCES

Ault, R. L. (1977). *Children's cognitive development: Piaget's theory and the process approach.* New York: Oxford University Press.

Bredekamp, S., & Copple, C. (1997). *Developmentally appropriate practice in early childhood programs.* Washington, DC: National Association for the Education of Young Children.

Charlesworth, R. (2000). *Experiences in math for young children* (4th ed.). Albany, NY: Delmar.

Cohen, D. H., & Stern, V. (1983). *Observing and recording the behavior of young children* (3rd ed.). New York: Teachers College Press.

Coody, B. (1992). *Using literature with young children* (4th ed.). Dubuque, IA: William C. Brown.

Fillmore, L. W. (1993, Summer). Educating citizens for a multicultural 21st century. *Multicultural Education,* 10–12, 37.

Kratcoski, A. M., & Katz, K. B. (1998). Conversing with young language learners in the classroom. *Young Children, 53*(3), 30–33.

Lay-Dopyera, M. & Dopyera, J. E. (1982). *Becoming a teacher of young children* (2nd ed.). Lexington, MA: D. C. Heath.

NAEYC. (1998). Learning to read and write: Developmentally appropriate practices for young children. A joint position statement of the International Reading Association (IRA) and the National Association for the Education of Young Children (NAEYC). *Young Children, 53*(4), 30–45.

Neuman, D. B. (1978). *Experiences in science for young children.* Albany, NY: Delmar.

Rasco, C. H. (1997). *Early childhood development and the America reads challenge* [On-line]. Available http://www.ed.gov/offices/OERI/ECI/newsletters/97fall/early1.html.

Read, K. H. (1976). *The nursery school: Human relationships and learning* (6th ed.). Philadelphia: W. B. Saunders.

Schickedanz, J. A. (1999). *Much more than the abc's.* Washington, DC: National Association for the Education of Young Children.

Seefeldt, C. & Galper, A. (1998). *Continuing issues in early childhood education* (2nd ed.). Upper Saddle River, NJ: Merrill.

Weiner, I. B., & Elkind, D. (1972). *Child development: A core approach.* New York: John Wiley & Sons.

CHAPTER 10

Professional Growth: *Success with Curriculum Management*

Curriculum Profile

Students who bravely ask questions find that they can advance important issues benefiting their college classmates. Toward the end of the semester, it is rewarding to interact with students who have progressed successfully through the course content. New words and concepts introduced at the beginning of the semester become part of your regular vocabulary. As you begin to "speak the language of Early Childhood Education," you do so with a commitment to the profession. During the initial teacher preparation period and during ongoing professional development, it is valuable to know how and where to access the volume of applicable knowledge for continued study and review as an Early Childhood educator.

Chapter Outline

Main Points of Curriculum Management
Benefits for Children, Families, and Staff
Will the Curriculum Plan Meet Program Guidelines?
Periodic Review—A Team Effort
Professional Preparation and Growth
Professional Commitment
Preparation
Professional Growth
Challenges for Early Childhood Educators

Study Guide

As you study the sections in this chapter, you should be able to:

- Learn the major points of curriculum management.
- Review curricular guidelines.
- Consider the value of the team effort in planning curriculum activities.
- Explore the significance of professional commitment.
- Understand professional training, growth, and child advocacy.

MAIN POINTS OF CURRICULUM MANAGEMENT

Perfecting your curriculum planning is essential to your development as an Early Childhood teacher. Planning with specific strategies will help you to secure a sense of predictability and confidence in your work with young children. These skills will increase the probability that your program will be one of quality.

Besides creating a secure and stable environment, when you plan and manage curriculum you maximize your time more efficiently. This increases opportunities for quality interaction among the staff and children. You will also find that you have more individualized time for the children and that your interaction with the families increases.

Benefits for Children, Families, and Staff

You have read about the importance of addressing the children's needs, allowing them to discover, to create, and to play. The preparation of a plan does necessitate that you consider the varied methods for presenting activities. You need to decide what curriculum approach best fits your program and the specific children enrolled in your program. You need to address quality standards. You will find a balance, within your own a perspective, that permits an inclusive framework with the use of a variety of approaches (Miller, 1999, p. 46).

Planning requires that the teachers meet regularly to collectively map out the way that the children's needs will be met most appropriately. The outcome of **team planning** is a balance of activities among the different curriculum areas and the Developmental Focus areas. Continuous review of the planned activities enforces a valuable aspect of curriculum planning: modification of activities in ways that will best meet the children's needs. Improved utilization of the facility and activity resources will also increase. When the teachers know what is expected of them, they are able to concentrate on supporting the children's needs. When parents know what is expected to happen, they know how they can best be of help. Planning also helps establish a common attitude among the staff members to work together to formulate a strategy with a common sense of purpose (Hildebrand & Hearron, 1997, p. 76).

Helping parents to appreciate their children by sharing and displaying your curriculum plans will be an additional benefit. Parents will begin to think differently about their children, and gain respect for how they learn and for you as a professional committed to promoting well-planned and validated activities. (Hildebrand & Hearron, 1997, p. 399).

Will the Curriculum Plan Meet Program Guidelines?

The **curricular guideline** designed for your school will affect the children directly. Guidelines will also influence the schedule and activities and determine the way in which the teachers interact with the children and their families. There is no consensus detailing which approach to curriculum planning is best for children. Instead, ideas about curriculum that you set will change as you and the teaching members of staff acquire new knowledge about child development and learning during early childhood. The guidelines of your program will also be impacted by events and changes in wider society (Click, 2000, p. 99).

Management tools, especially a manual containing the policies, procedures, and the curricular guidelines, will facilitate efficient management of the program and the curriculum (Sciarra & Dorsey, 1998, p. 470).

Periodic Review—A Team Effort

The presence of a team effort certainly has positive implications for the entire program. The team spirit is essential for creating strong interpersonal relations and is key for successful program planning. Because you are a teacher, you are part of an organization. This calls on you to work with colleagues (Arends, 1991, p. 381).

Planning requires that teachers meet regularly to collectively map out the way that the children's needs will be met most appropriately.

You may receive help from the director to become acquainted with your own style of interpersonal interaction. Welcome the program manager who visits your classroom daily to offer support. The director's sensitive feedback to your activity planning and implementation will help you achieve the curricular guidelines that you have formulated. Supportive staff will help you to become a major figure in the implementation of a caring environment for children and adults (Sciarra & Dorsey, 1998, p. 469).

Periodic review of long-range curriculum plans and activities will be most productive when those participating in the meeting know what to expect. Teachers, especially those with limited time, need to feel that their time is well spent. A prepared agenda contributes to the importance of the meeting and the collaborative planning process. Topics listed on an agenda tend to keep the discussion focused allowing input from more of the meeting participants. Think about this notion as you consider working as a team, "a vision can only become a force when people believe they can actually shape their future" (Senge, 1990, p. 231).

PROFESSIONAL PREPARATION AND GROWTH

You keep hearing that the more you learn about children, the more you will want to learn. While this thought applies to all subject areas, you as a teacher of young children must especially appreciate learning with a beginning glimpse into the educational perspectives and theories translated into teaching methods. Yet, have you thought about the way you learn? What motivates you to continue seeking knowledge? What should you know? There are numerous ways to energize your motivation for inquiry: collaborating with your peers in study sessions, scheduling unique staff meetings away from the center, and general curriculum sharing. The children will also further motivate you because their enthusiasm for learning will compel you to seek more answers and find better ways to meet their needs (Swick, DaRos, & Pavia, 1998/99, p. 67).

Professional Commitment

The two words, *professional* and *commitment*, go together. Textbooks and professional journals detail the significance of both. A professional is an individual who is in some way related to a profession and is engaged in an occupation as a career. An occupation requires special preparation and education, unlike a hobby or casual volunteer participation. An Early Childhood professional is engaged in the care and education of young children, ages newborn to eight years old, as a career and has committed to training and/or some type of certification that may include documented experience (Barnhart & Barnhart, 1990, p. 1661; Seaver, Cartwright, Ward, Heasley, 1979, p. 7). The commitment affirms learning as a continuous adventure with lifelong benefits.

Professional commitment begins with your own perception about your career. We want all teachers of young children to *want* to be there each day. Remember, this is as much fun as you make it! Yet you still need to continually clarify what is important and the responsibilities that you assume as an Early Childhood Education professional. Review your options: typical and available career paths, work requirements and compensation, and your skills and interest in young children and their families (Seaver, Cartwright, Ward, Heasley, 1979, p. 7).

The responsibilities you assume will be to the children, of course. You will also form a strong partnership with the children's parents. Teachers of young children are also parent educators. This implies that you are responsible for consistency between the children's homes and the program. The strong links you establish between the school and the children's homes will be advantageous for parent support and education. You will be competent as a professional when you help parents enjoy parenthood and feel competent about their parenting skills (Rodd, 1994, p. 148).

With the Early Childhood Education commitment to children and families in this society ranking as a priority, particular attention needs to be given to gender equity within the profession. Studies suggest that "men are likely to become more involved with children if appropriate opportunities" are provided. One strategy is to offer opportunities to men to participate in activities that may lead to Early Childhood care and education employment. It has also been suggested that the reactions to male involvement need to be addressed (Fagan, 1996, p. 65, 67, 68). Hiring and retraining men calls for programs to recognize the value of male teachers. The probability that male teachers will remain in programs may be related to what and how they feel in the setting. Are there posters of children with men, work uniforms modified to accommodate both men and women, and do in-service topics specifically refer to fathers and men? (Cunningham, 1999, p. 69).

Professional commitment encompasses your dedication to continue learning, appreciate others, model for young children, and respond to the needs of your co-workers. Professional satisfaction may be achieved with trusting and cooperative behaviors. Create a respectful setting by sharing resources and information with staff members (Katz & Ward, 1989, p. 33). One of the ways you can support staff, and future teachers, is to be a mentor. Once you have reached a level of confidence, share these abilities with a student teacher, a parent, or a volunteer. Demonstrate your commitment with ongoing advocacy for quality care and education.

Child advocacy gained prominence in 1990 (Hymes, 1991, p. 414) as a movement to connect knowledge about children and early education in ways that affect their lives (Seefeldt & Galper, 1998, p. 30). Support your colleagues in your own center and collaborate with teachers in other programs. Membership in one or more professional organizations connects you with many other professionals (Figure 10–1). Initiatives to improve the quality of life for children have created new organizations such as Stand for Children and Center for the Child Care Workforce. Participation opens professional opportunities for you to attend meetings and conferences. Larger organizations establish public policy and distribute information for you to share with parents and the local community groups as a professional and as an advocate for young children.

Preparation

Professional preparation for a career requires some form of preparedness, training, and experience in the occupational area. In Early Childhood Education, components of preparation include experience, training, and knowledge in child development, teaching and curriculum, health and safety, guidance, family relationships, diversity, and management (Taylor, 1997, p. 229). Access to educational preparation and employment requirements vary by state. Research, however, has made it clear that staff with formal credentials provide higher quality care and education for young children (NCEDL, 1999, p. 4). Early Childhood professionals who are knowledgeable about young children and quality child care understand that positive caregiving and language stimulation influence the children's cognitive development and their use of language (NICHD, 1997, pp. 1–2).

Points of entry into the profession vary, as do the listing and labeling of the positions on career ladders, such as teacher assistant, associate teacher, and Early Childhood teacher. The Child Development Associate Credential (CDA) provides competency-based training and evaluation and is administered by the Council for Early Childhood Professional Recognition. CDAs are awarded to candidates who

Professional commitment includes your dedication to young children.

FIGURE 10–1   Early Childhood Professional Organizations—Limited List

ACEI	Association for Childhood Education International 11501 Georgia Avenue, Suite 315 Wheaton, MD 20902 http://www.udel.edu/bateman/acei/
AMS	American Montessori Society 150 5th Avenue, Suite #203 New York, NY 10011 http://www.careguide.net/ams/home.html
AMI	Association Montessori Internationale 170 W. Scholfield Road Rochester, NY 14617–4599
ASCD	Association for Supervision and Curriculum Development 1250 N. Pitt Street Alexandria, VA 22314–1403 http://www.ascd.org/
CEC	Council for Exceptional Children Division of Early Childhood 1920 Association Drive Reston, VA 22091–1589 http://www.cec.org/
CDA	Council for Early Childhood Professional Recognition 1341 G. Street N.W. Washington, D.C. 20005–3105
NAEYC	National Association for the Education of Young Children 1509 16th Street N.W. Washington, D.C. 20036 http://www.naeyc.org
NAFDC	National Association for Family Day Care 725 15th Street N.W. Washington, D.C. 20005–2201
NCCA	National Child Care Association 1016 Rosser Street Conyers, GA 30012 http://www.nccanet.org/
SECA	Southern Early Childhood Association P.O. Box 56130 Little Rock, AR 72215–6130

meet the six core competency areas of the credential (Sciarra & Dorsey, 1998, p. 39). Two- and four-year colleges and universities offer certificates and degrees primarily with a sequence of classes for the teacher, including core courses about child development, family and community, curriculum, guidance, diversity, and inclusion.

Professional Growth

Professional growth is part of the commitment process. It may be a component of employment, necessary for renewal of certification and credentials, or your educational interest to improve caring and teaching strategies. Professional growth offers the chance to gather new curriculum ideas, acquire knowledge about current research, and to collaborate with others in the profession. The outcome of well-planned professional growth is the sense of fresh energy. Workshops, conferences, in-service training, and formal courses allow teachers to review and evaluate the process of lifelong learning.

It is recommended that professional development focus on the needs of the participating teachers. Did anyone conduct a survey to determine what the staff knows and wants to know? Professional development needs to be ongoing because application of new knowledge takes time. Professional growth should view the participants as "intellectuals, engaged in the pursuit of answers to genuine questions, problems, and curiosities." Do the planned professional development options encourage relationships with other teachers and suggest that you think about the perspectives (Vukelich & Wrenn, 1999, pp. 154–158), as well as ways to appropriately apply the information to your profession of Early Childhood?

CHALLENGES FOR EARLY CHILDHOOD EDUCATORS

At this time you are concentrating on your coursework and the application of that knowledge. However, you have been asked to think about what you want for children. The challenges facing teachers are great: bridging programs to benefit parents, family-friendly policies, accessibility to career preparation, compensation, and accountability for our programs. You can translate the challenges into a commitment to create more inclusive and caring places for children. As a teacher, you continuously model for the children, their families, and the community. Remain knowledgeable about children and how they behave and learn. Renew your understanding of the many ways to approach curriculum and activity planning. Appreciate the diversity of our cultures and prepare yourself to deliver knowledge with a variety of teaching methods. Endorse only those tools of the information age that are appropriate for use during the early years of childhood. Keep focused on your commitment to the profession and on being an advocate for curriculum that is meaningful for young children.

REVIEW

Early Childhood teachers who strive for quality programs for young children, their families, and communities face many challenges. Creating inclusive and caring programs requires that teachers have ongoing opportunities for inservice education and staff collaboration. Teachers who are given these opportunities are more likely to plan curriculum that will meet the children's needs appropriately. Team planning encourages positive staff interactions and directions for continuous curriculum review and organization. There are many points of entry into the field of Early Childhood. Preparation for this professional career requires some form of preparedness, including experience and academic study. Research clearly shows that staff with formal credentials provide higher quality care and education of young children. Professional growth, in the form of inservice workshops, conferences, and formal course work, allows teachers to review and evaluate in order to continue advocating for curriculum that is meaningful for young children.

KEY TERMS

child advocacy	professional growth
curricular guideline	professional
professional	preparation
commitment	team planning

RESPOND

1. Meet with a member of an Early Childhood professional organization. Discuss the benefits that the organization provides to members. Accompany, if possible, the member to a local meeting.
2. List your experiences and academic preparation in Early Childhood curriculum. List the areas in which you need workshops and/or course work. Research where this professional preparation will be offered during the next year.
3. Prepare a response to the negative remarks heard from persons outside the field of early childhood regarding the profession. List the remarks and thoughtful responses.
4. Log on to the following two Web sites. Provide the name, address, phone, and president's name for each professional organization.

    http://www.naeyc.org

    http://www.udel.edu/bateman.acei/

REFERENCES

Arends, R. I. (1991). *Learning to teach* (2nd ed.). New York: McGraw-Hill.

Barnhart, C. L., & Barnhart, R. K. (Eds.). (1990). *The world book dictionary.* Chicago: World Book.

Click, P. M. (2000). *Administration of schools for young children* (5th ed.). Albany, NY: Delmar.

Cunningham, B. (1999). Hiring and retaining male staff. *Child Care Information Exchange, 125,* 66–69.

Fagan, J. (1996). Principles for developing male involvement programs in early childhood settings: A personal experience. *Young Children, 51*(4), 64–70.

Hildebrand, V., & Hearron, P. R. (1997). *Management of child development centers* (4th ed.). Upper Saddle River, NJ: Merrill.

Hymes, J. L. (1991). *Early childhood education: Twenty years in review, a look at 1971–1990.* Washington, DC: National Association for the Education of Young Children.

Katz, L. G., & Ward, E. H. (1989). *Ethical behavior in early childhood education.* Washington, DC: NAEYC.

Miller, J. P. (1999). Making connections through holistic learning. *Educational Leadership, 56*(4), 46–48.

NCEDL. (1999). http://www.fpg.unc.edu/~ncedl/PAGES/wnew.htm. National Center for Early Development & Learning (1999 April 4).

NICHD. (1997). Results of NICHD study of early child care. http://www.hih.gov/nichd/html/news/re4top.htm. National Institute of Child Health and Human Development (1998, 25 April).

Rodd, J. (1994). *Leadership in early childhood: The pathway to professionalism.* St. Leonards, Australia: Teachers College Press.

Sciarra, D. J., & Dorsey, A. G. (1998). *Developing and administering a child care center* (4th ed.). Albany, NY: Delmar.

Seefeldt, C. & Galper, A. (1998). *Continuing issues in early childhood education* (2nd ed.). Upper Saddle River, NJ: Merrill.

Seaver, J. W., Cartwright, C. A., Ward, C. B., & Heasley, C. A. (1979). *Careers with young children: Making your decision.* Washington, DC: National Association for the Education of Young Children.

Senge, P. M. (1990). *The fifth discipline: The art & practices of the learning organization.* New York: Doubleday Currency.

Swick, K. J., DaRos, D., & Pavia, L. (1998/99). Inquiry as key to early childhood teacher education. *Childhood Education, 75*(2), 66–70.

Vukelich, C. & Wrenn, L. C. (1999). Quality professional development: What do we think we know? *Childhood Education, 75*(3), 153–160.

Taylor, B. J. (1997). *Early childhood program management: People and procedures* (3rd ed.). Upper Saddle River, NJ: Merrill.

APPENDIX A

Curriculum Activity Guides

Curriculum Activity Guide 1

Marble Painting

Goal: To allow children to experience painting with marbles

Curriculum Area	**Developmental Focus**	**Location/Interest Center**
Art	Affective—Aesthetic	Inside Art

Participants	**Time**	**Age Range**
1 to 4 children	5 to 10 minutes	3 and 4 years old

Materials

Marbles (large and small)
Box lids
Tempera paint, mixed medium thin, in open containers
Paper cut to fit box lid
Plastic spoons
Permanent marking pen

Preparation/Setup

1. Cut paper to fit box lids.
2. Mix paint to desired consistency.
3. Place 1 large and 1 small marble in each container with spoon.

Teaching Strategies

1. Write child's name on paper prior to activity.
2. Child uses spoon to place 2 marbles in lid.
3. Child rolls marble on paper by tilting lid.

Possible Outcomes

Concepts
You can paint in different ways.
Marbles roll.

Skills
Aesthetic pleasure
Introduction to new Art medium

Vocabulary
Marble, roll, paint

Curriculum Activity Guide 2

Planting Seeds

Goal: To allow children to observe the process of plant growth

Curriculum Area	**Developmental Focus**	**Location/Interest Center**
Science	Cognitive—Discovery	Outside Garden

Participants	**Time**	**Age Range**
1 to 4 children	5 to 10 minutes	Appropriate for all ages

Materials

Seeds (bean seeds work well)
Potting soil
Individual plastic flower pots (can use Styrofoam cups)
Water
Plastic spoons
Permanent marking pen

Preparation/Setup

1. Presoak beans for 2 to 3 hours (for quickest growth).
2. Gather materials, set up table outside.

Teaching Strategies

1. Talk to children about seeds. Discuss growing.
2. Child uses spoon to put potting soil in his or her pot.
3. Child places 1 to 2 seeds in the pot, covers with soil.
4. Teacher writes child's name on pot.
5. Child waters pot and places in sunny location.

Possible Outcomes

Concepts
Plants grow from seeds.
Seeds need soil, water, and sun to grow.

Skills
Exposure to Science concept of plant growth

Vocabulary
Seed, roots, plant, grow, soil

Curriculum Activity Guide 3

Body Tracing

Goal: To allow the child to experience body parts through a new medium

Curriculum Area	**Developmental Focus**	**Location/Interest Center**
Art	Affective—Emotional	Outside Art

Participants	**Time**	**Age Range**
Individual child	5 to 10 minutes	Appropriate for all ages

Materials
Butcher paper
Crayons or non-toxic felt pens
Masking tape

Preparation/Setup
1. Locate butcher paper, crayons, tape.
2. Clear area indoors or outdoors in a space appropriate for tracing.

Teaching Strategies
1. Teacher invites individual child to lay down on paper.
2. Teacher draws around child while naming body parts.
3. Teacher invites child to draw or paint their tracing.
4. Tracings can be taped on fence or building for child to complete.

Possible Outcomes

Concepts
My body has different parts.
No one else has my body.

Skills
Introduction to body part names
Develops sense of individuality

Vocabulary
Body, head, neck, arms, legs, trunk

Curriculum Activity Guide 4

Sociodramatic Play (Special Equipment)

Goal: To allow children to explore use of special equipment

Curriculum Area	**Developmental Focus**	**Location/Interest Center**
Social Understanding	Affective—Social	Outside Dramatic Play

Participants	**Time**	**Age Range**
1 to 4 children	10 to 20 minutes	4 and 5 years old

Materials
Pediatric wheelchairs
Pediatric crutches
Laminated pictures of authentic inclusion of children and adults with special needs

Preparation/Setup
1. Locate pictures of children and adults using special equipment, involved in activities.
2. Locate pediatric wheelchairs and crutches to borrow.
3. Set up Grouptime carpets.

Teaching Strategies
1. Introduce topic of special equipment at a Grouptime, using props and pictures.
2. Engage children in discussion of the necessity of special equipment.
3. Engage children in discussion of alike/different.
4. Model using the equipment with children, set up area outside for children to use.

Possible Outcomes
Concepts
Some people use special equipment to help them.
People who use special equipment can do many things.
I can see what it's like to try some special equipment.

Skills
Sense of empathy
Exposure to new concept

Vocabulary
Wheelchair, crutches, braces

Curriculum Activity Guide 5

Colors in Nature

Goal: The children will experience observing the colors in nature

Curriculum Area	**Developmental Focus**	**Location/Interest Center**
Science	Cognitive—Discovery	Unselected

Participants	**Time**	**Age Range**
5 to 8 children	10 to 20 minutes	Appropriate for all ages

Materials
Pictures of colors in nature (animals, plants, groundcovers, etc.)
Toilet paper rolls
Stapler
Hole punch
Yarn

Preparation/Setup
1. Locate and laminate pictures.
2. Gather materials for toilet paper roll "binoculars," assemble with two rolls stapled together, string yarn through holes for neck strap.
3. Set up for Grouptime.

Teaching Strategies
1. Teacher discusses colors in nature at Grouptime, shows pictures.
2. Teacher divides group into 3 to 4 (with adult)—assigns color to observe.
3. Children take nature walk with teachers, observing for "their" color.
4. Teachers facilitate discussion of colors in nature, why certain colors?

Possible Outcomes
Concepts
Most things in nature are browns or greens.
Many animals and insects are camouflaged to hide in nature.
Bright colors stand out in nature.

Skills
Observation skills
Differentiation skills
Introduction to nature

Vocabulary
Color, nature, camouflage, hide, color names

Curriculum Activity Guide 6

Listening Game

Goal: To give the child an opportunity to listen and repeat

| **Curriculum Area** | **Developmental Focus** | **Location/Interest Center** |
| Communication and Literacy | Cognitive—Language | Inside Circle |

| **Participants** | **Time** | **Age Range** |
| 5 to 8 children | 10 to 20 minutes | 3 and 4 years old |

Materials
Puppet (a parrot works well)
Carpet squares for Grouptime or circle game

Preparation/Setup
1. Set up area inside or outside for a small group game.
2. Gather all materials.

Teaching Strategies
1. Teacher gathers children and introduces puppet.
2. Teacher explains concept of "repeating."
3. One child invited up at a time to play repeating game with puppet.
4. Teacher can vary difficulty by whispering, rhyming, using silly sentences.

Possible Outcomes
Concepts
I can listen and repeat what I hear.
I can say silly things to the puppet.
Repeating is saying the same thing again.

Skills
Listening skills
Opportunity to verbalize
Introduction to concept of repetition

Vocabulary
Repeat, rhyme, listen, hear

Curriculum Activity Guide 7

Jumping Frog Obstacle Course

Goal: The children will have the opportunity to jump

Curriculum Area	**Developmental Focus**	**Location/Interest Center**
Movement	Physical—Large Motor	Outside Large Motor

Participants	**Time**	**Age Range**
5 to 8 children	10 to 20 minutes	Appropriate for all ages

Materials

Bicycle tires or hula hoops
Large mats (blue would be nice!)
Sign
Arrows or carpets to indicate starting point and direction

Preparation/Setup

1. Set up a "jumping frog" obstacle course with tires or hoops to jump into, mats to serve as "ponds" to jump into.
2. Make signs with drawings of frogs (or pictures taped on): "Jumping Frog Obstacle Course"; "Frog Pond—Jump In!!"

Teaching Strategies

1. Teacher will discuss how frogs like to jump, may model jumping.
2. Teacher invites children to try the "Jumping Frog Obstacle Course."
3. Children take turns jumping through the course like frogs.
4. Teacher encourages children verbally, "Look at this frog jump!"

Possible Outcomes

Concepts
Frogs jump.
Children can jump like frogs.

Skills
Large motor development
Following directions
Dramatic Play opportunity

Vocabulary
Jump, frog, obstacle course, leap

Curriculum Activity Guide 8

Storybook Reading

Goal: To allow children to explore family roles

Curriculum Area	**Developmental Focus**	**Location/Interest Center**
Social Understanding	Affective—Social	Inside Dramatic Play

Participants	**Time**	**Age Range**
1 to 4 children	20 to 30 minutes	Appropriate for all ages

Materials
Appropriate children's literature (consider illustrations, text, non-bias concerns)

Preparation/Setup
1. Set up area for storybook reading.

Teaching Strategies
1. Teacher introduces the book by discussing the cover—What do you think it will be about?
2. Teacher discusses title page, telling author and illustrator's name.
3. Teacher might discuss Art medium used in illustration (if known).
4. Teacher reads storybook, allowing for feedback.

Possible Outcomes
Concepts
Book covers can tell us something about the story.
Books have an author and an illustrator.
Books have a beginning, a middle, and an end.

Skills
Increased attention span
Exposure to language–literacy opportunity
Aesthetic appreciation for books

Vocabulary
Author, illustrator, cover, read

Curriculum Activity Guide 9

Family Mealtime: Exploring Breads

Goal: The children will have the opportunity to try a variety of breads

Curriculum Area	Developmental Focus	Location/Interest Center
Social Understanding	Affective—Social	Unselected

Participants	Time	Age Range
More than 8 children	10 to 20 minutes	Appropriate for all ages

Materials
Paper plates/napkins
Pictures of different breads
Sign for Parent Area

Preparation/Setup
1. Make sign or notice that you are planning to try a variety of cultural breads.
2. Laminate pictures, hang up sign.

Teaching Strategies
1. Teachers will invite families to contribute cultural breads to share with children.
2. Teacher and children will try various breads and discuss.
3. Teacher will use pictures to make a follow-up bulletin board for the breads tried.
Optional: Children can choose which ones they like best.

Possible Outcomes
Concepts
All cultures eat bread.
Breads have similarities and differences.
We can try different breads.

Skills
Sensory experience
Exposure to cultural diversity
Development of cultural identity

Vocabulary
Bread, tortilla, bagel, croissant, pan, pita, etc.

Curriculum Activity Guide 10

Sociodramatic Play: Becoming a Bus Driver

Goal: The children will have the opportunity to explore the role of bus driver

Curriculum Area	**Developmental Focus**	**Location/Interest Center**
Social Understanding	Affective—Social	Outside Dramatic Play

Participants	**Time**	**Age Range**
5 to 8 children	10 to 20 minutes	3 and 4 years old

Materials
Children's chairs (5 to 8)
Battery operated radio (optional)
Hand-held radio or walkie-talkie (optional)
Pennies or tokens/coffee can
Sign

Preparation/Setup
1. Set up chairs outside in configuration of bus—1 chair in front for a driver—2 rows behind.
2. Set up radio and walkie-talkies for "driver."
3. Cut hole in plastic lid of coffee can to accommodate pennies.
4. Make sign: "Come Ride the Bus."

Teaching Strategies
1. The children will role-play riding and driving the bus, using pennies as fare.
2. Teacher will facilitate children's enactment of bus-driving with interactive questioning, modeling, and supporting.

Possible Outcomes

Concepts
Bus drivers have an important job.
Boys or girls can grow up to be bus drivers.
You must pay a bus fare (money) to ride the bus.

Skills
Role playing skills
Dramatic play skills development
Social interaction skills

Vocabulary
Bus driver, riders, fare

Curriculum Activity Guide 11

Sociodramatic Play: Domestic Scene

Goal: To expose children to role-playing opportunity

Curriculum Area	**Developmental Focus**	**Location/Interest Center**
Social Understanding	Affective—Social	Inside Dramatic Play

Participants	**Time**	**Age Range**
1 to 4 children	20 to 30 minutes	Appropriate for all ages

Materials
Housekeeping props
Men's and women's clothing
Baby clothes, props, and dolls
Non-bias pictures of families and baby nurturing
Cultural clothing

Preparation/Setup
1. Locate appropriate non-bias pictures (laminate and display in Dramatic Play area).
2. Locate clothing and display in area.
3. Set up Dramatic Play area attractively.

Teaching Strategies
1. Introduce clothing commonly worn by both men and women, and by only men or only women at Grouptime.
2. Children freely explore materials and role play in area.

Possible Outcomes
Concepts
Boys and girls can pretend to be mommies and daddies.
Mommies and daddies take care of babies.
Sometimes we wear clothes that look the same and sometimes we do not.

Skills
Exposure to clothing differences
Development of accepting attitude toward differences
Opportunity to role play

Vocabulary
Mommy, daddy, baby, parents, adult, child

Curriculum Activity Guide 12

Free-Choice Activity Time

Goal: To allow children to make individual play choices

Curriculum Area	**Developmental Focus**	**Location/Interest Center**
Social Understanding	Cognitive—Critical Thinking	Inside Circle

Participants
More than 8 children

Time
20 to 30 minutes

Age Range
Appropriate for all ages

Materials
Carpets for Grouptime

Preparation/Setup
Set-up Grouptime area with carpets.

Teaching Strategies
1. Teacher discusses activity-time choices with children at Grouptime ("In the Art Area we have marble painting" . . ., etc.).
2. Teacher asks each child where they are going to play first.
3. Child verbalizes their choice and leaves to go and play.

Possible Outcomes

Concepts
I have lots of choices.
I can decide what kind of play I want to do.
I can play alone or with others.

Skills
Decision making
Socialization
Opportunity for autonomy

Vocabulary
Choice, play, interest center names

Curriculum Activity Guide 13

Introduction to Computer Use

Goal: To expose children to the computer and its use

Curriculum Area	**Developmental Focus**	**Location/Interest Center**
Communication and Literacy	Cognitive—Critical Thinking	Inside Computer

Participants	**Time**	**Age Range**
1 to 4 children	5 to 10 minutes	3 and 4 years old

Materials
Computer keyboard
Computer mouse
Mousepad
Sign-making materials

Preparation/Setup
1. Set up Grouptime next to computer and bulletin board (if possible).
2. Bring keyboard, mouse, and mouse pad to Grouptime.
3. Gather sign-making materials.

Teaching Strategies
1. Introduce the computer parts to children at Grouptime.
2. Discuss appropriate use of computers (no wet or dirty hands).
3. Involve children in making signs to discuss computer rules.
4. Post signs near computer.

Possible Outcomes
Concepts
Computers need special care.
Children can use computers.
Computer parts have special names.

Skills
Increased knowledge of computers
Exposure to new concept

Vocabulary
Keyboard, mouse, mousepad, computer

Curriculum Activity Guide 14

Parent Visit

Goal: To allow children to explore family roles

Curriculum Area	**Developmental Focus**	**Location/Interest Center**
Social Understanding	Affective—Social	Inside Dramatic Play

Participants	**Time**	**Age Range**
1 to 4 children	20 to 30 minutes	Appropriate for all ages

Materials

Survey of interests/talents of parents
Letter or note inviting parent to visit classroom (may specify to bring in cultural items)

Preparation/Setup

1. Review parent surveys and/or children's files.
2. Call or write note to parent.

Teaching Strategies

1. Welcome parent into classroom, inviting them to join or observe.
2. Introduce the parent to the children informally, as children approach.
3. Invite the parent (and child) to share what they've brought at Grouptime.
4. Observe the parent/child interactions.

Possible Outcomes

Concepts
Every family is different.
Every family is alike.
All children have families.

Skills
Exposure to new cultural information
Development of accepting attitude toward cultural differences
Expanding sense of community

Vocabulary
Visitor, specific cultural terms

Curriculum Activity Guide 15

Let's Help the Birds!

Goal: To allow the child to provide nesting materials for birds

Curriculum Area	Developmental Focus	Location/Interest Center
Science	Cognitive—Discovery	Outside Garden

Participants	Time	Age Range
1 to 4 children	5 to 10 minutes	Appropriate for all ages

Materials
Bird nests and/or pictures of bird nests
Plastic berry baskets
Yarn, thread, string, plastic "grass", tinsel, etc.

Preparation/Setup
1. Locate bird nests/pictures.
2. Tie yarn loop on basket for hanging.
3. Display yarns, threads, etc. on tray.

Teaching Strategies
1. Discuss birds and nest making, show examples.
2. Explain that birds look for materials for their nests.
3. Child pushes yarns, strings, etc. through holes in basket, leaving ends dangling free.
4. Teacher assists children in hanging baskets from trees.

Possible Outcomes
Concepts
Birds make nests.
Nests can be made from many things.
We can help the birds.

Skills
Fine motor skill
Introduction to Science concept
Appreciation for nature

Vocabulary
Bird, nest, nesting

Curriculum Activity Guide 16

Manipulatives

Goal: To allow the child an opportunity to interact with manipulatives

Curriculum Area	**Developmental Focus**	**Location/Interest Center**
Movement	Physical—Small Motor	Inside Manipulative

Participants	**Time**	**Age Range**
1 to 4 children	5 to 10 minutes	Appropriate for all ages

Materials
Variety of manipulatives in tubs or on trays such as puzzles, stacking cubes, and matching colors

Preparation/Setup
1. Offer attractive manipulatives on shelves.
2. May decide to put out a tub or tray on table to stimulate interest.

Teaching Strategies
1. Children work independently (with a tray) or together (with a tub) of manipulatives.
2. Teacher facilitates exploration while allowing independent use.
3. Children are encouraged to put away materials when finished.

Possible Outcomes
Concepts
I can put things together and take them apart.
I can work by myself or with my friends.

Skills
Fine motor
Eye–hand coordination
Cooperation

Vocabulary
Manipulative, stacking, sorting

Curriculum Activity Guide 17

Let's Look It Up!

Goal: To allow the child to discover information about an interest

Curriculum Area	**Developmental Focus**	**Location/Interest Center**
Science	Cognitive—Discovery	Inside Quiet—Reading

Participants	**Time**	**Age Range**
1 to 4 children	5 to 10 minutes	Appropriate for all ages

Materials
Science reference books
Science software for computer
Variety of insect/bug visiting containers

Preparation/Setup
1. Teacher is always prepared for spontaneous sharing of Science materials.
2. Pull out appropriate reference materials, containers, as needed.

Teaching Strategies
1. Child brings in an insect or butterfly, wants to know about it.
2. Teacher tells child that they will "look it up" together.
3. Teacher facilitates child placing insect in a safe viewing container.
4. Teacher and child look it up together.
5. Teacher and child cooperate to make a sign.
6. Release insect safely.

Possible Outcomes
Concepts
I can discover more about my interest.
Nature is fragile, we must be respectful.
I can let something go back to nature.

Skills
Introduction to reference, computers
Stimulates curiosity

Vocabulary
Reference, look up, discover, release

Curriculum Activity Guide 18

What Kind of Muffin?

Goal: The children will have the opportunity to make a choice about a muffin

Curriculum Area	**Developmental Focus**	**Location/Interest Center**
Health, Safety, Nutrition	Affective—Social	Unselected
Participants	**Time**	**Age Range**
More than 8 children	10 to 20 minutes	Appropriate for all ages

Materials

Recipe and materials for plain muffins
Bowls of seeds, nuts, dried fruit, wheat germ, chopped fresh fruit, etc.
Paper muffin/cupcake cups

Preparation/Setup

1. Set up for a Cooking activity.
2. Assemble all materials.

Teaching Strategies

1. Children and teacher wash hands.
2. Children help make plain muffins.
3. Each child chooses 2 items to add to their muffins.
4. Teacher labels child's muffin paper, bakes muffins.
5. Children get to eat their muffins at a snacktime, comparing choices.

Possible Outcomes

Concepts
Muffins can be changed by adding different ingredients.
Children can make choices for themselves.

Skills
Decision-making skills
Social interaction
Nutrition information exposure

Vocabulary
Muffin, choice, nuts, seeds, fruit, etc.

Curriculum Activity Guide 19

Cultural Pattern Match

Goal: The children will have the opportunity to explore cultural patterns

Curriculum Area	**Developmental Focus**	**Location/Interest Center**
Social Understanding	Cognitive—Critical Thinking	Inside Manipulative

Participants	**Time**	**Age Range**
Individual child	Under 5 minutes	3 and 4 years old

Materials

Tray, mat outlined
Small containers for fabric swatches
Cultural fabrics with distinct patterns

Preparation/Setup

1. Locate and cut fabrics with distinct patterns into uniform size.
2. Outline and laminate a mat for the activity tray.
3. Set up tray with containers and fabrics.

Teaching Strategies

1. Teacher sets out activity tray on shelf.
2. Children explore the properties of the fabric, matching and comparing.
3. Teacher can facilitate by asking open-ended questions.
4. Teacher can reinforce learning by explaining **where** the fabrics originate from.

Possible Outcomes

Concepts
All cultures use fabrics.
Fabrics from different parts of the world are unique.
There are many beautiful patterns and fabrics around the world.

Skills
Differentiation/discrimination skills
Observational skills
Exposure to cultural diversity

Vocabulary
Pattern, fabric, culture, names of countries or cultures

Curriculum Activity Guide 20

Hands, Eyes, and Nose Tell Me

Goal: The children will have the opportunity to use their senses

Curriculum Area	**Developmental Focus**	**Location/Interest Center**
Science	Cognitive—Discovery	Unselected

Participants	**Time**	**Age Range**
1 to 4 children	5 to 10 minutes	3 and 4 years old

Materials

Sensory table
Fresh herbs (basil, mint, dill, etc.)
Blindfold
Large bowls (4)

Preparation/Setup

1. Purchase herbs.
2. Set up sensory table with herbs mixed in together in four bowls (1 for each child).

Teaching Strategies

1. Teacher invites children to the sensory table to explore herbs.
2. Children are invited to sort the herbs by sight.
3. Children are challenged to use the blind fold to sort herbs by feel and smell.
4. Teacher facilitates children's exploration by discussion of herbs and senses.

Possible Outcomes

Concepts
Herbs have a different smell, look, and feel.
People use herbs to cook.
Herbs can be distinguished by their appearance, feel, and smell.

Skills
Sensory exploration
Differentiation
Mathematical skill development—comparison, sorting

Vocabulary
Herbs, names of each herb, smell, touch, see

Curriculum Activity Guide 21

Art Appreciation

Goal: To allow children an opportunity to develop aesthetic appreciation of art

Curriculum Area	Developmental Focus	Location/Interest Center
Art	Affective—Aesthetic	Inside Art

Participants	Time	Age Range
1 to 4 children	10 to 20 minutes	Appropriate for all ages

Materials
Art reproduction posters, calendar art, or art books
Corresponding art medium (watercolor, chalk, etc.)
Paint smocks, table cover

Preparation/Setup
1. Familiarize yourself with Art medium used in example.
2. Locate and set up appropriate Art materials.
3. Cover table, provide paint smocks.

Teaching Strategies
1. Teacher introduces artist's work, describes medium used.
2. Children examine artist's work, discuss.
3. Children explore Art medium on their own work.
4. Display children's work and artist's work together.

Possible Outcomes
Concepts
I am an artist.
I enjoy the work of artists.
Different Art mediums create different looks.

Skills
Exposure to quality artwork
Decision making skills
Aesthetic appreciation

Vocabulary
Artist, medium

Curriculum Activity Guide 22

The Three Bears: Creative Dramatics

Goal: To allow children an opportunity to dramatize a familiar story

Curriculum Area	**Developmental Focus**	**Location/Interest Center**
Creative Dramatics	Affective—Social	Inside Dramatic Play

Participants	**Time**	**Age Range**
1 to 4 children	10 to 20 minutes	3 and 4 years old

Materials

A "Three Bears" storybook
Three chairs
Three plastic bowls and spoons
Three mats, or blankets to serve as beds

Preparation/Setup

1. Locate props.
2. Set up Dramatic Play area as for the bear's house.

Teaching Strategies

1. Teacher reads a "The Three Bears" storybook at Grouptime.
2. Teacher explains that props are available in Dramatic Play area to act out the story.
3. Children use props to freely act out story.

Possible Outcomes

Concepts
We can act out stories.
We can take turns playing parts.

Skills
Social interaction
Cooperation
Opportunity for affective development

Vocabulary
Actor, drama

Curriculum Activity Guide 23

We All Have Families

Goal: To allow children to explore concept of family

Curriculum Area	**Developmental Focus**	**Location/Interest Center**
Social Understanding	Affective—Social	Inside Circle

Participants	**Time**	**Age Range**
5 to 8 children	10 to 20 minutes	Appropriate for all ages

Materials

Books, pictures of variety of families (authentically inclusive, representing diverse and mixed groups)
Lined paper for dictation
Plain paper for drawing
Marking pens

Preparation/Setup

1. Locate books, pictures.
2. Set up materials for extension of Grouptime at Art table.

Teaching Strategies

1. Teacher introduces concept of families at Grouptime, shares book and/or pictures.
2. Discuss the children's family make-up, similarities, differences.
3. Extend Grouptime at art table, with opportunity to draw family.
4. Take child's dictation about their drawing.

Possible Outcomes

Concepts
We all have families.
Families are alike and different too.

Skills
Exposure to concept
Development of self-identity
Acceptance of difference

Vocabulary
Family, family names, same, different

Curriculum Activity Guide 24

Neighborhood Field Trip

Goal: To allow children to explore their neighborhood

Curriculum Area	**Developmental Focus**	**Location/Interest Center**
Social Understanding	Affective—Social	Unselected

Participants	**Time**	**Age Range**
More than 8 children	20 to 30 minutes	Appropriate for all ages

Materials
Field trip backpack (emergency cards, first aid kit, tissues, 2-way radio, etc.)

Preparation/Setup
1. Make prior arrangements with neighborhood business.
2. Arrange for maximum staffing, parent help.
3. Secure all necessary signed permission slips.
4. Set up for Grouptime to discuss trip.

Teaching Strategies
1. Teacher will discuss field trip with children, prewarning about expected behaviors, what they will see, etc.
2. Teachers and parents hold hands with children on walk.
3. One teacher facilitates and leads discussion.
4. Children cooperate to prepare group thank you dictation project.

Possible Outcomes

Concepts
There are businesses in our neighborhood.
We can walk safely together.

Skills
Social understanding
Social interaction
Exercise

Vocabulary
Neighborhood, business, walk

Curriculum Activity Guide 25

Lotto Game (Individual)

Goal: To allow child to individually explore concept of matching

Curriculum Area	**Developmental Focus**	**Location/Interest Center**
Mathematics	Cognitive—Critical Thinking	Inside Manipulative

Participants	**Time**	**Age Range**
Individual Child	Under 5 minutes	3 and 4 years old

Materials

Lotto game on tray (Example is matching pictures of sand toys)

Preparation/Setup

1. Make or purchase lotto game with gameboard and matching cards.
2. Make a placemat for tray with outlines for board and cards.

Teaching Strategies

1. Child plays matching game, exploring concept.
2. Teacher facilitates child's free exploration of lotto game by limited interaction, as appropriate.
3. Child replaces pieces on tray, returns to shelf.

Possible Outcomes

Concepts
I can match.
Items that look the same are matching.

Skills
Cognitive skills
Exposure to concept of matching
Mathematics skill—one-to-one correspondence

Vocabulary
Match, same, lotto

Curriculum Activity Guide 26

Lotto Game (Small Group)

Goal: To allow child to participate in a group matching game

Curriculum Area	**Developmental Focus**	**Location/Interest Center**
Mathematics	Cognitive—Critical Thinking	Inside Manipulative

Participants	**Time**	**Age Range**
1 to 4 children	5 to 10 minutes	3 and 4 years old

Materials

Lotto game with four game boards and corresponding cards (Example is matching pictures of pets)

Preparation/Setup

1. Make or purchase lotto game with gameboard and matching cards.
2. Make a placemat for tray with outlines for board and cards.

Teaching Strategies

1. Teacher invites children to play a matching game.
2. Each child is given a game board.
3. Teacher describes a card, waits for child to find on board.
4. Children collect "matches" until board is filled.

Possible Outcomes

Concepts
I can match.
I can play a game with my friends.
Items that look the same are matching.

Skills
Listening skills
Cognitive skills
Exposure to concept of matching
Social interaction

Vocabulary
Match, same, lotto

Curriculum Activity Guide 27

Obstacle Course

Goal: The children will have an opportunity to try an obstacle course

Curriculum Area	**Developmental Focus**	**Location/Interest Center**
Movement	Physical—Large Motor	Outside Large Motor

Participants	**Time**	**Age Range**
5 to 8 children	10 to 20 minutes	Appropriate for all ages

Materials
Mats
Tires
Tunnels
Steps, or movable climbers
Freestanding shapes to climb through
Directional arrows

Preparation/Setup
1. Locate all obstacle course materials.
2. Set up an obstacle course, considering the developmental level of the children.
3. Take special care to consider safety, placing mats under higher components.
4. Set up arrows and/or small carpets to designate beginning and end.

Teaching Strategies
1. Teacher will supervise obstacle course area to facilitate safe use.
2. Children can be reminded about taking turns, waiting safely.
3. Teacher uses language to facilitate child's movement vocabulary.

Possible Outcomes
Concepts
I can climb, crawl, jump, etc.
I can try new activities.

Skills
Gross motor development
Sense of achievement

Vocabulary
Climb, crawl, jump, obstacle course

Curriculum Activity Guide 28

Bean Bag Toss

Goal: The children will have an opportunity to toss a bean bag through a target

Curriculum Area	**Developmental Focus**	**Location/Interest Center**
Movement	Physical—Large Motor	Outside Large Motor

Participants	**Time**	**Age Range**
1 to 4 children	5 to 10 minutes	Appropriate for all ages

Materials
Bean bags (3 for each child)
Boxes, baskets, or pre-made target (bucket or box)
Small carpets for waiting children

Preparation/Setup
1. Set up an area outside with targets and carpets for child to stand on while throwing (can be done inside in rainy weather).
2. Set 3 bean bags on each carpet for each child.

Teaching Strategies
1. Invite children to try throwing bean bags at the target (bucket or box).
2. Carpets can be moved closer or farther from the target to accommodate developmental levels of children.

Possible Outcomes
Concepts
I can throw.
I can aim.

Skills
Hand–eye coordination
Perceptual–motor skill

Vocabulary
Bean bag, toss, aim

Curriculum Activity Guide 29

Eyedroppers and Soap Suction

Goal: The children will have an opportunity to use an eyedropper

Curriculum Area	**Developmental Focus**	**Location/Interest Center**
Movement	Physical—Small Motor	Inside Manipulative

Participants	**Time**	**Age Range**
Individual child	5 to 10 minutes	3 and 4 years old

Materials

Plastic eyedroppers
Water with food coloring added in small container
Plastic soap suction holders
Small sponge
Tray

Preparation/Setup

1. Prepare a placemat for tray, outlining all materials.
2. Place materials on tray, place tray on shelf or table.

Teaching Strategies

1. Teacher may need to introduce use of eyedropper.
2. Child squeezes water into eyedropper, placing one drop on each suction cup of the soap holder.
3. When finished, child uses sponge to wipe up water and get it ready for the next child.

Possible Outcomes

Concepts
I can use an eyedropper.
Squeezing the top of an eyedropper pulls the water up.

Skills
Fine motor development
Increased attention span
Concentration

Vocabulary
Eyedropper, squeeze, pull

Curriculum Activity Guide 30

Tweezers and Ice Cube Trays

Goal: The children will have an opportunity to use tweezers

Curriculum Area	**Developmental Focus**	**Location/Interest Center**
Movement	Physical—Small Motor	Inside Manipulative

Participants	**Time**	**Age Range**
Individual child	5 to 10 minutes	3 and 4 years old

Materials
Tray
Plastic ice cube tray
Tweezers
Items to pick up (beans, plastic spiders, pom-poms, etc.) in container

Preparation/Setup
1. Make a placemat for tray, outlining materials.
2. Set up all materials on tray.
3. Items to pick up can change with focus or theme.

Teaching Strategies
1. Encourage child to use tweezers to pick up items and place in compartments of ice cube tray.
2. Child uses tweezers to return items to container when finished.

Possible Outcomes
Concepts
I can use tweezers.
Tweezers are a tool used to pick up very small items.

Skills
Fine motor development
Perceptual motor development
Concentration

Vocabulary
Tweezers, squeeze, small

Curriculum Activity Guide 31

Height Strips

Goal: The children will have an opportunity to experience concept of height

Curriculum Area	**Developmental Focus**	**Location/Interest Center**
Health, Safety, Nutrition	Cognitive—Discovery	Inside Art

Participants	**Time**	**Age Range**
1 to 4 children	10 to 20 minutes	Appropriate for all ages

Materials
Cash register paper rolls
Children's marking pens
Scissors
Adult permanent marker
Optional: tape measure

Preparation/Setup
1. Clear a long table and set out marking pens.
2. Locate paper rolls, scissors.

Teaching Strategies
1. Teacher holds up paper roll to child, informally measuring height.
2. Teacher draws a line across to designate height, writes child's name above.
3. Child draws on his/her strip with markers.
4. Hang on a bulletin board to compare heights.
5. Introduce measuring tape to children who show interest.

Possible Outcomes
Concepts
I am getting taller.
I am taller than some children and shorter than others.
The length of the paper shows my height.

Skills
Mathematical concepts
Creative expression

Vocabulary
Height, tall, measure

Curriculum Activity Guide 32

Trampoline and Stethoscope

Goal: The children will have opportunity to explore heartbeat and exercise

Curriculum Area	**Developmental Focus**	**Location/Interest Center**
Health, Safety, Nutrition	Physical—Large Motor	Outside Large Motor

Participants	**Time**	**Age Range**
1 to 4 children	10 to 20 minutes	3 and 4 years old

Materials

Small trampoline
Carpets for waiting children
Working stethoscope

Preparation/Setup

1. Set up trampoline in safe area outside, away from equipment, trikes.
2. Locate stethoscope.

Teaching Strategies

1. Teacher sits children down for exercise activity, explains how to jump safely.
2. Teacher helps children to feel their heartbeat and listen with stethoscope before exercise.
3. Children jump on trampoline, then listen again.
4. Teacher facilitates understanding of exercise/heartbeat.

Possible Outcomes

Concepts
My heart beats faster when I exercise.
Jumping is an exercise that makes my heart beat faster.
A stethoscope monitors heartbeat.

Skills
Large motor development
Concept of health exercise

Vocabulary
Heartbeat, exercise, trampoline, stethoscope

Curriculum Activity Guide 33

Dial 911

Goal: The children will be exposed to the concept of 911 Emergency

Curriculum Area	**Developmental Focus**	**Location/Interest Center**
Health, Safety, Nutrition	Cognitive—Critical Thinking	Inside Circle
Participants	**Time**	**Age Range**
5 to 8 children	10 to 20 minutes	4 and 5 years old

Materials

Touch-tone phones
Small red circle stickers
Bulletin board with a phone enlarged

Preparation/Setup

1. Make a bulletin board with 911 and phone face enlarged.
2. Locate touchtone phones (not connected).
3. Set up for Grouptime.

Teaching Strategies

1. Teacher will introduce concept of **emergency** at Grouptime.
2. Teacher will discuss calling 911.
3. Teacher will discuss possible scenarios and model them for group.
4. Children will practice dialing 911, teacher acts as operator.
5. Phones placed in Dramatic Play area for continued practice.

Possible Outcomes

Concepts
I can use the phone in an emergency.
There are special people who can help me in an emergency.
Phones are not toys.

Skills
Exposure to important safety concept
Role-playing opportunity

Vocabulary
911, emergency, dial

Curriculum Activity Guide 34

Medicine Is Not Candy

Goal: The children will be exposed to the concept of medicine vs. candy

Curriculum Area	**Developmental Focus**	**Location/Interest Center**
Health, Safety, Nutrition	Cognitive—Critical Thinking	Inside Circle

Participants	**Time**	**Age Range**
5 to 8 children	10 to 20 minutes	3 and 4 years old

Materials

Vitamin bottles (children's)
Prescription medicine bottles
Construction paper and pens for sign

Preparation/Setup

1. Locate all materials, place on tray or in bag or covered plastic box for Grouptime.
2. Set up carpets for Grouptime.

Teaching Strategies

1. Teacher discusses medicine, assesses children's knowledge.
2. Teacher discusses safety of dispensing medicine—who can do it; adult supervision.
3. Children can help teacher make a sign about medicine—"Medicine Is Not Candy."

Possible Outcomes

Concepts
Medicine is not candy.
Only adults can give children medicine; adults supervise.
Medicines can make you sick if you take too much.

Skills
Exposure to important safety concept
Differentiation skill

Vocabulary
Medicine, adult supervision

Curriculum Activity Guide 35

Individual Snack

Goal: The children will make their own healthy snack

Curriculum Area	**Developmental Focus**	**Location/Interest Center**
Health, Safety, Nutrition	Cognitive—Critical Thinking	Unselected

Participants	**Time**	**Age Range**
Individual child	5 to 10 minutes	Appropriate for all ages

Materials

Snack items for each child (peanut butter and celery, crackers with cream cheese, etc.)
Cooking smocks
Utensils for spreading, cutting, etc.
Cooking chart
Paper plates

Preparation/Setup

1. Prepare a visual Cooking chart with pictures of each step.
2. Sanitize Cooking table.
3. Set out Cooking smocks—1 for each child at activity.

Teaching Strategies

1. Children and teacher wash hands and come to Cooking table.
2. Each child prepares their snack and places on paper plate for snacktime.
3. Teacher uses opportunity to discuss healthy eating habits.

Possible Outcomes

Concepts
I can make my own snack.
Healthy foods help us grow.

Skills
Fine motor development
Perceptual–motor development
Exposure to nutrition concepts

Vocabulary
Snack, spread, prepare, healthy

Curriculum Activity Guide 36

Food Collage

Goal: The children will make collages of their favorite healthy foods

Curriculum Area	**Developmental Focus**	**Location/Interest Center**
Health, Safety, Nutrition	Cognitive—Critical Thinking	Inside Art
Participants	**Time**	**Age Range**
5 to 8 children	10 to 20 minutes	3 and 4 years old

Materials

Magazine pictures of food (can be precut)
Scissors
Glue and glue applicators
Paper plates

Preparation/Setup

1. Cover table and set out Art smocks.
2. Arrange all magazine pictures on a tray.
3. Set out glue, scissors, etc. for each child.

Teaching Strategies

1. Children can look through magazine pictures, cut out food pictures.
2. Children glue pictures of favorite healthy foods on paper plates.
3. Teacher facilitates discussion of healthy foods.

Possible Outcomes

Concepts
Healthy foods help us grow.
I like healthy foods.

Skills
Decision making opportunity
Differentiation
Fine motor development

Vocabulary
Healthy foods, vegetable, fruit, etc.

Curriculum Activity Guide 37

Bath Scrubber Toss

Goal: The children will have an opportunity to practice a perceptual motor skill

Curriculum Area	**Developmental Focus**	**Location/Interest Center**
Movement	Physical—Large Motor	Outside Large Motor

Participants	**Time**	**Age Range**
1 to 4 children	10 to 20 minutes	4 and 5 years old

Materials

Baths scrubbers (netting with cords removed)
Plastic gallon milk cartons, or purchased scoops

Preparation/Setup

1. Cut bottom off of plastic milk cartons, leaving handle intact.
2. Locate bath scrubbers, remove cords.
3. Set out a scrubber/carton combination for 1 to 4 children

Teaching Strategies

1. Teacher will model tossing up the scrubber, catching it in carton.
2. Children can practice the skill individually.
3. When competent, they can throw scrubber between pairs, or as a group game.

Possible Outcomes

Concepts
I can catch
I can throw

Skills
Perceptual–motor development
Hand-eye coordination
Socialization

Vocabulary
Catch, throw, toss

Curriculum Activity Guide 38

Coloring to Music

Goal: The children will have an opportunity to experience music combined with art

Curriculum Area	**Developmental Focus**	**Location/Interest Center**
Music and Rhythm	Affective—Social	Inside Art

Participants	**Time**	**Age Range**
1 to 4 children	5 to 10 minutes	4 and 5 years old

Materials

Butcher paper to cover table (round is preferable)
Felt pens/markers
Instrumental music with varying tempo/rhythms
CD or cassette player

Preparation/Setup

1. Cover table with paper and set out markers in center—use no chairs.
2. Set up CD/cassette player nearby.

Teaching Strategies

1. Teacher puts on music, and children draw to the rhythm.
2. Children freely walk around table, drawing to the music.
3. Teacher can facilitate discussion of tempo—fast/slow, etc.
4. Group art project can be displayed for all to enjoy.

Possible Outcomes

Concepts
Music has different tempos.
I can draw with the music's rhythm and tempo.

Skills
Music appreciation
Aesthetic enjoyment
Social interaction

Vocabulary
Music, art, tempo, rhythm

Curriculum Activity Guide 39

Balance Beam

Goal: The children will have an opportunity to walk on a balance beam

Curriculum Area	**Developmental Focus**	**Location/Interest Center**
Movement	Physical—Large Motor	Outside Large Motor

Participants	**Time**	**Age Range**
1 to 4 children	5 to 10 minutes	Appropriate for all ages

Materials

Balance beam—height appropriate for developmental age of children
Arrows or carpets to designate beginning and direction

Preparation/Setup

1. Set up balance beam outside in safe place, away from trike area (grass preferable).
2. Set out carpets with arrows.

Teaching Strategies

1. Teacher supervises balance beam area, making sure one child at a time attempts.
2. Teacher can facilitate younger or unsure children by offering a finger to balance.

Possible Outcomes

Concepts
I can balance.
I can move in one direction.

Skills
Kinesthetic ability development
Coordination
Large motor development

Vocabulary
Balance, direction, balance beam

Curriculum Activity Guide 40

Hopping Like a Popcorn Kernel

Goal: The children will have the opportunity to pretend to be popcorn

Curriculum Area	**Developmental Focus**	**Location/Interest Center**
Creative Dramatics	Affective—Social	Inside Circle

Participants	**Time**	**Age Range**
5 to 8 children	10 to 20 minutes	Appropriate for all ages

Materials
Air popcorn popper
Popcorn
Clean white sheet
Carpets for Grouptime

Preparation/Setup
1. Set up area for Grouptime.
2. Locate popcorn popper, popcorn, take to Grouptime.
3. Locate sheet.

Teaching Strategies
1. Teacher readies children for Grouptime with songs, fingerplays, etc.
2. Teacher introduces popcorn popper—asks the children what they think will happen.
3. Teacher spreads out sheet, begins popping corn directly onto sheet at Grouptime.
4. Children observe and taste cooled popcorn, discussing the experience.
5. Sheet is put away, and children pretend to be small and pop like popcorn kernels.

Possible Outcomes
Concepts
Popcorn pops open from the kernel.
Popcorn makes a sound when it pops open.
Popcorn has a distinct smell.
Children can pretend to be popcorn.

Skills
Sensory experience
Role-playing opportunity
Social interaction

Vocabulary
Popcorn, kernel, pop, popper, hop

Curriculum Activity Guide 41

Dancing with Scarves

Goal: The children will have an opportunity to dance creatively with scarves

Curriculum Area	**Developmental Focus**	**Location/Interest Center**
Music and Rhythm	Physical—Large Motor	Outside Dramatic Play

Participants	**Time**	**Age Range**
1 to 4 children	10 to 20 minutes	Appropriate for all ages

Materials

Basket or tub of assorted colorful scarves
Instrumental CD/cassette with player
Optional: Large mounted mirror

Preparation/Setup

1. Set up in Music area (outside is preferable for space).
2. Designate area for up to 4 participants.

Teaching Strategies

1. Teacher puts music on and invites children to experiment with dancing and scarves.
2. Teacher may facilitate by modeling dancing with children.
3. Teacher can enhance childrens' experience by commenting on tempo, rhythm, etc.

Possible Outcomes

Concepts
I can dance.
Music makes me move and dance.

Skills
Large motor development
Socialization
Music appreciation

Vocabulary
Music, dance, instrument

Curriculum Activity Guide 42

Oatmeal Box Drums

Goal: The children will have an opportunity to beat a rhythm on a drum

Curriculum Area	**Developmental Focus**	**Location/Interest Center**
Music and Rhythm	Physical—Large Motor	Outside Large Motor

Participants	**Time**	**Age Range**
1 to 4 children	10 to 20 minutes	Appropriate for all ages

Materials

Oatmeal boxes (children can pre-decorate with paint, markers)
Instrumental CD/cassette with player

Preparation/Setup

1. Set up an area outside for 4 children to experience drums.
2. Locate an appropriate CD/cassette with rhythmic tempo.

Teaching Strategies

1. Teacher invites children to experiment with "drums."
2. Teacher facilitates the children's experience by joining and modeling.
3. Teacher can vary the instrumental selection to provide different tempos.

Possible Outcomes

Concepts
I can beat a drum.
Music has a rhythm.

Skills
Following directions
Music appreciation

Vocabulary
Drum, beat, rhythm

Curriculum Activity Guide 43

Grouptime with Rhythm Sticks

Goal: The children will have an opportunity to use rhythm sticks at a Grouptime

Curriculum Area	**Developmental Focus**	**Location/Interest Center**
Music and Rhythm	Physical—Large Motor	Inside Circle

Participants	**Time**	**Age Range**
5 to 8 children	5 to 10 minutes	Appropriate for all ages

Materials
Rhythm sticks—2 for each child
Small carpets for Grouptime

Preparation/Setup
1. Set up carpets for Grouptime.
2. Locate rhythm sticks, place in pillowcase, bag, or music box.

Teaching Strategies
1. Settle down children for Grouptime, with active songs, fingerplays.
2. Explain that we will be trying a new instrument.
3. Model the rhythm stick, emphasizing that we will be playing together.
4. Pass out rhythm sticks.
5. Lead children in simple—complex rhythms.

Possible Outcomes
Concepts
We can make music together.
I can follow directions.

Skills
Cooperation
Following directions
Introduction to concept of rhythm

Vocabulary
Rhythm, beat, listen, musical instrument

Curriculum Activity Guide 44

Exploring Feelings

Goal: The children will have an opportunity to identify and explore feelings

Curriculum Area	**Developmental Focus**	**Location/Interest Center**
Social Understanding	Affective—Emotional	Inside Circle

Participants	**Time**	**Age Range**
5 to 8 children	10 to 20 minutes	Appropriate for all ages

Materials
Pictures of various adults and children depicting different emotions
Small unbreakable mirrors
Grouptime small carpets

Preparation/Setup
1. Laminate pictures.
2. Locate mirrors—one per child.
3. Set up carpets for Grouptime.

Teaching Strategies
1. Teacher settles down group with active songs and fingerplay(s).
2. Teacher assesses children's knowledge of emotions—discusses pictures.
3. Teacher engages children in interactive questioning (What do you think is happening here?).
4. Teacher and children model same emotion while looking in their mirror.

Possible Outcomes
Concepts
Everyone has feelings.
It's OK to feel mad or sad sometimes.

Skills
Language opportunity
Emotional development
Socialization

Vocabulary
Happy, sad, angry, mad, worried, feelings, emotions

Curriculum Activity Guide 45

Puppetry (Making Friends)

Goal: The children will have an opportunity to experience puppets discussing friendship

Curriculum Area	**Developmental Focus**	**Location/Interest Center**
Creative Dramatics	Affective—Emotional	Inside Circle

Participants	**Time**	**Age Range**
5 to 8 children	10 to 20 minutes	Appropriate for all ages

Materials

Puppets—two preferably a boy and a girl puppet
Pillowcase or bag
Grouptime carpet squares

Preparation/Setup

1. Locate puppets and place in pillowcase.
2. Set up carpets for Grouptime.

Teaching Strategies

1. Teacher settles down children with active songs and fingerplay(s).
2. Teacher tells children she has some special friends that came to group today.
3. Teacher introduces each puppet (one has difficulty making friends).
4. Involve the children in problem-solving how he/she could make friends.

Possible Outcomes

Concepts
I like puppets.
Everyone wants a friend.
There are special ways to make friends.

Skills
Social interaction
Concept of social skills
Emotional development

Vocabulary
Friends, share, join, puppets

Curriculum Activity Guide 46

When I Was a Baby

Goal: The children will have the opportunity to consider their growth

Curriculum Area	**Developmental Focus**	**Location/Interest Center**
Social Understanding	Cognitive—Critical Thinking	Inside Circle

Participants	**Time**	**Age Range**
5 to 8 children	10 to 20 minutes	3 and 4 years old

Materials

Baby items—bottles, bibs, diapers, baby food containers, etc.
Baby doll
Pictures of babies, families nurturing babies
Optional: Book about growing up
Large paper, teacher marker

Preparation/Setup

1. Set up carpets for Grouptime.
2. Locate all materials.

Teaching Strategies

1. Teacher settles down children with active songs, fingerplay(s).
2. Teacher brings out baby props, discusses their use.
3. Teacher elicits discussion of growing bigger, writes children's responses on paper.
4. Teacher hangs paper "All by Myself" with responses.

Possible Outcomes

Concepts
I am getting bigger.
I used to be a baby.

Skills
Social understanding
Sense of identity

Vocabulary
Baby, grow, family

Curriculum Activity Guide 47

Litter Patrol

Goal: The children will have the opportunity to beautify the area around their school

Curriculum Area	**Developmental Focus**	**Location/Interest Center**
Social Understanding	Affective—Social	Unselected

Participants	**Time**	**Age Range**
More than 8 children	20 to 30 minutes	3 and 4 years old

Materials
Plastic or paper bags with handles
Waterless sanitizing handwash

Preparation/Setup
1. Set up carpets for Grouptime.
2. Locate bags and handwash.

Teaching Strategies
1. Teacher prepares children for a field trip at Grouptime.
2. Teacher discusses litter, and discusses "litter patrol."
3. Teacher discusses safety issues—no cigarettes, glass, gum, etc.
4. During field trip, children are supervised carefully.

Possible Outcomes
Concepts
I can help clean up my neighborhood.
Litter hurts our environment.

Skills
Exposure to concept of environment
Social responsibility
Social interaction

Vocabulary
Litter, environment, clean

Curriculum Activity Guide 48

Comparing Children's Illustrators

Goal: The children will have an opportunity to examine and compare illustrators

Curriculum Area	**Developmental Focus**	**Location/Interest Center**
Art	Affective—Aesthetic	Inside Circle

Participants	**Time**	**Age Range**
5 to 8 children	10 to 20 minutes	3 and 4 years old

Materials

Children's literature books two to three each by two illustrators
Small carpet squares for Grouptime

Preparation/Setup

1. Locate and familiarize yourself with books.
2. Set up carpets for Grouptime.

Teaching Strategies

1. Teacher settles down Grouptime with songs and fingerplay(s).
2. Teacher discusses illustration and shows books.
3. Teacher discusses different mediums used by illustrators.
4. Teacher leads children to examine and compare the two.
5. Optional: Set up Art activity with both mediums.

Possible Outcomes

Concepts
Illustrators are artists.
Artists use different mediums.

Skills
Aesthetic development
Art appreciation
Differentiation

Vocabulary
Artist, illustrator, paint, draw

Curriculum Activity Guide 49

Music Appreciation: Many Instruments

Goal: The children will have the opportunity to experience diverse music and instruments

Curriculum Area	Developmental Focus	Location/Interest Center
Music and Rhythm	Affective—Aesthetic	Inside Circle

Participants	Time	Age Range
5 to 8 children	10 to 20 minutes	Appropriate for all ages

Materials
Diverse selections of instrumental music on CD/cassettes
CD/cassette player
Variety of instruments—including castanets, drums, cajun banjo, other cultural instruments
Optional: Pictures of some of the instruments

Preparation/Setup
1. Locate music, set up in Grouptime area.
2. Locate instruments, set up near Grouptime area.
3. Familiarize yourself with the music and instruments.
4. Laminate pictures, if used.

Teaching Strategies
1. Teacher settles down children with active songs, fingerplay(s).
2. Teacher invites children to listen to music they may not have heard before.
3. Teacher discusses music and instruments from around the world.
4. Children are invited to explore the instruments provided and play along with music.
5. Teacher can take dictation about the music and display with laminated pictures.

Possible Outcomes
Concepts
Music is played all over the world.
Different cultures play different music.
Children can make music with instruments.

Skills
Music appreciation
Aesthetic appreciation
Social understanding of cultural diversity

Vocabulary
Music, world, play, names of instruments

Curriculum Activity Guide 50

Tissue Paper and Starch Art

Goal: The children will have the opportunity to experience tissue paper/starch art

Curriculum Area	**Developmental Focus**	**Location/Interest Center**
Art	Affective—Aesthetic	Inside Art

Participants	**Time**	**Age Range**
1 to 4 children	10 to 20 minutes	3 and 4 years old

Materials

Tissue paper, various colors
Liquid laundry starch
Small containers, short wide brushes
Paper

Preparation/Setup

1. Cut or tear tissue paper into small pieces.
2. Put starch into small containers, add brushes.
3. Cover table, set out art smocks.

Teaching Strategies

1. Children cover their paper with starch, using brushes.
2. Children place tissue paper on wet paper, overlapping as desired.
3. Dry flat if possible, as tissue paper colors drip.

Possible Outcomes

Concepts
I am an artist.
Colors can mix to make other colors.

Skills
Color awareness
Aesthetic pleasure
Art appreciation

Vocabulary
Tissue paper, starch, art, color

Curriculum Activity Guide 51

Tire Track Art

Goal: The children will have the opportunity to paint with toy cars

Curriculum Area	**Developmental Focus**	**Location/Interest Center**
Art	Affective—Aesthetic	Inside Art

Participants	**Time**	**Age Range**
Individual child	5 to 10 minutes	3 and 4 years old

Materials
Tempera paint, mixed medium thin
Paper—large is best
Aluminum pie pans
Small cars, trucks with interesting tire tracks

Preparation/Setup
1. Locate all materials, cover table, set out Art smocks.
2. Pour small amount of tempera into pie pan to cover bottom.
3. Place 2 to 3 small cars/trucks in each pan.

Teaching Strategies
1. Children use cars/trucks to drive across and paint their paper.
2. Teacher can facilitate discussion of different tracks.
3. Hang to dry—Teacher may write "Tire Track Art" to inform parents.

Possible Outcomes

Concepts
There are different ways to paint.
Car tires can make tracks.

Skills
Creativity
Aesthetic pleasure
Small motor development

Vocabulary
Tire, tracks, art

Curriculum Activity Guide 52

Nature Collage

Goal: The children will have the opportunity to create a collage with natural materials

Curriculum Area	**Developmental Focus**	**Location/Interest Center**
Art	Affective—Aesthetic	Inside Art

Participants	**Time**	**Age Range**
1 to 4 children	10 to 20 minutes	3 and 4 years old

Materials
Sturdy paper or thin cardboard
Glue and glue applicators
Natural materials—sticks, leaves, moss, pine needles, etc.

Preparation/Setup
1. Children can collect materials on a nature walk, or teacher can collect.
2. Cover table, set out Art smocks.
3. Display nature materials on tray on center of table.
4. Set out glue and applicator for each child.

Teaching Strategies
1. Children glue natural materials on their paper.
2. Teacher can facilitate discussion of materials.
3. This can also be done as a group project—large piece of cardboard.

Possible Outcomes

Concepts
There are interesting and beautiful items in nature.
I am creative.
Collecting means gathering and bringing back items.

Skills
Aesthetic development
Creativity
Introduction to Science concepts

Vocabulary
Collage, leaves, acorns, seeds, etc.

Curriculum Activity Guide 53

Grocery Store

Goal: The children will have the opportunity to interact in a Grocery Store Interest Center

Curriculum Area	**Developmental Focus**	**Location/Interest Center**
Social Understanding	Affective—Social	Inside Dramatic Play

Participants	**Time**	**Age Range**
1 to 4 children	10 to 20 minutes	3 and 4 years old

Materials

Plastic food, empty food containers
Grocery bags, sacks
Toy cash register and/or small calculators, paper and pencils
Shower curtain backdrop
Scale for weighing food

Preparation/Setup

1. Using a white shower curtain liner, draw a grocery store scene with permanent markers.
2. Collect empty food containers from parents, staff.
3. Set up Dramatic Play area with all props.

Teaching Strategies

1. Children interact in familiar grocery store setting, buying and selling food.
2. Teacher can facilitate children's writing of signs and labels for foods.
3. Children use paper and pencil to write up receipts.

Possible Outcomes

Concepts
I know about grocery stores.
Grocery stores are also called markets.

Skills
Social understanding
Social interaction
Literacy and Mathematics skill development

Vocabulary
Grocery, buy, sell, cash register, scale

Curriculum Activity Guide 54

Making New Friends ("I'm Thinking of a Friend")

Goal: The children will have the opportunity to consider their uniqueness

Curriculum Area	**Developmental Focus**	**Location/Interest Center**
Social Understanding	Affective—Social	Inside Circle

Participants	**Time**	**Age Range**
5 to 8 children	10 to 20 minutes	3 and 4 years old

Materials
Carpets for Grouptime

Preparation/Setup
1. Set up area for Grouptime.

Teaching Strategies
1. Teacher readies children for Grouptime with songs, fingerplays.
2. Children initiates activity "I'm thinking of a friend . . ." (who likes to build, who likes to sing, who likes to climb in the loft—emphasizing traits shared by many.
3. Teacher facilitates children's discovery that they share many traits.
4. Teacher ultimately describes a trait unique to one child.

Possible Outcomes

Concepts
We are all alike in some ways and different in others.
Children can have many different friends.

Skills
Listening skills
Prediction skills
Social interaction

Vocabulary
Friend, same, different

Curriculum Activity Guide 55

Talking and Showing

Goal: The children will have the opportunity to participate in group problem-solving

Curriculum Area	**Developmental Focus**	**Location/Interest Center**
Social Understanding	Affective—Social	Inside Circle

Participants	**Time**	**Age Range**
5 to 8 children	10 to 20 minutes	3 and 4 years old

Materials
Carpets for Grouptime
Puppets, dolls, or flannel pieces

Preparation/Setup
1. Set up for Grouptime.
2. Locate materials.

Teaching Strategies
1. Using materials, teacher tells a story about a common classroom conflict, such as two children wanting the same tricycle.
2. Children are invited to interact and help the characters problem-solve.
3. Teacher facilitates input from children and they discuss possible solutions to conflict.
4. Children help decide the best strategy for solving the problem.

Possible Outcomes
Concepts
Everyone has conflicts some time.
Conflicts can be solved by using words and cooperating.
Angry feelings can be channeled into words.

Skills
Problem-solving
Social interaction
Decision making

Vocabulary
Problem, conflict, solve, cooperate, resolve

Curriculum Activity Guide 56

Fix-It Shop

Goal: The children will have the opportunity to role play a repair shop

Curriculum Area	**Developmental Focus**	**Location/Interest Center**
Social Understanding	Affective—Social	Inside Dramatic Play

Participants	**Time**	**Age Range**
1 to 4 children	10 to 20 minutes	3 and 4 year olds

Materials

Broken small appliances (cords removed)—check for sharp edges, safety
Small tools, primarily screwdrivers with short handles
Sign: "Fix-It Shop"

Preparation/Setup

1. Locate small appliances (note request in parent newsletter).
2. Set up table with tools and appliances.
3. Loosen screws throughout to facilitate children's success.

Teaching Strategies

1. Teacher discusses repair, Fix-It Shop.
2. Children work on taking apart and putting together appliances.
3. Parts may be saved for a Group Junk Sculpture later on.

Possible Outcomes

Concepts
I can take things apart.
I can pretend to be a repair person.

Skills
Hand–eye coordination
Fine motor development
Social understanding

Vocabulary
Repair, Fix-It Shop, tool names

Curriculum Activity Guide 57

Growth Sequence

Goal: The children will have the opportunity to use an activity focusing on growth sequence

Curriculum Area	**Developmental Focus**	**Location/Interest Center**
Social Understanding	Cognitive—Critical Thinking	Inside Manipulative

Participants	**Time**	**Age Range**
Individual child	Under 5 minutes	3 and 4 years old

Materials

Uniform-size pictures of growth sequence from baby to old age
Placemat for tray
Container to hold pictures

Preparation/Setup

1. Locate and laminate picture cards, sequence of 3 to 5.
2. Outline placemat with place for cards in sequence and container.
3. Place activity tray on shelf.

Teaching Strategies

1. Child takes activity tray from shelf and puts pictures in order of growth sequence.
2. Teacher can facilitate language development, discussing "baby," "teenager," etc.
3. Child replaces pictures to container and replaces tray to shelf.

Possible Outcomes

Concepts
There is a sequence to growth.
Babies grow up.
Children get bigger.

Skills
Ordering skills
Social understanding

Vocabulary
Growth, baby, child, teenager, adult, older adult

Curriculum Activity Guide 58

Telephone Partners

Goal: The children will have the opportunity to interact with each other by "telephone"

Curriculum Area	**Developmental Focus**	**Location/Interest Center**
Communication and Literacy	Cognitive—Language	Inside Dramatic Play

Participants	**Time**	**Age Range**
1 to 4 children	5 to 10 minutes	Appropriate for all ages

Materials
Two telephones with cords removed
Small table and 2 chairs
Pictures of people talking on telephones
Materials to make a sign

Preparation/Setup
1. Set up small table with two telephones so that children will be facing each other.
2. Locate pictures and laminate.
3. Make a sign: "Let's Talk on the Telephone!"

Teaching Strategies
1. Children can freely choose to use the telephones to talk to one another.
2. Teacher can enhance conversation and language development by asking interactive questions, "Did you tell him about . . .?", "I wonder if you asked _____ about . . .?"

Possible Outcomes
Concepts
I can pretend to talk on a telephone.
Telephones help people communicate with each other when they are not close to each other.

Skills
Language development
Social interaction

Vocabulary
Telephone, talk, conversation

Curriculum Activity Guide 59

Flannel Board Story Retelling

Goal: The child will have an opportunity to retell a story with a flannel board

Curriculum Area	**Developmental Focus**	**Location/Interest Center**
Communication and Literacy	Cognitive—Language	Inside Circle

Participants	**Time**	**Age Range**
1 to 4 children	5 to 10 minutes	3 and 4 years old

Materials
Storybook
Corresponding flannel board story pieces
Flannel board

Preparation/Setup
1. Set up area for small group storytelling opportunity.
2. Locate all materials.

Teaching Strategies
1. Teacher reads story to small group of children.
2. Teacher introduces flannel pieces, involving children in identifying them.
3. Children have opportunity to retell the story, using flannel pieces.

Possible Outcomes

Concepts
I can remember a story.
I can use flannel board pieces to tell a story.

Skills
Memory skills
Social interaction
Literacy development

Vocabulary
Story, flannel board, remember

Curriculum Activity Guide 60

Storytelling

Goal: The children will have the opportunity to tell a story

Curriculum Area	**Developmental Focus**	**Location/Interest Center**
Communication and Literacy	Cognitive—Language	Inside Quiet—Reading

Participants	**Time**	**Age Range**
Individual child	5 to 10 minutes	3 and 4 years old

Materials
Children's lined paper
Permanent marker
Clipboard

Preparation/Setup
Locate paper and put on clipboard.

Teaching Strategies
1. Teacher invites child to tell a story, and he or she will write it down.
2. Child should be positioned next to teacher to see writing appropriately.
3. Child dictates a story, with teacher writing it **verbatim.**
4. When finished, teacher reads back story to child.

Possible Outcomes
Concepts
I am a story teller.
My words can be written down.

Skills
Language development
Literacy development
Imagination and creativity

Vocabulary
Story, tell, write, dictate

Curriculum Activity Guide 61

Story Sequence

Goal: The child will have an opportunity to explore story sequence

Curriculum Area	**Developmental Focus**	**Location/Interest Center**
Communication and Literacy	Cognitive—Language	Inside Quiet Reading

Participants	**Time**	**Age Range**
Individual child	Under 5 minutes	3 and 4 years old

Materials

Story sequence card with beginning, middle, end (familiar stories work best at first)
Placemat with outline for each section
Tray

Preparation/Setup

1. Outline placemat and place on tray with story sequence cards.
2. Set activity tray on shelf.

Teaching Strategies

1. Child uses activity tray, placing cards in order of sequence of a story.
2. Teacher facilitates child's understanding by asking questions, "Which one do you think is the beginning?"
3. Child replaces all materials and returns tray to shelf.

Possible Outcomes

Concepts
Stories have a beginning, a middle, and an ending.

Skills
Sequence development
Literacy development

Vocabulary
Beginning, middle, ending

Curriculum Activity Guide 62

Labeling Science Share Items

Goal: The child will have an opportunity to communicate about Science share items

Curriculum Area	**Developmental Focus**	**Location/Interest Center**
Communication and Literacy	Cognitive—Language	Science

Participants	**Time**	**Age Range**
Individual child	5 to 10 minutes	Appropriate for all ages

Materials
Trays
Paper and Marking Pens

Preparation/Setup
1. Welcoming teacher ready to check and accept appropriate share item when child arrives.
2. Materials should always be ready for spontaneous Science share items from home.

Teaching Strategies
1. Child brings in Science item from home for Science shelf at school.
2. Teacher facilitates communication about item.
3. Teacher writes down child's words about item, where they found it, etc.
4. When possible, add Science reference materials to tray to expand information.

Possible Outcomes
Concepts
I can talk about my Science share item.
My teacher will help me learn more about it.

Skills
Communication/language development
Science concepts
Sense of discovery

Vocabulary
Science, share, look up

Curriculum Activity Guide 63

Word Card Letter Match

Goal: The child will have an opportunity to explore letters and words

Curriculum Area	**Developmental Focus**	**Location/Interest Center**
Communication and Literacy	Cognitive—Critical Thinking	Literacy

Participants	**Time**	**Age Range**
Individual child	Under 5 minutes	3 and 4 years old

Materials
Stickers of simple familiar words (cat, dog, ball, etc.)
Rubber letters
Card stock
Container for letters, cards

Preparation/Setup
1. Cut cards in a uniform size.
2. Place a sticker on each card, outline letters of corresponding word.
3. Select rubber letters to correspond with word, separate colors for each word.
4. Set out 2 cards on each tray, with letters in container.

Teaching Strategies
1. Child chooses letters to match with letters on word card.
2. Teacher facilitates child's literacy development by naming letter names, reading word.
3. Child replaces activity on shelf.
4. Teacher rotates words appropriately, as children become confident.

Possible Outcomes
Concepts
Words are made of letters.
I can match the letters in these words.

Skills
Letter recognition
Literacy development

Vocabulary
Letters, alphabet, words

Curriculum Activity Guide 64

Letter Writing

Goal: The child will have an opportunity to write a letter

Curriculum Area	**Developmental Focus**	**Location/Interest Center**
Communication and Literacy	Cognitive—Critical Thinking	Inside Quiet—Reading

Participants	**Time**	**Age Range**
Individual child	5 to 10 minutes	3 and 4 years old

Materials
Children's lined paper
Permanent marker
Envelope
Children's markers

Preparation/Setup
1. Have materials ready for appropriate time.
2. Set up materials in a writing center and at arrival location.

Teaching Strategies
1. If a child is having separation difficulties, teacher can suggest writing a letter to parent.
2. Teacher takes dictation from child about why they are feeling sad, etc.
3. Child is encouraged to decorate envelope, paper, as desired.
4. Child puts letter in cubby to take home.

Possible Outcomes

Concepts
I can communicate my feelings.
I feel better when I talk about my feelings.

Skills
Language development
Emotional outlet
Communication facilitation

Vocabulary
Letter, write, feelings, dictation

Curriculum Activity Guide 65

Sorting Seashells

Goal: The child will have an opportunity to explore and sort seashells

Curriculum Area	**Developmental Focus**	**Location/Interest Center**
Mathematics	Cognitive—Critical Thinking	Inside Manipulative

Participants	**Time**	**Age Range**
Individual child	Under 5 minutes	3 and 4 years old

Materials

Sorting tray with numerous compartments
Assortment of seashells, 2 to 3 each of various types

Preparation/Setup

1. Locate all materials.
2. Set up sorting tray with all shells in large compartment.

Teaching Strategies

1. Child takes activity from shelf and sorts shells by type and/or size.
2. Teacher can facilitate child's experience by discussing attributes of shells.
3. Child replaces all materials, returns activity to shelf.

Possible Outcomes

Concepts
I can sort shells.
Sorting means to match the shells that look the same.

Skills
Differentiation skills
Mathematical development

Vocabulary
Alike, different, shells, sort, match, same

Curriculum Activity Guide 66

What's Our Favorite Apple?

Goal: The children will have an opportunity to graph apple preferences

Curriculum Area	**Developmental Focus**	**Location/Interest Center**
Mathematics	Cognitive—Critical Thinking	Inside Circle

Participants	**Time**	**Age Range**
5 to 8 children	5 to 10 minutes	3 and 4 years old

Materials
Apples, green, red, yellow
Cutting board, knife
Napkins
Large paper, divided in three
Red, yellow, green markers

Preparation/Setup
1. Locate all materials.
2. Set up area for Grouptime.

Teaching Strategies
1. Children and teachers wash hands.
2. Teacher discusses apples, differences, similarities.
3. Teacher draws green, red, and yellow apples on large paper.
4. Teacher cuts apples and lets each child eat a slice of each color apple.
5. Teacher and/or children graph their favorite apple on chart.

Possible Outcomes
Concepts
We all like different apples.
We can tell which apple is the favorite by looking at our chart.
Apples are different colors and have different shapes.

Skills
Mathematical skill
Social interaction

Vocabulary
Apples, favorite, chart, graph

Curriculum Activity Guide 67

Measuring/Pouring Rice

Goal: The children will have an opportunity to explore measuring and pouring

Curriculum Area	**Developmental Focus**	**Location/Interest Center**
Mathematics	Cognitive—Discovery	Sensorial

Participants	**Time**	**Age Range**
1 to 4 children	5 to 10 minutes	3 and 4 years old

Materials

Sand and water table, set up with 3 tubs
Rice
Measuring cups, spoons

Preparation/Setup

1. Rice.
2. Set up sand and water table with rice in 3 tubs, measuring cups and spoons in each.

Teaching Strategies

1. Children explore the rice by measuring and pouring.
2. Children discover mathematical concepts by experiential use of materials.
3. Teacher may facilitate experience by communicating with child.

Possible Outcomes

Concepts
I can measure and pour rice.

Skills
Mathematical skill development
Tactile experience
Social interaction

Vocabulary
Rice, measure, pour

Curriculum Activity Guide 68

Grass Seed Growing on Sponge

Goal: The children will have an opportunity to observe grass growing on a sponge

Curriculum Area	**Developmental Focus**	**Location/Interest Center**
Science	Cognitive—Discovery	Science
Participants	**Time**	**Age Range**
5 to 8 children	5 to 10 minutes	3 and 4 years old

Materials
Tray
Grass seed
Sponges
Squirt bottle with water

Preparation/Setup
Assemble all materials on tray.

Teaching Strategies
1. Teacher works with small group to discuss growing grass seeds.
2. Children wet sponge with squirt bottle.
3. Children sprinkle ample grass seeds on top of sponge and water again.
4. Children observe grass seed on Science shelf as they begin to grow.
5. Can use children's scissors to cut after seed grows.

Possible Outcomes
Concepts
Grass grows from seeds.
Grass needs water to grow.

Skills
Science concept development
Prediction skills
Social interaction

Vocabulary
Grass, sponge, water, grow

Curriculum Activity Guide 69

Milk Tasting

Goal: The children will have an opportunity to taste a variety of milks

Curriculum Area	**Developmental Focus**	**Location/Interest Center**
Science	Cognitive—Discovery	Sensorial

Participants	**Time**	**Age Range**
1 to 4 children	5 to 10 minutes	Appropriate for all ages

Materials
Milks (regular, buttermilk, goat milk, chocolate milk)
Small disposable cups
Small pitchers, identical
Labels for pitchers

Preparation/Setup
1. Locate milks.
2. Place milks in small pitchers, label each.
3. Place all milks, cups on tray.
4. Check children's allergy chart.
5. Set up table for 4 children to taste.

Teaching Strategies
1. Teacher invites children to come to a milk-tasting activity.
2. Children are given each milk to taste, ending with chocolate milk.
3. Children are encouraged to voice their preferences.

Possible Outcomes
Concepts
Milks taste different.
I like some milks more than others.

Skills
Differentiation skills
Science concept
Social interaction

Vocabulary
Milk, taste, sour, sweet

Curriculum Activity Guide 70

Ice Melt

Goal: The children will have an opportunity to explore properties of ice

Curriculum Area	**Developmental Focus**	**Location/Interest Center**
Science	Cognitive—Discovery	Science

Participants	**Time**	**Age Range**
1 to 4 children	5 to 10 minutes	3 and 4 years old

Materials
Large blocks of ice in tubs
Rock salt in small containers
Eyedroppers
Water dyed with food coloring in small containers (2 primary colors)

Preparation/Setup
1. Freeze water in large blocks, or purchase.
2. Locate and set out all materials.

Teaching Strategies
1. Child sprinkles rock salt on ice and uses eyedropper to squirt water.
2. Child observes ice melting and colors mixing.
3. Teacher facilitates experience by discussing observations.

Possible Outcomes

Concepts
Ice melts.
Salt makes ice melt faster.
Colors mix to make new colors.

Skills
Science concept development
Color-mixing opportunity
Observation skills

Vocabulary
Ice, melt, salt, colors

APPENDIX B

Reproducible Sample Forms

Developmental Focus Area Approach

Week _____   Teacher _____   Group/Classroom _____

Curricular Guidelines:

Physical   Affective and Aesthetic   Cognitive and Language

Monday

Tuesday

Wednesday

Thursday

Friday

Curriculum Area Approach

Week _____   Teacher _____   Group/Classroom _____

Curricular Guidelines:

Art   Creative Dramatics   Health, Safety, Nutrition

Communication and Literacy   Mathematics   Movement

Music and Rhythm   Science   Social Understanding

Grouptime

Theme

Date: Review:

Curriculum Planning Form

Week _____   Teacher _____   Group/Classroom _____

Curricular Guidelines:

Theme/Unit/Project:

————————————————— **Developmental Focus** —————————————————

Physical (P)   Affective and Aesthetic (A)   Cognitive and Language (C)

————————————————— **Activities in Curriculum Areas** —————————————————

Art   Creative Dramatics   Health, Safety, Nutrition

Communication and Literacy   Mathematics   Movement

Music and Rhythm   Science   Social Understanding

Grouptime

Date: Review:

Curriculum Activity Guide

Title:

Goal:

Curriculum Area	**Developmental Focus**	**Location/Interest Center**
Participants	**Time**	**Age Range**

Materials

Preparation/Setup

Teaching Strategies

Possible Outcomes

Concepts

Skills

Vocabulary

Interest Center Guide

Interest Center

				Theme	
Art	Cooking	Literacy	Quiet Reading	Outside Art	Outside Large Motor
Block	Computer	Manipulatives	Science	Outside Circle	Outside and/Water
Circle	Dramatic Play	Music/Rhythm	Sensorial	Outside Garden	Trike Path

Interest Center Guidelines   **Approximate Age Range**

Developmental Focus   Physical   Affective and Aesthetic   Cognitive and Language

Curriculum Area

Interest Center Materials

  Constant

  Featured

Preparations/Setup

Teaching Strategies

Possible Outcomes for the Child or Children

  Concepts

  Skills

  Vocabulary

Child Participation   **Date**

Glossary

activity. An enriching experience planned and offered for children in an Early Childhood setting.

activity goal. A statement that describes the purposes of an activity. The goal relates the information that the teachers would like the children to experience.

aesthetic development. Developing awareness and responsiveness to beauty and the surroundings.

affective development. The growth and changes in young children's social and emotional behaviors.

age-appropriate. Experiences in Early Childhood settings that are suitable for the participating children.

age range. The chronological age span of the children for whom the activities are planned.

Art. A curriculum area encouraging relaxation, exploration, and pleasure with varied experiences ranging from art appreciation to painting and molding.

assessment. Ongoing observation and documentation of children that provides information about their needs and interests while contributing to curriculum planning decisions.

assessment methods. Data about children collected informally (notes, conversation, participation) and formally (checklists, logs, time sampling).

authentic inclusion. An aspect of curriculum for young children that values their culture, families, and abilities while avoiding separate, add-on activities.

best practices. Teaching strategies, experiences, and settings suitable to meet the developmental, age, individual, cultural, and linguistic needs of the young children enrolled in an Early Childhood program.

child advocacy. Promotion of positive issues relating to children and their well-being, education, and families.

child-initiated. Curriculum that is focused on meeting the needs of young children by encouraging their active learning with opportunities for choices within a planned environment.

clustering. Organizing activities for young children to pattern the experiences to progress from the simple to the more complex.

cognitive. Relates to knowledge and how knowledge is acquired. Combines with language to create one of the three Developmental Focus areas.

cognitive development. Growth of knowledge and understanding, including mental abilities and language acquisition.

Communication. Ability to relate feelings and ideas. Communication and Literacy form a curriculum area for young children.

concepts. Single ideas about an object or subject written and spoken simply for a child's understanding. One of the elements of a Curriculum Activity Guide.

Cooking. Part of the curriculum area of Nutrition that helps children to appreciate different foods and experience pleasure in food preparation.

Creative Dramatics. Adapted as a general term to organize four categories of activities that contribute to affective and aesthetic development of young children: Dramatic Play, Guided Drama, Puppetry, and Sociodramatics.

creativity. A process of developing expressive abilities encouraged with appreciation of new views, ways, and ideas.

culturally and linguistically appropriate. Programs sensitive and responsive to each child's family culture and language; offers appropriate experiences building children's confidence and tolerance for diversity.

curiosity. Self-motivated interest and inquiry about surroundings, people, and events. Teachers encourage natural curiosity of young children within flexible settings.

curricular guideline. An idea or a plan that defines an intended direction of the curriculum that a program has for the children, staff, and parents. Educational beliefs, commitment to children, and goals of a center influence the guidelines.

curriculum. Broadly refers to all the school or program-related experiences that affect the children. Specifically, the organized experiences and activities planned to meet the children's developmental needs.

Curriculum Activity Guide. A form, or template, to document activities and guide the direction of planned experiences in a program for young children.

curriculum area. Subject or content area organizing experiences by discipline, such as Art, Language, Mathematics, Music, Physical Education, Science, and Social Studies.

curriculum plan.   A written guide documenting the proposed activities designed to meet the needs and interests of the enrolled children.

curriculum resources.   Family and community members who contribute time, cultural enrichment, and occupational information and equipment to enhance the learning opportunities for the children.

daily schedule.   A framework of suggested time, and activities, including free-choice blocks of time, meeting transition and routine needs. Provides a guide, carries out program goals, and meets children's needs.

development.   Individualized sequence of changes and patterns of growth within physical, affective and aesthetic, and cognitive and language areas.

developmental age.   Each child's individual patterns of growth influenced by their unique heredity and life experiences.

developmentally appropriate practices (DAP).   Activities designed to respond to the unique needs and interests of the enrolled children, emphasizing each child's age and developmental level.

Developmental Focus Approach.   An approach to curriculum design emphasizing the development of the whole child with consideration of developing skills.

Developmental Focus areas.   Areas of growth and behavior categorized by professionals for the study and understanding of an increasing volume of knowledge about children. Developmental Focus areas are referenced in this volume within three domains: physical, affective and aesthetic, and cognitive and language.

discovery.   The occurrence of a behavior resulting from a child's natural interest to try out unstructured and flexible materials; allows the child to arrive at a new level of understanding.

Dramatic Play.   Voluntarily observing, participating, and playing in creative activity using imaginary objects and imitating people and surroundings.

Early Childhood Education.   The study and education of young children from infancy though the primary grades; includes programs, experiences, and services and strategies to facilitate the development of young children.

elements.   The term used to refer to the parts of an activity that is planned for young children, including title, goal, materials, etc.

emergent.   Curriculum offering activities and experiences that naturally flow from the children's interests and needs.

emotional development.   Growth and expression of feelings, self-worth, and preferences influenced by heredity, culture, language, region, and era.

environment.   Surroundings, conditions, and the locations where care and learning for young children may take place; the indoor and outdoor classrooms.

equity.   Fair access to programs, facilities, and educational opportunities with respect to diversity and differences.

expectation.   Anticipated behavior of children within an age range.

experiences.   Planned and unplanned developmentally appropriate activities creating the core of the curriculum and meeting program goals.

exploration.   Curiosity and self-motivated activity to investigate an object or idea; leads to discovery and learning.

extended-day activities.   Before- and after-school programs offered for primary and school-age children.

fundamentals.   Basic ideas that organize curriculum concepts throughout the textbook; offer a general guide and a conceptual framework.

Grouptime.   A teacher-guided activity bringing children together in circle time with a specific goal, such as introduction of a new idea or to enjoy social interaction.

guidelines.   Beliefs and values of the program staff who influence everyday interaction with children, daily experiences, and the curriculum.

Guided Drama.   Pantomime or acting out of a poem, short story, or rhyme.

harmony.   Peaceful understanding and appreciation of differences and diversity.

Health.   Wellness, physical well-being, and fitness.

healthy habits.   Activities planned to familiarize children with routine practices that facilitate physical well-being and fitness.

inclusive.   Programs for young children that promote non-bias behaviors with experiences and opportunities for children with different abilities and from diverse backgrounds.

inclusive settings.   An environment prepared to respond to the great diversity of children, cultures, languages, and abilities.

individually appropriate.   Experiences suitable for a child's ability, temperament, patterns of growth, family culture, and current need and interest.

individualizing curriculum.   The process of adapting experiences to the changing needs and interests of a child as growth and behavior change.

indoor places.   Flexible child-centered space and equipment arranged inside.

integrated.   Curriculum that offers activities and experiences that are balanced among the Developmental Focus areas and across the curriculum.

integrating activities.   Experiences for children are balanced among the Developmental Focus areas and across the curriculum areas.

interactive questioning.   Encouraging and expanding children's language through appropriate and sensitive questions, body movements, and verbal responses.

Interest Centers. Delineated areas for specialized activity within an environment.

Interest Center Guide. Form to document the experiences within a delineated activity area.

language. Communication, including gestures, movements, and words; is tied to thinking, beliefs, and emotions.

language development. Acquisition of communication skills; influences thinking and is a cognitive achievement.

large movement. Activity or motion propelled by the gross (large) body muscles.

Learning Centers. Designated areas of activity; also referred to as Interest Centers.

Literacy. Reading and writing skills; early exposure to print benefits young children when experiences are appropriate and positive.

Location/Interest Center. Area for a specific activity. One of the elements listed on the Curriculum Activity Guide.

locomotor. Moving oneself from one location to another.

manipulative. Material or an object encouraging activity and small motor development. A puzzle is a manipulative.

materials. Supplies needed to prepare curriculum activities, or those used by the children during curriculum experiences.

Mathematics. Curriculum area of learning about numbers, size, and amount. Encourages exploration and discovery about arranging, comparing, ordering, and measuring.

modifying activities. Formal and informal review of planned experiences by staff to identify the necessary changes required for the activities.

Montessori Method. Environments typically meet the individual needs of young children; appreciation for children's sensitive periods of development; planned environment emphasizes learning through senses.

movement. Use of muscles to allow a range of small or large activity to change the position or place of the body or body parts. Also refers to a curriculum area.

movement and perceptual motor development. Acquisition of specific motor skills through active participation in physical activity encouraging coordination, balance, and control of large and small muscles; promotes sensorial and discriminating skills.

movement skills. Sequential development of large and small muscles allowing capabilities in walking, running, climbing (large motor), and holding, pouring, and reaching (small motor).

multi-age grouping. The grouping or placement of children of different ages in settings where they participate for either partial or full-day scheduling in the same classroom and area.

multiple intelligence theory. Howard Gardner's theory identifying seven-plus different capacities of intelligence. Appropriate experiences encourage children to think about objects and ideas in many different ways.

music and rhythm skills. Participation and appreciation of songs, instruments, rhymes, fingerplays, and dancing.

non-bias curriculum. Program and experiences promoting positive understanding of diversity of cultures, languages, genders, differing abilities, religions, and classes.

Nutrition. Healthy awareness of food and meal preparation. A component of the curriculum area of Health, Safety, and Nutrition; emphasizes healthy living habits and wellness behaviors.

Nutritional Awareness. Education outlining activities that help children enjoy food preparation and mealtime while emphasizing lifelong healthy habits.

observe/review/plan. Individualizing curriculum with collection of data about each child; identifying behavioral changes and preparing activities and experiences to meet the identified needs.

outdoor places. Natural surroundings with activity providing opportunities for learning; especially accommodating for large movement and gardening.

parents and technology. Teachers provide information about computers, software, and Internet access linking the school and home settings.

parents as resources. Family members contribute their time, sharing their culture, hobbies, and occupations; enriches the curriculum learning experiences.

participants. One of the elements of an activity identified on the Curriculum Activity Guide. Recommended number of children participating for that listed activity.

physical development. The dimension of growth that relates to basic physiological changes and growth.

play. Spontaneous, unrestricted, and joyful response to the environment. Helps children learn about their world, acquire competencies, and resolve challenges and conflict.

possible outcomes. Description of the behavior that a child may be expected to achieve after participating in the specific activity. May include concepts, skills, and vocabulary. One of the elements of the Curriculum Activity Guide.

preparation/setup. Making ready the materials needed for an activity; includes the suggested steps. One of the elements of the Curriculum Activity Guide.

professional accountability. Continuous professional development experiences to ensure that program goals support Early Childhood Education principles and maintain balance of activities to meet the needs of enrolled children.

professional commitment. Perception about career, responsibility to children and families, and dedication to continued learning.

professional growth. Acquiring new information related to child development, curriculum, research; collaborating with others in the field.

professional preparation. Education, training, and experiences in an occupational field. Early Childhood preparation includes experience, training and knowledge in child development, teaching and curriculum, health and safety, and guidance, family relationships, diversity, and management.

Project Approach. Curriculum that evolves around a theme or topic, such as gardening, and integrates learning experiences across content areas over a period of time.

Puppetry. Use of a figure resembling a person or animal used by teachers to present new ideas, encourage creativity, explore emotions, and enjoy movement.

respect. Positive regard and honor for diversity of culture, language, gender, religion, and class.

Safety. A component of the curriculum area of Health, Safety, and Nutrition; encourages safe practices and accident prevention.

Science. Information about the world divided into two fields (biological and physical); includes study about growing and living elements of the world and causes and effects of matter, energy, and space.

sensitive. Respectful recognition and representation of all identities and abilities.

sensorial. Discovery and exploration of materials using one's senses in concrete experiences. Sensory education is a major aspect of the Montessori Method.

settings. The surroundings, the conditions, and the locations where care and education of children take place. These environments also include the buildings and play spaces.

shelving. Flexible, low storage throughout indoor and outdoor spaces. Holds selected curriculum materials accessible to children.

skills. Developed abilities in body movement, thinking, and social and emotional behaviors.

small motor abilities. Children's innate fine movement capacities that occur with maturation.

small movement. Pouring, placing, holding, stacking, reaching, and assembling; engages children's fine (small) muscles.

social development. Acquisition of skills that enable children to react and interact with others as they mature and begin to understand the point of view of others.

Social Understanding. Appropriately planned activities help children develop self-awareness and skills to react and interact positively with others.

Sociodramatics. Children voluntarily engage in activity by pretending to be someone or something, while acquiring negotiation skills during interaction.

storage. Places to keep materials, supplies, and equipment that are important to the operation of programs for young children.

teacher-guided. Two primary teacher-guided experiences in an Early Childhood setting occur: to introduce new materials for an activity and to gather children for Grouptime.

teaching strategies. The recommended action for the teacher who is guiding an activity; may suggest sequence in guiding the child's participation. One of the elements of the Curriculum Activity Guide.

team planning. Collaborative effort of the staff working together to arrange and facilitate the curriculum.

technology. Tools such as computers; opens access to information and utilization for multimedia projects. Software to run the technological tools should meet appropriate guidelines.

Thematic Approach. Curriculum activities organized around a theme, such as My Family; balances experiences among the curriculum areas.

theme. Unit of study around a topic such as "pets;" sets a general framework allowing children to explore and enjoy theme-related experiences balanced among the curriculum areas.

theoretical perspectives. Ideology explaining and predicting behavior of children developed by educators and psychologists; includes behavioral, cognitive, developmental, ecological, maturational, and psychodynamic.

title. The first element of the Curriculum Activity Guide naming and describing the activity.

type of program. Some Early Childhood programs offer care and/or learning to infants and toddlers, some to preschoolers, and some to school-age children for extended-day programs. Categories include cooperative, employer-supported, child care, enrichment/compensatory, family child care, preschool/nursery, training/lab, and faith-based.

value of play. Benefits of active learning by doing, practicing, and pretending. Translates to courage, curiosity, commitment, self-acceptance, optimism, gaiety, cooperation, and emotional maturity.

vocabulary. A possible outcome listed on the Curriculum Activity Guide; words related to the activity to be used appropriately in conversation with the children participating in the activity.

webbing. Creating and recording the ideas suggested by children during "brainstorming" session; contributes to activity planning related to a project topic or theme.

whole child. Supporting the development of each child in all areas of growth (physical, affective and aesthetic, cognitive and language) while respecting each one's individuality.

Index